Stability and Change in Guale Indian Pottery, A.D. 1300–1702

Rebecca Saunders

THE UNIVERSITY OF ALABAMA PRESS
Tuscaloosa and London

1 2 3 4 5 6 7 8 9 • 08 07 06 05 04 03 02 01 00

Cover design by Ken Botnick

∞

The paper on which this book is printed meets the minimum requirements of American
National Standard for Information Science–Permanence of Paper for Printed Library
Materials, ANSI Z39.48–1984.

Library of Congress Cataloging-in-Publication Data

Saunders, Rebecca, 1955–
    Stability and change in Guale Indian pottery, A.D. 1300–1702 /
Rebecca Saunders.
        p.   cm.
    Includes bibliographical references and index.
    ISBN 0-8173-1012-6 (pbk. : alk. paper)
    I. Title.   1. Guale pottery.   2. Guale Indians—Antiquities.
3. Guale Indians—Social conditions.   4. Sea Islands—Antiquities.
5. Amelia Island (Fla.)—Antiquities.
E99.G82 S38   2000
975.8'733—dc21

                                                99-006821

British Library Cataloguing-in-Publication Data available

Stability and Change
in Guale Indian Pottery,
A.D. 1300–1702

Contents

List of Figures

List of Tables

Acknowledgments

This study was accomplished with an extraordinary level of cooperation from a number of remarkable individuals and institutions. The research could not have begun were it not for Dr. George and Dottie Dorion and Gus and Marion Heatwole, who owned the adjacent lots on Amelia Island where the missions of Santa Catalina de Guale de Santa María and Santa María de Yamassee were unearthed. Those individuals gave permission to excavate on their respective properties without any legal requirement to do so. The Dorions went so far as to postpone house construction for five years while we completed our work. Mitch and Beanie Wenigman, who owned the adjoining lot, provided housing and lab space for several seasons. All of these people bolstered our spirits with their interest in, and enthusiasm for, our research.

The mission on the Dorion lot was initially investigated by Piper Archaeological Research, Inc. (now Janus Research). Ken Hardin, president of that company, designed the first field seasons at the site that I directed, secured funds from the Dorions, and arranged for Dr. Clark Spencer Larsen to analyze the human remains. In so doing, Ken initiated a program of institutional cooperation that remained a hallmark of this project. After two field seasons, Ken recognized that the work would require more long-term effort than a contracting company could afford, and he relinquished the project to the Florida Museum of Natural History. Ken never lost his own appreciation for the potential of the site, however, and has been helpful throughout the long years it has taken to complete the work.

Public interest in the sites on Amelia Island was immense. Although the site was within the Amelia Island Plantation, a restricted residential development, the number of people who visited the site each day began to impinge on our ability to concentrate. Deon Jaccard of the Amelia Island Museum of

History came to our rescue. We instituted a series of weekly site tours using Amelia Island Museum volunteer interpreters. The Amelia Island Plantation management, especially James Restor, graciously allowed visitors to take advantage of these tours. In the ensuing years, special tours were instituted for schoolchildren in the region. In one season, more than two thousand children visited the site.

All told, there were seven field seasons on Amelia Island. These were financed in part by two Historic Preservation Grants provided by the Bureau of Historic Preservation, Florida Department of State, assisted by the Historic Preservation Advisory Council. The Dorions and the Heatwoles also contributed funds.

Too many crew members have come and gone to list them all here, but there were a number of repeaters who formed the backbone of the excavation. Those folks were (and are) Tina Bassett, Brack Barker, Boots Lewis, James McGill, Kathleen Richert, Vicki Rolland, Donna Ruhl, and Susan Simmons. There was also a multitude of lab personnel. Again, several individuals deserve special mention—Gianna Browne, Radai Cintron, Tracey Garbade, Joe Hock, Penny Melville, Vicki Rolland, Deb Sommerer, and Joyce Walker.

While work was under way on Amelia Island, we became aware of another long-term mission excavation of yet another Santa Catalina (the predecessor of the one on Amelia Island) on St. Catherines Island, Georgia. That research was being conducted by David Hurst Thomas of the American Museum of Natural History. The relevancy of that project to our own work was immediately apparent, and an Amelia Island contingent soon infiltrated American Museum of Natural History crews (and vice versa). Dave has been supportive of all aspects of this research. He helped to secure funds from the Edward John Noble Foundation for the excavation and analysis of the Meeting House Fields site and offered me an American Museum of Natural History Study Grant to analyze the collections of materials previously excavated at the St. Catherines Island, Georgia, mission. Other individuals from the American Museum have enlightened and enlivened the last few years, including Lorann Pendleton, Deb Peter, and Joe Jimenez—oh, and David Hurst Thomas III (please pass the baby). Royce Hayes, superintendent of St. Catherines Island, supplied every imaginable logistical support for excavations at the mission and at Meeting House Fields and provided many outstanding island dinners.

This project owes much to the efforts of Jerald T. Milanich, a fixture in Florida archaeology. When one looks at current research in Mission Period archaeology in Florida, it seems that almost every project owes something to his long involvement in the field. I appreciate the opportunity to have worked with him. Input from the other members of my Ph.D. dissertation committee, Drs. Kathleen Deagan, Michael V. Gannon, Prudence M. Rice, and David Hurst Thomas, enhanced this work.

Many thanks to Judith Knight of the University of Alabama Press, who, with blinding speed, got the original work reviewed, revised, and into production. Kathy Swain edited the revised version for the press and is responsible for improving the language and organization of the sometimes intractable text, not to mention the tables. Thanks also to Mary Lee Eggart of the Cartographic Section of the Department of Georgraphy and Anthropology at Louisiana State University, who drafted or redrafted most of the figures, and to Radai Cintron, who drew the pottery pipes depicted in Chapter 5.

Finally, thanks to all those who provided support of many kinds during the dissertation research and during the process of revising the dissertation into this book. You know who you are. And thanks, Mom and Dad, for everything.

Stability and Change
in Guale Indian Pottery,
A.D. 1300–1702

1

Pottery and Culture Change

This work is a study of change in the pottery made by the late pre-Columbian and Mission period Guale (whälē) Indians of the Georgia and northeast Florida coasts (Figure 1.1). Technological and stylistic attributes of Guale pottery are compared across time and space, beginning in the late pre-Columbian period and ending in 1702, the date of the demise of the Spanish mission system on the Atlantic coast. As such, the research deals with three previously defined pottery assemblages. The first two, Irene phase (circa A.D. 1300–1600) and Altamaha phase assemblages (circa A.D. 1600–1690), from the central and northern Georgia coasts, are associated with the pre-Columbian and early Mission period Guale Indians, respectively. The last assemblage, San Marcos (circa A.D. 1650–1763?) assemblages of the St. Augustine phase, appeared in what is now southern Georgia and northeastern Florida at the time of the immigration of the Guale and Yamassee to that region in the mid-seventeenth century (Worth 1995).

What follows is a description of technological and stylistic attributes of those pottery types from a series of discrete temporal contexts. A consideration of the changes in attribute values over time and space, in concert with relevant historical and ethnohistoric data, should help explain when Irene assemblages qualitatively changed and became Altamaha assemblages. The characteristics of Altamaha assemblages are then compared to San Marcos assemblages to determine which pottery attributes changed and which remained stable over the years of declining population and the nucleation of peoples in the later Mission period. Taken together, these data will be used to assess the extent to which the disruption of the traditional

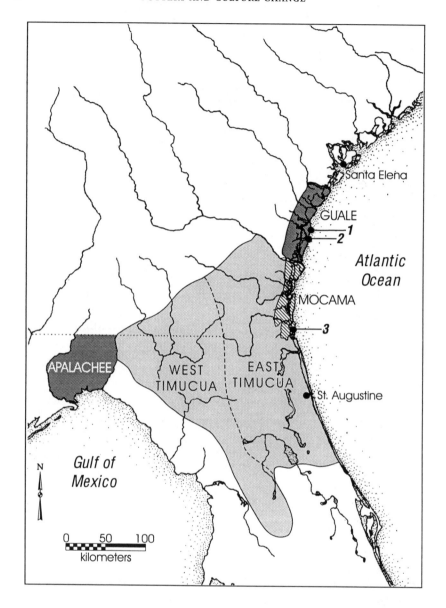

1.1. Location of the Major Linguistic Groups and Key Sites in Northern *La Florida*. Key: 1 = Meeting House Fields; 2 = Santa Catalina de Guale; 3 = Santa Catalina de Santa María.

production and social systems of the Guale Indians in the Mission period affected pottery production.

This study begins with a review of general theories of ceramic change and the results of previous research into Native American pottery in (principally Spanish) colonial contexts. Chapter 2 presents a social history of the Guale. Using archaeological and ethnohistoric data from *La Florida*,[1] I review relevant aspects of traditional Guale settlement and subsistence patterns and social structure. A brief history of contact and the development of the mission system follows. The imposition of the mission system on the native inhabitants interfered with indigenous traditions; the resultant changes and their effect on pottery production and iconography are the focus of the chapter.

The next chapters provide a review of the type descriptions of the pottery involved (Chapter 3) and the attributes chosen for this study of change (Chapter 4). Attributes were chosen on the basis of the type descriptions developed and refined for late Irene, Altamaha, and San Marcos assemblages and from other studies of pottery from single and multicomponent sites associated with the Guale. Both technological and stylistic attributes are considered, though stylistic aspects are emphasized. In particular, I examine the evolution of the curvilinear Irene phase filfot cross with its fine land and grooves to the bold carving in San Marcos rectilinear stamped motifs.

Once the relevant attributes are described, the methodology for the analysis of the assemblages studied is explained (Chapter 4). Chapter 4 includes a discussion of the coding system used, how attributes were assessed and measured, and how the data are displayed in subsequent chapters.

The data for this research come from three Guale sites. The earliest pottery examined is from middle to late Irene phase (circa A.D. 1350–1580) components at the Meeting House Fields site on St. Catherines Island, Georgia. This assemblage provides baseline data from which to monitor the changes known to have occurred in the pottery in the succeeding Mission period. Criteria for the selection of this site for the research and the results of the analysis of the pottery from the site are presented in Chapter 5.

The next set of pottery collections comes from the Spanish buildings at the mission site of Santa Catalina, also on St. Catherines Island, Georgia (Chapter 6). At that site, pottery from pre-1597 contexts in the *convento* (the residence of the friars) are compared with both the Meeting House Fields materials and later postrebellion (1604–1680) context pottery at the mission to determine the rate of change in attributes from Irene to Altamaha pottery. Once that determination is made, pottery collections from the later contexts—a church, a kitchen, and the late convento—are examined to see whether pottery attributes are correlated with structure function. The determination of the extent to which these "contexts of use" are associated with distinct assemblages of form or decoration is crucial to an understanding of the change in Guale pottery as a whole.

Many of the Guale Indians associated with the Santa Catalina mission in Georgia (along with some other groups) were moved to Amelia Island, Florida, in 1684 (Worth 1995:194). Mission Santa Catalina was reestablished on that island and remained inhabited until 1702 when it was attacked and burned by British forces from South Carolina. Analysis of the pottery from three contexts—a possible kitchen, the convento, and the church of the Santa Catalina mission on Amelia—are analyzed in the same way as the material from St. Catherines Island (Chapter 7). Finally, the assemblages from the Georgia and Florida incarnations of Santa Catalina are compared. Results of this analysis provide the first detailed study of the differences between Altamaha and San Marcos pottery. The Amelia Island materials can also be used to address the question of changes in pottery assemblages consequent to population nucleation.

It is unfortunate that few pottery collections from Mission period aboriginal village contexts are available because these would be the most appropriate contexts to compare with the village refuse of the Irene phase site. The pueblo associated with the Santa Catalina mission on St. Catherines Island has been tested with a mechanical auger, but the ceramic analysis has not been published. The Wamassee Head site, immediately southeast of the mission compound, was tested by Lewis Larson in 1959 and by the American Museum of Natural History in 1980 (Thomas 1987:105, 113). Altamaha phase pottery from Larson's excavations was analyzed by Brewer (1985). Her findings are incorporated into this discussion. The village presumably associated with the Santa Catalina mission on Amelia Island (but possibly associated with the earlier Yamassee Indian mission of Santa María) was tested in 1971, and the pottery recovered was reported (Hemmings and Deagan 1973). Although their methodology differed from that used at the mission and their analysis was not as detailed, Hemmings and Deagan had some results that can be compared with those from the mission compound (see Chapter 7).

Taken together, these assemblages provide geographical, temporal, and contextual control over attribute changes in Guale Indian pottery. In contrast to many other cases of aboriginal pottery in colonial contexts (reviewed below), there were conspicuous changes in Guale Indian pottery after contact. The thrust of this work, facilitated by the series of tightly dated components, was to determine the timing and rate of these changes and to correlate them with other changes in Guale culture during the Mission period.

Before examining the specific archaeological contexts used in this analysis, I reviewed past approaches to the understanding of pottery change. The review underscores the fact that pottery production and use are embedded in the technological, sociological, and ideological subsystems of a society but that no single medium can be expected to "reflect" directly any of these subsystems in all situations (see Arnold 1985; Hodder 1982).

General Theories of Pottery Change

Some researchers have argued that there is a conservative pragmatism in traditional potters that precludes much dramatic change in their wares (Foster 1960; cf. Rice 1987:460). Nevertheless, over time, pottery does change, and as one of the primary sources of data in the archaeological record, it is incumbent upon us to explain under what circumstances changes occur. Certainly, change does not appear to affect pottery uniformly through time or space. Instead, as Binford (1962) suggested some time ago (alluding to material culture in general), process(es) of change are dependent on the way an item functioned in society—as a technomic, sociotechnic, or ideotechnic artifact or in some combination of these subclasses. Changes in technomic, utilitarian artifacts can be related to environmental variables; sociotechnic artifact change can be correlated with change in the structural aspects of society, and ideotechnic artifacts respond to ideological or cosmological aspects. Binford noted that style crosscuts all three subclasses and, anticipating Wobst (1977), observed that style *functions* to provide "a symbolically diverse yet pervasive artifactual environment promoting group solidarity and serving as a basis for group awareness and identity. This pansystemic set of symbols is the milieu of enculturation and a basis for the recognition of social distinctiveness" (Binford 1962:25). Binford related change in stylistic attributes to "changes in the structure of sociocultural systems either brought about through processes of *in situ* evolution, or by changes in the cultural environment to which local sociocultural systems are adapted" (Binford 1962:25). Although Binford did not discuss pottery change directly in this classic work on the "systemic approach," it can be noted here that pottery production and use incorporates technomic, sociotechnic, ideotechnic, and stylistic elements so that the entire adaptive milieu must be considered when approaching pottery change.

Kubler (1961:15) used a somewhat similar "systemic approach" when he retrodicted that in Spanish colonial contexts in Latin America, the utility of any particular native behavior was "closely linked" with its survival. Consequently, religious beliefs and the art symbolizing their expression were particularly vulnerable to rapid extermination. Although Kubler's explanation was uninformed by more recent research into the functional uses of style, he (Kubler 1961:34) nevertheless offered a viable and testable hypothesis for the survival of material culture in conquest situations:

> In respect to colonial action, differing graduated scales can be suggested for the survival of various items in the cultural repertory. The scales vary according to the magnitude of the intrusion. Most likely to weather a great displacement in the hands of a few stragglers would be useful plants and animals (index 5). Useful crafts would be next most likely to attain perpetuation if any one survived (index 4). Then, useful symbolic knowledge such as language, explanatory myths or animalistic accounts (index 3). Aesthetic symbols would come next, in the arts of time and space (index 2). Religious beliefs: the accounting of the unknown in nature and in perception would have the lowest value (index 1).

Thus, in Kubler's approach, pottery should survive, but the aesthetic symbols or religious iconography used as decoration would be unstable. Kubler's addendum, that the order of abandonment is reversed when considering the acquisition of traits by subjugated populations (so that religion is the first to be adopted) has been disproved (see, for example, Spicer 1961).

Other factors that might figure in the retention or abandonment of pottery types and/or attributes have also been explored. For instance, in his cross-cultural examination of the causes of stability and change in pottery production, Nicklin (1971; see also Arnold 1985) stressed the cultural context of pottery production. Pottery is less likely to change if the context was production for use on a seasonal basis than if production was stimulated by market demands, though under certain circumstances the market may also contribute to conservatism. Population pressure (Arnold 1985; Rice 1984) and depopulation (Rice 1984) can force changes in the mode of production and in stylistic aspects of pottery. In one of the more comprehensive treatises on change, Rice (1984) isolated seven major factors—resources, efficiency, diet, ritual behavior, value systems, status of potters and organization of production, and market demand—each with separate variables that might influence stability or change in ware characteristics.

In the last decade or so, there has been little emphasis on the description and explication of pottery change in the literature. A 1992 review of archaeological research on style (Hegmon 1992) does not even mention change. This situation may have resulted from the ascendancy of the postprocessualists and their emphasis on the more static problem of the meaning and uses of style rather than stylistic change. Although some works by postprocessualists have discussed changes in symbolic meaning through time (e.g., Emerson 1997), such studies tend to be highly particularistic; only the cultural evolutionists have continued to formally discuss and describe change in material culture attributes at the level of high- and middle-range theory (Braun 1995; Durham 1990; Hill 1985; Maschner 1996; but see Plog 1995). Thus, in Carr and Neitzel's (1995:9; also see Carr 1995a, 1995b) exhaustive, hierarchical "unification" of the multiple approaches to style, selectionist theory, coupled with concepts and vocabulary provided by processualism, provides the "umbrella framework for integrating many processes that determine material style and its change or stability over time. These processes include natural selection, cultural selective processes that do not involve choice, and cultural selective processes that do involve choice." However, in analyzing a single instance of change, Carr and Neitzel (1995:10) note that explication must consider: (1) the phenomenological level of explanation (ecosystem, society and culture, and/or the individual, each of which has different factors that affect style), and (2) four logical types of causal factors: (a) dynamic processes; (b) constraints and conditions that define, promote, or discourage these processes; (c) the local history that triggers the processes; and (d) the regulating structures that permit the survival of the system by controlling processes.

The interplay of many of these causal factors is apparent in the results of previous research of pottery change in Spanish colonial contexts. Although few studies have the unified rigor of Carr's (1995a, 1995b) research design, in a number of instances, researches have alluded to some, though never all, of both the phenomenological level of explanation and the four causal factors.

Pottery Change in Spanish Colonial Contexts

Conventional wisdom has it that the change from Irene phase pottery to that of the Altamaha and St. Augustine (San Marcos pottery) phases reflected the simplification or "deculturation" (*sensu* Smith 1987) of the

Guale brought about by the ravages of epidemic disease and other de-structive consequences of Spanish colonization. This "deculturation" could have resulted from many of the social changes wrought in the colonial milieu. Theoretically, the transmission of both the technology of pottery manufacture *and* design style and content could have been interrupted by population loss and/or changes in marriage patterns and residence rules (Deagan 1985:295; see also Hann 1988:245–246 for changes in Apalachee pottery). Simplification in design execution might also be linked with increased labor demands on Native Americans in mission contexts. Finally, Hann (1988:246; see also Willey 1982:489) noted "a decline in the aesthetic quality of mission-era pottery, but . . . it was expected because this feature was intimately linked with aboriginal tribal lore and religion."

The fact that any or all of these factors produced an entirely different pottery type out of the late pre-Columbian Irene phase pottery makes the case of Guale pottery one of a few demonstrable examples of ceramic change correlating with historic change. Indeed, in contrast to Binford's expectation that change in stylistic attributes would be directly related to changes in the cultural environment, many researchers (e.g., Charlton 1968; Cusick 1989; Tschopik 1950) studying historically known groups of Native Americans in Spanish colonial contexts found only minor changes in tradi-tional pottery manufacture and decoration (except where the indigenous population died out altogether and the pottery disappeared completely; see, for example, Smith 1986). Studies in other historical contexts, for instance Adams's (1979) analysis of African pottery, have also failed to correlate ceramic change with known tumultuous events, casting doubt on the ability of archaeology to perceive social change on the basis of changes in material culture.

Two studies of pottery change in the context of Spanish-Amerindian contact have been particularly influential. Despite severe depopulation for both the Aymara (Tshopik 1950) and the Aztec (Charlton 1968), pottery change appeared limited to a decrease in the frequency of burnishing for both groups, the addition of infrequent colono-ware forms for the Aymara, and the loss of a ceramic type for the Aztec. As Rice (1984:270) noted when discussing these works, in both areas pottery factories were established and Native Americans began to produce wheel-thrown, kiln-fired glazed wares for Spanish consumption. Because the Spanish did not rely on native wares for their own use, Spanish influence on these wares was negligible. More recently, however, Charleton and Fournier (1993) have described a process of ceramic change in urban and, to a lesser extent, rural areas of central Mexico. The introduction of Spanish ceramics was followed by the stimulation and elaboration of native ceramics with borrowing of selected Spanish attributes. Ultimately, "the indigenous ceramic tradition became less complex and converged with a Hispanic ceramic tradition that was also less complex and variable than that in the Iberian Peninsula" (Charleton and Fournier 1993:211). In the Aymara area, however, Chucuito pottery (the pre-Columbian type) continued to be used by the Aymara and by mestizos. Tshopik (1950:206) added that in the case of the mestizo "aristocracy," the use of native utilitarian wares was restricted to the kitchen, whereas serving wares were imported glazed wares and glassware. A remarkably similar dichotomy existed in the mestizo households of St. Augustine (Deagan 1983, 1988; and see below).

Evidence of significant change in Native American pottery in Spanish colonial contexts is also available from the Caribbean. Cusick (1989:33–34; see also Deagan 1988) has summarized what is known about changes in Taino pottery after contact: "In contrast to what was noted in the cases of the Aymara and Aztec, pottery making among the Taino undergoes rapid changes immediately after conquest, changes which include not only the introduction of new methods of making pottery, but the modification or disappearance of native potting traditions."

Garcia-Arevalo (1990, following Foster 1960; see also Deagan 1983) characterized changes in Taino pottery in terms similar to those used by Charleton and Fournier for central Mexico. He distinguished two "phases" of change in post-contact Taino pottery: the contact phase, a period of informal control of the conquest culture over the recipient culture, and the conquest phase, during which control became more formal and change more directed by the conquest culture. In the initial contact phase, the Taino were stimulated to copy Spanish earthenware forms, sometimes producing aberrant forms different from either Taino or Spanish precedents (Garcia-Arevalo 1990:278). During the later conquest phase (circa 1515–1530), Taino pottery "again changed dramatically, marked by artistic impoverishment, and the disappearance of the richly symbolic iconographic traits that characterized Antillean pottery in precontact times. This loss can be explained by Spanish hostility toward elements that were inspired by Taino magico-religious belief and mythology, and that were contrary to the goals of Catholic evangelization" (Garcia-Arevalo 1990:278).

Because the pottery studied by Garcia-Arevalo came from Spanish as opposed to Indian towns, the pottery was hypothesized to have had a utilitarian function only and to have been adapted to Spanish culinary needs. Vessels were thicker, and, owing to changes in cooking techniques and fuels and the introduction of new foods, vessels were more heavily sooted (Garcia-Arevalo 1978). The pottery also had simpler surface finishes. Because of the aforementioned loss of ritual and artistic functions, vessel surfaces were most often left plain, lacking the elaborate incising and punctation, adornos, and handles of the pre-Columbian pottery.

Similar results were reported by Smith (1986) for Puerto Real in Haiti. At that Spanish town (1503–1580), pre-Columbian aboriginal wares were replaced first by plain wares and then by a type of colono-ware, designated Christophe Plain, purportedly made by African peoples brought to Hispaniola as slaves. Other instances of simplification in response to contact or conquest have also been noted in contexts as widely separated as Venezuela (Deagan 1985) and North Dakota (Deetz 1965).

Cusick (1989:34–35) suggested that the relative rapidity of social change might account for the co-occurrence of societal and ceramic change in the Caribbean as opposed to other areas. As Cusick noted, however, all the Caribbean assemblages studied and discussed above come from Spanish towns. In contrast, changes in the pottery studied by Cusick from the aboriginal town of En Bas Saline in Haiti were subtle indeed, consisting solely of a decline in the thoroughness of burnishing and a shift from carinated to unrestricted bowls (Cusick 1989:178). No aberrant forms appeared at En Bas Saline; the town ceased to exist by 1520.

Cusick's study indicates that there may be a difference in pottery changes and/or in the rates of change depending on whether aboriginal pottery was produced for Spanish use (or for Native American women in Spanish households), as is likely in the context of Spanish towns in the Caribbean, or whether it was produced for native use.[2] This point is relevant to the case of Spanish missions of the Southeast, in which, *presumably*, Native Americans affiliated with a mission supplied its friars with pottery. To date, however, with the exception of frequencies of colono-wares, there have been no observed differences in Altamaha or San Marcos pottery in, for example, St. Augustine versus mission sites versus aboriginal habitation sites; this question has never been formally studied.

Nowhere were the demographic consequences of Spanish colonization as severe as in Hispaniola, where the native population was wiped out by 1520. Demographic collapse is demonstrated in the abandonment of native towns such as En Bas Saline and the appearance of African-influenced "colono-wares" in Spanish towns such as Puerto Real. Although vitiated to a certain extent by geographic and historical circumstances (Deagan 1988:198–199), demographic decline was also quite severe in northeast Florida (Deagan 1990b; Dobyns 1983; Hann 1986a). Unlike in the Caribbean, however, the Spanish in *La Florida* could draw on a large, interior population reservoir, and they actively encouraged immigration into Timucua by converted Guale and unconverted Yamassee (Worth 1995:18–20).[3] The arrival of these peoples, whose pre-Columbian and Mission period pottery was so distinct from Timucuan wares, is evident in Timucua by 1650. By 1700, the frequency of the San Marcos pottery in St. Augustine was three times that of the Timucuan St. Johns pottery, perhaps reflecting the demise of the latter group (Deagan 1990b:306). After 1711, other Indian groups, such as the Apalachee, Jororo, Costa, Western Timucua, and South Florida Indians sought refuge in St. Augustine (Deagan 1990b:306). Although one might expect increasing heterogeneity in the pottery assemblages of St. Augustine after 1711, in fact San Marcos wares continued to increase in frequency in domestic sites in St. Augustine throughout the First Spanish period, whereas the frequency of "other" pottery (non-Timucuan, non-Guale) remained virtually unchanged (Deagan 1990b:307).

Furthermore, according to Deagan (1990b:307), Guale pottery was unaltered by Spanish colonization. She noted: "One of the most interesting features of the Indian pottery found in the Spanish sites is that the great majority of it is unmodified from its traditional forms—neither shape nor decoration show European influence in most cases. This is an important observation, because it demonstrates, first, that traditional Amerindian crafts persisted in a largely unaltered form through the entire colonial period, and, second, that there did not appear to be any serious directed effort on the part of the Spaniards to influence change in favor of Spanish tastes."[4]

Deagan's analysis considered only change within the San Marcos type. If one takes the long view and considers San Marcos the derivative of Irene phase wares, changes are more apparent. As will be demonstrated in the following chapters, a bolder, rectilinear stamped design replaced a fine land and groove curvilinear one, and there were changes in rim form and treatment. New, or at least reemphasized, finishing techniques and new forms were incorporated into pottery assemblages used by both the Spanish and the Native Americans. Once established, however, the San Marcos type appears to have been extremely stable through many social perturbations, disappearing only with the removal of the Spanish-allied Indians to Cuba at the end of the First Spanish period. Thus, the situation in the Spanish towns of *La Florida* contrasts markedly with that in the Caribbean. In the Caribbean, urban settings resulted in dramatic change in native pottery production, whereas in Florida the urban setting in St. Augustine appears to have maintained or even fostered stability in aboriginal pottery.

Nevertheless, it is inaccurate to characterize pottery change in *La Florida* as monolithic. Different contexts of use produced very different assemblages. For instance, although no adequate comparison between assemblages of San Marcos pottery from mission contexts and St. Augustine exists, it is generally believed that San Marcos pottery exhibited more formal change at missions (e.g., Deagan 1990a:239, 1990b:308). In those relatively remote outposts, poverty and isolation made Spanish tablewares difficult to acquire. Native Americans may have been required to produce most of the pottery suitable for Spanish serving dishes and perhaps even some required for Catholic services.

In contrast, in St. Augustine the high incidence of Guale female–Spanish male intermarriage (Deagan 1990b) created a situation (similar to that in the Peruvian highlands) in which traditional utilitarian wares continued to be produced and used by Guale women, whereas serving dishes and tablewares, more visible status objects, were European (Deagan 1983; 1988). Indeed, zooarchaeological studies have shown that the typical diet in St. Augustine incorporated much of the pre-Columbian native foodways (Deagan 1983; Reitz and Scarry 1985; Scarry and Reitz 1990). Another factor that may have contributed to stability in this urban setting is that Native American pottery, presumably San Marcos (based on census data and pottery type frequencies), was sold in the markets of St. Augustine (Bushnell 1994:115; K. Hoffman 1997:26). It is unclear what the basis of production for these market wares was, but what little information is available suggests that production was informal and on an individual, entrepreneurial basis. Whether standardization like that often seen in production-for-market contexts, or even simplification like that observed by Garcia-Arevalo for the Caribbean, resulted from the sale of San Marcos wares in St. Augustine (and elsewhere?) remains to be studied.

Further evidence that different contexts will produce dramatically different assemblages is available in K. Hoffman's (1990:127–130) study of the pottery assemblage from the Convento de San Francisco, the province house of the Franciscan order in St. Augustine. In a series of discrete contexts dated between 1588 and 1702, Hoffman demonstrated that the frequency of "nonlocal" wares eclipsed that of both St. Johns and San

Marcos wares by 1702. Hoffman attributed the increase in nonlocal wares to the collapse of the mission system and the consolidation of peoples in St. Augustine. This collapse, however, was almost invisible in the domestic contexts of urban St. Augustine. In addition, and in contrast to remote mission sites, colono-ware forms were quite rare at the Convento de San Francisco. This was most likely because Spanish majolicas were relatively abundant (constituting 12 to 13 percent of all ceramics) throughout the time periods analyzed. It appears that the province house was well supplied with elite wares and had little need to supplement European serving vessels with colono-wares.

The foregoing summary indicates that the study of pottery change is complex and multifaceted. The perspective from *La Florida* is that one of the more crucial controls for an understanding of change will be contexts of use, where *contexts* can be defined at a scale as large as the socioeconomic system and as small as an activity area within a site. A comparison of the assemblages from a mestizo household, a mission convento, and the province house, for instance, might be very different because individuals in each context had differential access to the "world cultural system" (South 1988, 1990). Structure function or activity area within institutional compounds should also determine to a large extent the composition of the assemblage—one would expect a mission church to have a different assemblage than a mission kitchen.

South (e.g., 1977) has long sought pattern recognition in artifact assemblages to determine structure function and ethnic/class identity; here known functions and/or occupants are used to explicate differences in pottery assemblages. In addition, the notion of contexts of use owes much to Binford's (1962) formulation of technomic, sociotechnic, and ideotechnic functions of material culture; majolicas, colono-ware plates, and Guale Indian cooking jars function differently in the system, as do the designs on their surfaces.

With these ideas in mind, it is useful to review the contexts of pottery use and manufacture among the Guale described above. The following archaeological and ethnohistorical summary of the pre-Columbian and Mission period Guale emphasizes factors that would affect ceramic ecology and technological, formal, and stylistic attributes of pottery produced by a society under continuous stress to adapt to changing infrastructural, structural, and ideological circumstances.

2

Archaeological and Ethnohistoric Perspectives on the Guale Indians

Primary accounts of the contact period Guale are few but informative. The most useful documents are those of the French expeditions along the coast—those captained by Jean Ribault in 1562 and by René Laudonnière in 1564 (see below). These works, in combination with later sources, have been used to produce a fairly extensive literature on Guale ethnohistory (e.g., Bushnell 1994; Crook 1978, 1986; Jones 1978; Larson 1978, 1980a; Milanich 1999; Saunders 2000a; Thomas 1987, 1993; Worth 1995). In addition, there are a few synthetic treatments on the archaeology of Irene phase site settlement and subsistence patterns that can be used in conjunction with early documents to provide a tentative reconstruction of prehistoric and contact period lifeways (Crook 1986; DePratter and Howard 1980; Larson 1978, 1980a; Pearson 1978, 1980).

Pre-Columbian Settlement and Society

Much about late Prehistoric and Historic period lifeways of the Guale is still under debate, including such basic information as diet and health. The reconstruction presented below is likely to change in some details, but it represents the consensus, or lack thereof, at present.

The Guale Coast

Archaeological evidence indicates that Irene phase sites were confined to a narrow coastal strip of maritime live oak forest on the barrier islands and adjacent mainland in Georgia north of the Altamaha River (Figure 2.1). The interior pine barrens constrained settlement west toward the interior, though the interior boundary "was neither fixed nor inflexible," and "the Guale were in close contact with related peoples" (Jones 1978:186). As for the southern boundary, Pearson (1978:55; see also Smith 1984) noted that no Irene phase sites are reported south of the Altamaha River. Milanich (1986:61) also placed St. Simon's Island and the south side of the Altamaha River estuary outside the area of significant Guale habitation (cf. Crook 1986:42). Some evidence, however, indicates that Irene pottery was traded further south to contemporaneous Savannah phase peoples who used Irene pottery principally as a mortuary ware (Milanich 1986).

The southern boundary of Irene phase occupations corresponds to the linguistic and political boundary described as existing between the historic Guale and the Timucuan Mocama. "The Irene phase appears to be the archaeological equivalent of the historic Guale" (Pearson 1978:55). Despite increasing skepticism over the identification of ethnic groups with material culture (see, for example, Hegmon 1992:527), the equivalence of the distribution of Irene ceramics and the ethnohistorically described Guale is accepted by more recent researchers. Indeed, the other major social groups in *La Florida,* the Timucuan chiefdoms (Worth 1998a:2) and the Apalachee (Hann 1988), are also coextensive with distinct ceramic assemblages.

The northern boundary of Guale territory is under some dispute, as is the ethnic affiliation of the peoples in the Port Royal area. Some historians believe the boundary extended as far north as Edisto Island (Bushnell 1994:60; Jones 1978:186–187), thus including the Port Royal–area polities— the Orista and Escamacu—with the Guale. Others cite the Savannah River as the northern extent (Hann 1987:2–4) and align the Port Royal natives with interior tribes (Swanton 1946). Some archaeologists contend that the boundary changed through time. In this scenario, Irene peoples may have settled as far north as Edisto Island in the Irene I phase (A.D. 1300– 1450). However, after A.D. 1450, the northern boundary contracted and did not extend as far north as the Savannah River (Anderson 1989:119– 120; 1994:326; Braley 1990:99; Thomas 1993:41–42). Garrison's (personal communication, 1999) report of a structure on Skidaway Island dating to 1σ cal A.D. 1430–1495 may represent one of the latest Irene occupations in the area (see Chapter 5).

Sociopolitical Organization

Archaeological and ethnohistoric data indicate that Irene phase peoples were organized into complex chiefdoms. These regionally organized societies had at least two centralized, hierarchical decision-making levels that coordinated activities among village communities (Anderson 1994:7). At

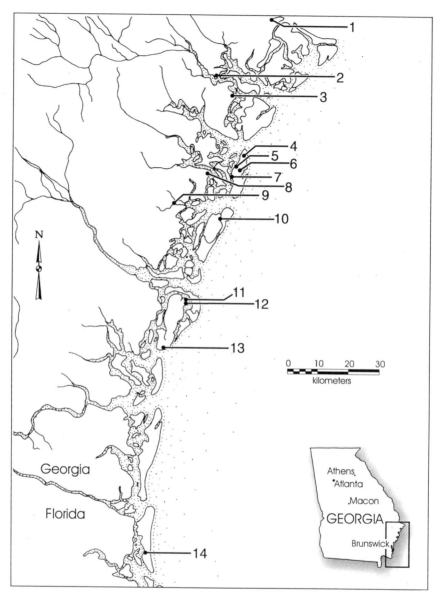

2.1. The Guale Coast with Irene Period Sites. Key: 1 = Irene; 2 = Seven Mile Bend; 3 = Red Bird Creek; 4 = Marys Mound; 5 = Meeting House Fields; 6 = Johns Mound; 7 = Santa Catalina, Georgia/Wamassee Head; 8 = Harris Neck Wildlife Refuge; 9 = Pine Harbor; 10 = Bourbon Field; 11 = Couper Field/Indian Field; 12 = Taylor Mound; 13 = Kent Mound; 14 = Santa Catalina, Florida.

the highest level, reigning at the largest, most elaborate mound complex (or council house—see below), was the paramount chief. This individual maintained control over other villages through lesser chiefs, many of whom may have been related to the paramount chief through the matriline. Jones (1978:200, 202–209) suggested a variation of this pattern for the Contact period, in which some Guale chiefdoms had two, coequal principal towns. Thus, along the northern coast, the Guale-Tolomato chiefdom was ruled by two coequal chiefs, one of whom resided in Guale and the other in Tolomato. Jones (1978) thought that dual chiefdoms also existed for Asao-Talaxe and Espogache-Tupiqui (Figure 2.2).

The Guale, like all other Southeastern tribes, were matrilineal; thus chiefly power was inherited from a mother's brother through her to her son. Paramount chiefs, and, to a lesser degree, lesser chiefs, were accorded a good deal of pomp and circumstance by their subjects, which served to reinforce traditional social ranking (Worth 1995:12). This was true of Southeastern chiefs in general (see, for example, Smith and Hally 1992) and is depicted in de Bry's engravings of Laudonnière's watercolors of the Timucuan peoples immediately south of the Guale (Alexander 1976). Chiefs, surrounded by an entourage, were carried on litters to important events. Men, and women as well (Worth 1998a:9), possessed badges of office that both signified and conferred power, and their subjects treated them with deference and devotion. Chiefs practiced polygyny, sometimes sororal polygyny. Researchers are divided over the extent to which polygyny was practiced by commoners. Jones (1978:202) believed it limited to "important leaders," whereas Larson (1978:125) thought it "popular and widespread." Chiefs were entitled to tribute—foodstuffs such as deer and organic and inorganic sumptuary items—that was passed up through the ranks and redistributed during ceremonial feasting presided over by the chief and, perhaps, a "sorcerer" (see Milanich and Sturtevant 1972:41).

The chief and other *principales* benefitted from the *sabana* system, as did the population in general:

> Once or twice a year the commoners of an Indian town prepared and planted two kinds of fields: individual fields for the cacique, the *principales,* the medicine man or woman, the interpreter, the ballplayers, and anyone else they saw fit to support, and one large communal field whose harvest would function as the town's reserve against famine, provide food for widows, orphans, and travelers, finance feasts, and ration those who were busy with construction

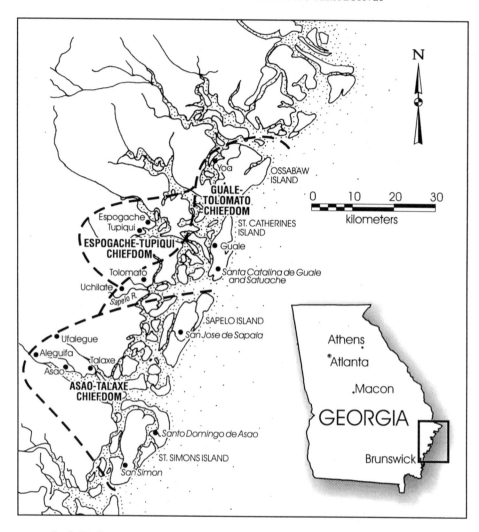

2.2. Dual Chiefdoms in Guale (from Jones 1978; by permission).

projects, long-distance trade, or military campaigns for the defense or the honor of the town (Bushnell 1994:111).

Although he commanded respect from the population, the chief shared decision-making power with the other principal men. According to Laudonnière (1975:14), "The men do nothing without assembling and counseling together thoroughly before arriving at a decision. They meet together every morning in the great public house where the king is and where he sits on a seat higher than all the others. . . . If there is business to transact, the king calls the priests and also the elders and asks their advice." The power of the chief, then, was mostly that of persuasion; alliances between chiefs were those of convenience. In fact, competition between chiefs, often resulting in small-scale warfare, appears to have been more common than alliance. The inability of most Native American chiefdoms to field any concerted resistance against the "European invasion" is a reflection of this competition and the self-interest that motivated most chiefs (Saunders 1998).

Despite the hierarchical social structure and the apparent food surplus, the Irene chiefdoms were neither as hierarchically organized nor as nucleated as their forebears in the preceding Savannah phase (Pearson 1980:179; cf. Crook 1986). Nor were they as involved in the politico-religious Southeastern Ceremonial Complex as their contemporary inland relatives (Cook and Pearson 1989:149).[1] In fact, except at the type site, Irene phase sites lack most late Mississippian traits, including platform mounds. Indeed, the Irene site platform mound (built predominantly during the Savannah phase) was abandoned in the early Irene phase in favor of a council house (Caldwell and McCann 1941); the latter suggests a more egalitarian social structure (Saunders 2000a).[2] The absence of Mississippian traits along the coast has been attributed to a lesser reliance on maize horticulture by these coastal peoples, either necessitated by poor soils (Larson 1978, 1980a; Pearson 1978:57) or afforded by abundant estuarine resources.

Settlement and Subsistence

The subsistence pattern of the Guale has been debated (Jones 1978; Saunders 2000b; Thomas 1987, 1993). Principally on the basis of correspondence of the early Jesuit priests in *La Florida,* Larson (1980a) and Crook (1978, 1986) proposed that the majority of the Guale engaged in a shifting seasonal subsistence and settlement pattern. In the early winter, matrilineages lived adjacent to the estuary where they exploited molluscs, estuarine fish, and deer. In the spring, when swidden plots had to be prepared, the population was more dispersed, and one or two nuclear families might work the same plot in the oak forest. Crook hypothesized subsistence stress at this time, when stored foods such as maize were becoming exhausted. Molluscan resources and estuarine fish were still exploited, however. In June, large schools of anadromous fish arrived, and by July the first harvest could be brought in. Matrilineages converged into strategically located, permanent town sites, where the chief and his retinue had remained throughout the year. Populations dispersed again in the fall to the oak forests where they subsisted on deer and the oak and hickory nuts that attracted them.

Jones (1978) has argued that this model of residential mobility is based on poor historiography. Jesuit letters to superiors in the Old World had to justify the failure to make any inroads into the "heathenism" in *La Florida*. According to Jones (1978:179), Guale horticulture was productive enough, in combination with other resources, "to account for the presence of permanent towns, a chiefdom level of social organization, temporary federations of chiefdoms under centralized leadership, and long distance trade networks." If the Indians retired to the woods in the winter, it was only to rid themselves of the Spanish. According to Jones, documents from sources other than disgruntled friars suggest bounteous harvests and year-round settlements of *dispersed towns*. Jones (1978:192) takes for his definition of these settlements a description by Sandford of Orista in 1666—ninety years after any effective Spanish control in that area: "The Towne is scituate on the side or rather in the skirts of a faire forrest, in which at several distances are diverse feilds of maiz with many little houses straglingly amongst them for the habitations of the particular families." Jones cites similar descriptions for Santa Elena, St. Catherines Island, and Fort George Island. Although these descriptions are relatively late, a dispersed settlement pattern was also suggested by Oviedo (1959 IV:326, 327) in his contemporary narrative of the ill-fated 1526 Ayllón expedition; in the area of Sapelo Sound, the Spanish saw only "a few scattered Indian houses, like rural farmsteads in Spain."

Archaeological sites recognized as late Irene occupations conform only partially to the ethnohistoric description. The Meeting House Fields site (Chapter 5), like most late Irene sites, is composed of discrete middens thought to represent the refuse from individual households. The middens are irregularly distributed but occur within a fairly confined area. There is no indication of horticultural activities among these middens, though there have been no studies specifically directed toward this question. Small, isolated sites, the possible manifestations of those "straggling" houses, are usually considered seasonal, special purpose extraction sites (see Pearson's model below). Indeed, dispersed occupation areas such as those described by Oviedo and Sandford would have very low archaeological visibility; few surveys have broad enough coverage yet fine enough data recovery methods to ferret out such occupations.

As might be expected for a chiefdom, sites appear to have been organized hierarchically. Pearson (1977b, 1979, 1980) identified sixty-one sites with Irene phase components on Ossabaw Island, just north of St. Catherines Island. These were clustered into four size classes. Pearson found that site size was correlated with environmental factors and postulated a settlement hierarchy (which has been criticized by Crook 1986:47–48). The single Class I site was large (140,000 square meters), had multiple burial mounds, contained pre–Irene phase components, and was correlated with advantageous environmental parameters (mixed oak-hardwood forest) (Pearson 1979, 1980, cf. 1977b). Pearson suggested that this site was a permanent, year-round settlement. Class II sites were more numerous (n = 7) and smaller (26,000–56,000 square meters), but still large with respect to the rest of the sites on the island. They generally did not have burial mounds and were sometimes found in locations other than the most environmentally advantageous. Pearson was reluctant to assign a function to these sites (1979:135), noting only that they made up the second level of the settlement hierarchy. Six of the Class III (n = 19; size range 6,600–18,000 square meters) sites had burial mounds, but the mounds were small—less than a meter in height. Pearson (1979:135–138) suggested that some of these sites might have been occupied seasonally to exploit a limited range of resources but that others, including all those with burial mounds, represented permanent settlement expansion into less advantageous resource areas. The smallest sites (n = 34; 1–5,000 square meters), Class IV sites, were considered seasonal extractive sites. Pearson's site hierarchy has some similarities with Crook's model; however, more sedentism is suggested by Pearson's archaeological data than is found in Crook's ethnohistoric reconstruction.

Because the ethnohistoric record is biased and internally inconsistent (Saunders 2000a), the argument over late prehistoric and contact period subsistence must be resolved with zooarchaeological studies of site seasonality and subsistence patterns and with human skeletal studies, including stable isotope analysis. Only two seasonality and subsistence studies based on fine-screened samples have been done on Irene phase sites (Braley et al. 1986; Russo 1991).[3] Vertebrate and invertebrate data from the pre-Columbian component at the Harris Neck site indicated year-round occupation (Braley et al. 1986:119); invertebrate data from the Meeting House Fields site also indicated year-round occupation. Meeting House Fields is a large site (more than 71,400 square meters) and may represent a Class II site in Pearson's settlement model (no mounds have been associated with the site; see Chapter 5) or the permanent town sites of Crook's model. Both site size and mound association are more problematic for the multicomponent, somewhat disturbed Harris Neck site (Braley et al. 1986:25–26, 53–61).[4] Seasonality for the full range of site types remains to be tested.

As far as the degree of reliance on maize is concerned, paleobotanical remains suggest little maize consumption. Burned maize cobs and/or kernels are not common on Irene sites; pollen is poorly preserved in sandy, coastal soils. However, stable isotope analysis on two human skeletal remains from South End mound, an early Irene phase site on St. Catherines Island, suggest maize consumption at higher levels ($\delta^{13}C = -13.3$) than in samples from twelve burials from the preceding St. Catherines phase on the island ($\delta^{13}C = -14.2$).[5] This is in contrast to early Irene phase burials from the Irene site, which show a dramatic decline in maize consumption ($\delta^{13}C = -16.7$) prior to site abandonment (Hutchinson et al. 1998:Table 2). These data suggest that maize did contribute significantly to the coastal Guale diet. However, in order to resolve the issue of maize reliance, stable carbon isotope analysis on middle and late Irene phase skeletal samples from numerous contexts will be necessary.

Organization of Labor

According to Hudson (1976:259), two pairs of structural oppositions ruled the organization of labor in Southeastern societies: men as opposed to women, and a cold season as opposed to a warm season (see also, for example, Adair 1930:448). The division between the sexes was so complete that men and women were often seen as separate species; day-to-day activities kept men and women apart from each other (Hudson 1976:260). Europeans were appalled to report that women performed the bulk of the subsistence activities: "The little work that is done among the Indians is done by the poor Women, while the men are quite idle, or at most employed only in the Gentlemanly Diversions of Hunting and Fishing" (Byrd 1929, quoted in Silver 1990:44). Hudson (1976:267) stated: "The principal occupations of the men were hunting, the ball game, politics, war, and the ceremonies connected with the entire round of social life."

Laudonnière (1975:15) was not specific about the various roles of males and females in agriculture. Presumably referring to cultivation of the *sabana,* he noted, "When the land is to be sown, the king commands one of his men to assemble his subjects every day to labor, during which time the king causes the supply of the drink already mentioned [black drink] to be made for them." De Bry's engravings of Laudonnière's watercolors indicate men tilling soil and women doing the planting. Men likely also did the initial heavy clearing. Apparently, as in most swidden agriculture, little field maintenance was necessary after the initial sowing (Laudonnière 1975:15), but fields did have to be protected from animal predation.

Pottery Production and Use

Most important to this discussion, pottery making—from clay collection to firing—was done by the women (Swanton 1946).[6] Among the modern Catawba, who continue to make pottery very much like that found on archaeological sites associated with their ancestors, pottery is generally produced in the early spring to late fall (Arnold 1985:95, Table 3.2; Fewkes 1944). However, Fewkes (1944:72) noted that the weather did not impose a serious drawback to production throughout the year because, at least in modern times, vessels could be dried indoors. Vessel construction, not including the procurement of the clay and the preparation of the paste, took about two hours (Fewkes 1944:95). Firing took another four hours (Fewkes 1944:95), but the fact that several pots could be fired at once must be factored into that figure. Vessel forms included jars for cooking stews, brewing black drink, and storing food. Casuela-form bowls were used for toasting cassina leaves (Hann 1996:97) and for serving. Pottery sherds were reused as hones, which are particularly prevalent on Irene phase sites, and gaming disks.

Women executed the incised designs on pottery (Speck 1909; Swanton 1946); there is no mention in primary or secondary sources as to which sex might have carved the oblong to rectangular wooden paddles used to stamp vessels.[7] Given the broad range of their duties (Hudson 1976:258–269, 285, 295) and their involvement in all other aspects of pottery manufacture, women most likely carved the paddles unless the paddles had some other function unrelated to pottery decoration.

Some evidence suggests that pottery designs (or other attributes) may have been used to signal clan or tribal affiliation or some other level of social organization. Hally et al. (1990:133) noted that each identifiable chiefdom in the interior Southeast (for which adequate data were available) can be distinguished by the associated pottery assemblages at the phase level. For the historic Seminole, Weisman (1989:45; and see Sears 1959) suggested that the limited repertoire of simple rim decorations might correlate with the *huti,* the matrilocal unit formed by related women.

Of design in general, and pottery design in particular, Speck (1909:54) commented that, among the Catawba, "as regards the artistic expression of this tribe, it seems that, in general, special conventional decorations symbolizing concrete objects are confined to a few articles of clothing such as neckbands, sashes, hair ornaments, leggings, and carry-pouches. The whole field is permeated with a strong religious significance. Decorations of a like sort with a still more emphatic religious meaning are found on pottery, though rarely, as well as on other objects."

Implications

The degree of sedentism, residence rules, and the organization of labor all potentially affect pottery production (Arnold 1985). If the Guale did shift residences throughout the year, as Crook envisioned, pottery production would have been limited by climactic considerations and also might have to be scheduled for seasons in which all the resources necessary for pottery production were nearby (Arnold 1985:123). With canoes, though, the Guale were fairly mobile, and shifting residences probably did not affect pottery production to any great extent.

Plog (1980) has discussed the relationship between sedentism and pottery assemblages in Southwestern assemblages; his concepts can be extended to the Southeast. Thus, if the Guale occupied a series of different settlements throughout the year, emphasizing different resources at each, we might expect to find a different assemblage of vessel forms for seasonal sites having different functions and different food processing needs. In addition, because certain surface treatments and designs are often restricted to particular vessel forms (Arnold 1984; Friedrich 1970; M. Hardin 1984), seasonal settlements may have entirely different formal and/or decorative assemblages from one another. At present, Pearson's (1977b, 1979, 1980) study is the only research addressing this problem along the Guale coast. His data (Pearson 1979:127–131, cf. 1977b:105–119) indicated that pottery attributes did not correlate with site types, suggesting that possible biases like those enumerated above will not be a problem for Irene phase sites.

Sedentism is also related to specialization and trade. Full-time pottery production emerges only in the context of fully sedentary societies, both because scheduling conflicts are reduced and because demand is increased in more populous, sedentary societies (Arnold 1985). Specialization, particularly in the production of elite or ritual wares, might also stimulate or maintain trade networks. However, there is no evidence of specialization in pottery production among the pre-Columbian Guale. Braley (1990:101) has isolated one possible Irene phase mortuary ware, a small carinated jar, but in general, even in mortuary contexts, jars and bowls placed with burials are indistinguishable from village pottery. In fact, the presence of heavy sooting and broken rims on much of the pottery placed with individuals in the Kent Mound (Cook 1986) and Johns Mound (Larsen and Thomas 1982) suggests that it *was* village pottery (though such vessels may have been used for ceremonial feasting). The absence of specialization in pottery production is not indirect proof of shifting settlements, however. As Arnold (1985) has shown, specialization is correlated with sedentism, but sedentism does not invariably result in specialization.

In contrast to specialized production, which tends to result in standardization, trade in pottery may increase the heterogeneity of ceramic assemblages. There is little archaeological evidence for widespread importation or export of Guale utilitarian pottery per se, though it has been mentioned by Jones (1978:197). The amount of trade *involving* pottery (the contents of pots) has not been tested with any analysis of subtypical variation or paste characteristics. However, the interrelatedness of the chiefdoms, the probability that there was some system of tribute in pre-Columbian times, and evidence of informal networks in the documentary record suggest that it was frequent.

Residence rules and the organization of labor have been observed or hypothesized to affect design execution and transmission. The "social archaeologists" who struggled to find evidence of lineage and residence patterns in pottery design in the 1970s and early 1980s theorized that if pottery was made by women, residence was matrilocal (cf. Jones 1978:201–202), and pottery was constructed, decorated, and fired by women in a single social or residential unit (all of which may have been true for the Guale), then a relatively homogeneous assemblage should result because there is little opportunity for extra-local designs to appear (e.g., Deetz 1968; M. Hardin 1977; see review in Plog 1983). Irwin (1974:371) hypothesized a similar scenario for the interpretation of the distribution of paddle-stamped motifs in the Solomon Islands. Conversely, if residence is patrilocal, women would be "imported," along with construction techniques and design repertoires peculiar to her nuclear family or lineage. In this case, pottery attributes would be expected to be more heterogenous. Other results of early research into learning and interaction indicated that designs are more likely to be borrowed (and assemblages more heterogenous) in the context of ad hoc work groups than if women are engaged in pottery production alone or only with members of their own lineage (Friedrich 1970; M. Hardin 1977). More recent studies (see review in Hegmon 1992:526–527) have found that learning contexts may not be good predictors, in and of themselves, of stylistic homogeneity. The degree of influence of the production context appears to be more strongly associated with the location of the design in the hierarchical analysis—whether designs are isochrestic, symbolic, or ideographic (*sensu* Plog 1995:372; Weissner 1985).[8]

The extent to which subsistence patterns, residence rules, the organization of labor, production specialization, and trade patterns were altered in the Mission period may help to explain the changes observed in Guale Indian pottery from the late pre-Columbian through the Mission period. These changes will be explored by way of a brief narrative of the historical developments along the Guale coast from contact through the end of the Mission period. This discussion is necessarily a synopsis; works referenced below contain more information on specific subjects.

The Guale and European Colonization

The Guale of the northern and central Georgia coast were among the first Southeastern groups to come into contact with the Spanish and French colonists seeking "Chicora," a land "abounding in timber, vines, native olive trees, Indians, pearls, and at a distance inland, perhaps gold and silver" (Hoffman 1984:419). The slave raids sponsored by Lucas Vásquez de Ayllón and Juan Ortiz de Matienzo in the early 1520s did not directly affect the Guale; those raids were on their northern neighbors, the coastal Sioux (Hoffman 1984:420–421; Jones 1978:180). However, given the ease of coastal communication, the Guale were probably well informed about the intruders.

In 1526, Ayllón established the colony of San Miguel de Gualdape in the "land of Gualdape." The colony was probably on Sapelo Sound (Hoffman 1990; Saunders 2001; cf. Jones 1978:181), though over the years other researchers have argued for locations further north among the Siouan peoples (Swanton 1922) or as far south as the Altamaha River (Hann 1990b:9). Ayllón's 1526 expedition was ambitious. His complement consisted of six vessels and some six hundred men and women, including African American slaves and Dominican friars.[9] The endeavor was, however, short lived. The loss of one of the main cargo ships along with all of its cargo prior to the choice of a settlement location, internal rebellion, Ayllón's own death, and, perhaps, the chill of the Little Ice Age, resulted in the abandonment of the colony just two months after it was founded (Hoffman 1990).

Ayllón's people had little contact with Native Americans in the area. None were described in the reconnoitering of the Guale coast. In the aforementioned description of a dispersed settlement pattern in Oviedo, no inhabitants were seen. Oviedo (1959 III:629) and Garcilaso de la Vega (1993:65–66) give conflicting versions of a single, but apparently devastating, interaction on the part of the colonists. Some men, up to two hundred according to Garcilaso, abandoned the colony on the coast and took up residence at a pueblo "3 leagues inland." It is unclear how long the Spaniards resided there, but they eventually wore out their welcome and were slain. Colonists remaining at the coastal colony were subsequently attacked by this same group. According to Garcilaso, most of the colonists were killed or wounded, and this precipitated the abandonment of the colony. As noted, there are numerous discrepancies between Oviedo's and Garcilaso's accounts, not the least of which is whether Ayllón was alive at the time and when, precisely, in the short history of the colony these events transpired (Hoffman 1990:77). Nevertheless, some nugget of truth is probably lodged in the tale, and it indicates, as in earlier encounters along the Florida peninsula, that Native Americans were not afraid to deal harshly with these strange intruders. Other evidence of interaction includes the presence of axes, a jet rosary, and trade beads, presumably from San Miguel, at Cofitachequi, where they were seen by members of the de Soto expedition (Jones 1978:180; Smith 1968:240).

The year 1526 may also have marked the arrival of the first European epidemic along the Atlantic coast (Jones 1978:194; contra Dobyns 1983). The 1526 epidemic *may* have spread inland as far as Cofitachequi; disease was cited by the de Soto expedition as the reason for the abandonment of several villages around Cofitachequi by 1540 (Smith 1968:63). This narrative evidence of an early inland epidemic brought about by contact with the Ayllón colony has been cited by numerous authors (e.g., Jones 1978; Smith 1987) but questioned by DePratter (1994:215–217). A recent critical reevaluation of the possibility of epidemics introduced by the de Soto expedition (Ramenofsky and Galloway 1997) would also seem to indicate a high probability of disease transmission by the Ayllón expedition.

The consequences of the spread of Old World diseases through New World populations have been discussed by numerous modern researchers. Milner (1980), Dobyns (1983), Hann (1986a), Larsen (1994), Ramenofsky (1987), Smith (1987), Silver (1990), Galloway (1995), Johnson and Lehmann (1996), and Ramenofsy and Galloway (1997), to name a few, have all examined the evidence with respect to the Southeast. These researchers stress that "virgin soil" epidemics have the potential for a 60 to 90 percent mortality rate. These rates were once applied across the board for the Southeast. However, it now appears that epidemic disease was "a patchwork affair" (Larsen 1994:109). In particular, interior tribes that became less centralized in the late prehistoric, like those that became the Chickasaw (Johnson and Lehmann 1996) and the Choctaw (Galloway 1995), were not affected until long after contact (see also Larsen 1994:122–123). The Guale coastal settlement pattern, if dispersed, would mitigate against rapid disease transmission. However, the sociopolitical structure, from the daily meetings of the principal men to social events that brought the dispersed population together, would encourage the spread of diseases, as would the sharing of bowls and the dipping of drinks or food with contaminated utensils.

Other behaviors may also have contributed to the spread of disease. Like other Native Americans, the Guale likely adopted the pig as a food source—at Johns Mound on St. Catherines Island, an Altamaha phase burial intrusive into the mound was accompanied by the partial skeletal remains of a pig (Larsen and Thomas 1982:298). Swine are reservoirs for brucellosis, leptospirosis, trichinosis, anthrax, tuberculosis, and taeniasis/cysticercosis, and some of these diseases can be transmitted to deer and turkeys, which then also act as reservoirs (Ramenofsky and Galloway 1997:271, 273). These data suggest that populations along the southeastern Atlantic coast could have been reduced by 90 percent by the end of the sixteenth century (Ramenofsky 1987:171), that is, before effective missionization ever began. However, there is *no* archaeological evidence for this. The only hard evidence for epidemics in Guale outside of Mission cemeteries consists of mass graves in a mound at the Pine Harbor site (Cook 1980a:40–41); two of these could be dated with inclusive European artifacts to the late sixteenth or early seventeenth century. This site is discussed in more detail in Chapter 8.

Indeed, Guale societies appeared to be flourishing when the French attempted to settle in the 1560s. Jean Ribault established Charlesfort on Parris Island in Port Royal Sound, South Carolina, in May 1562. The fortification, inhabited by thirty men, survived two winters, largely through the beneficence of the natives of region, that is, the Orista, the Guale, and the Escamacu. These groups supplied the hapless French with corn, maize flour, and beans on several occasions—an important point when considering questions of aboriginal seasonality, sedentism, and food surpluses. The French abandoned the fort shortly before it was destroyed by the Spanish in the summer of 1564.

In spite of increasing resistance from the native inhabitants, the French and the Spanish continued to vie for control of the Guale coast (Hann 1986b; Ross 1923, 1924), attesting to the perceived importance of the area (Hoffman 1984, 1990). The Spanish eventually won nominal control of the territory with the establishment of St. Augustine in 1565 and Santa Elena in 1566. However, the French continued to trade with the Indians along the Savannah River into the early seventeenth century (Ross 1924), and

French and British pirates harassed Spanish mission settlements until the Guale coast was abandoned in 1684 (Worth 1995).

Missionization

The history of the missionization of *La Florida* has been recounted by numerous scholars (Bushnell 1994; Gannon 1965; Geiger 1937; Hann 1988, 1991; Matter 1972; Milanich 1995; Oré 1936; Sturtevant 1962; Worth 1995, 1998a, 1998b). Several watersheds in that history are important for this study of Guale social change and pottery production. The first missionaries to *La Florida* were the Jesuits, who disembarked in St. Augustine in 1567. The Jesuits failed to make any conversions, and the order retreated in 1570. The Franciscans who followed also had little success until after the turn of the century (Jones 1978:183). Indeed, the last quarter of the sixteenth century saw innumerable skirmishes between the Guale and Spanish colonists, including two organized revolts, one in 1576 and the other in 1597. Both revolts were followed by scorched-earth reprisals by the Spanish; the reprisals created famine and disease throughout the Guale coast. The 1597 Juanillo rebellion, which was fought, ostensibly, because Franciscan friars opposed the succession to chief of the polygynous Juanillo (Oré 1936), was one of but a few documented planned and cohesive attacks by a federation of chiefdoms in the history of *La Florida*. Thomas (1993:17) considered the revolt the climax of "27 years of nearly uninterrupted rebellion against excessive and repeated Spanish demands for food and continued military harassment." During the Juanillo rebellion, all of the Guale missions were destroyed and five of six Franciscan friars killed (Quinn 1979:73). The rebellion failed when twenty-six (Quinn 1979:73, cf. p. 72) Guale canoes containing four hundred men forged past their southern border into Mocama, where the insurgents were repulsed by natives at San Pedro de Mocama. Juanillo and his followers escaped and hid among relatives in the interior until 1601. At that time, exhausted by hunger and pestilence, a chief of Asao-Talaxe led a federation of other Guale chiefs in a successful attack on the leaders of the 1597 rebellion (Jones 1978:184) and turned them over to the Spanish. The failure of the revolts, the unprecedented (by aboriginal standards) harshness of the Spanish reprisals, and the toll of epidemic disease led to an ostensible capitulation on the part of the Guale. The ensuing years saw peace and the reestablishment of the missions on the Georgia coast (Figure 2.3).

When missionization began in *La Florida*, the Spanish had some forty years' experience in the conversion and "civilization" of the indigenous

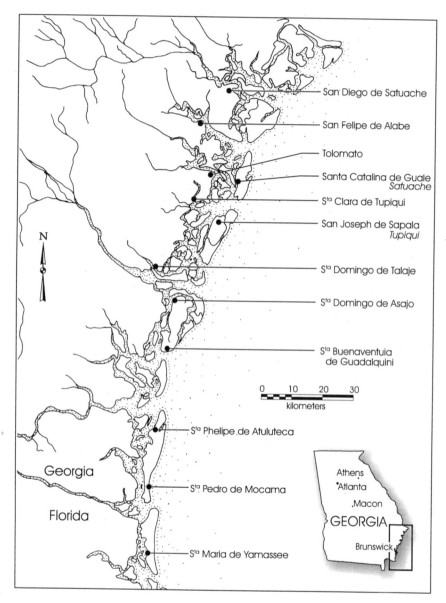

San Diego de Satuache

San Felipe de Alabe

Tolomato

Santa Catalina de Guale
Satuache

Sᵗᵃ Clara de Tupiqui

San Joseph de Sapala
Tupiqui

Sᵗᵃ Domingo de Talaje

Sᵗᵃ Domingo de Asajo

Sᵗᵃ Buenaventuia
de Guadalquini

N

0   10   20   30
kilometers

Sᵗᵃ Phelipe de Atuluteca

Georgia

Florida

Sᵗᵃ Pedro de Mocama

Sᵗᵃ Maria de Yamassee

Athens
•Atlanta
.Macon
GEORGIA
Brunswick

2.3. Compilation of Locations of Franciscan Missions in *La Florida* circa 1650–1700.

populations of the Caribbean and twenty to thirty years' experience in parts of Latin America. In *La Florida*, as elsewhere, pacification was to be accomplished by "reducing" the scattered populations to mission towns. However, because missions in *La Florida* were initially established in population centers, *reducción* may not have been necessary (Deagan 1985:303; Hann 1988:28; Saunders 1992). Still, the entire missionized population should have lived *"bajo campana,"* or "below the bell," no farther than half a league (approximately 2.75 kilometers/1.5 miles) from the mission bell tower (Bushell 1994:96). Whether most Guale actually abandoned their hypothetical dispersed settlement pattern to live permanently under the purview of the missions remains to be demonstrated with adequate survey data. In support of settlement changes, Larsen (1994:124–127) found a dramatic increase in periosteal reactions in Mission Santa Catalina as compared with prehistoric populations—an indication of population nucleation and "deplorable living conditions." Larsen (1994:140) also found evidence for increased sedentism in the mission population.

In return for the benefits of a Catholic education, settled life, and Spanish protection from enemies, neophytes were expected to spend much of their time laboring for the Spanish. For Native Americans throughout Spanish Florida, labor included not only the cultivation of crops that supported both the mission enterprise and the Spanish military and civilian populations but also the construction of mission buildings and secular structures and fortifications both at the missions and in St. Augustine. In the absence of decent roads and an adequate supply of draft animals, natives became beasts of burden. They were expected to transport goods from *ranchos* and missions as far away as Tallahassee to St. Augustine as well as from northern coastal missions along the coastal road to St. Augustine (Bushnell 1994:113–114; see also Larsen 1990:16–17). Increases in osteoarthritis and changes in bone shape may reflect the increased labor demands in Guale mission populations (Larsen 1994:128).

In Guale, as elsewhere, the friars co-opted the *sabana* system, requiring each village to plant an additional field to provide for the sustenance of the friars and to help cover the costs of maintenance and ornamentation of churches, including the purchase of those items they deemed necessary for a Catholic service (Bushnell 1994:111).[10] The Guale were also required to keep a ferry service running between the barrier island missions and St. Augustine; this method of transportation was preferred over the road mentioned above. The ferry service route included a ten- to twelve-league portage from the south bank of San Pablo Creek to the relocated town of Tolomato. The Guale were paid for this service. "In the late 17th century, the rental for a canoa to carry Indian corn from Amelia Island down to the haulover was 8 reales, plus the paddlers' rations and the wages of 1 real a day" (Bushnell 1994:113).

Despite documentary evidence of continued high mortality rates among the mission inhabitants and innumerable defections to the British (Bushnell 1994; Saunders 1998; Worth 1995, 1998b:134), the missions on the Georgia coast endured until the 1680s. The work force was supplemented by Yamassee immigrants. The Spanish, desperate for labor, encouraged this "multiethnic" group to settle in *La Florida,* even though they remained unconverted (Worth 1995). With the establishment of Charleston in 1670, however, the international rivalry over the Atlantic coast heated up once again. In 1680, the northernmost Spanish mission, Santa Catalina de Guale on St. Catherines Island, Georgia, was attacked by natives allied with the British. Subsequent events precipitated the Spanish withdrawal from the Georgia coast in 1684 (Worth 1995 and Bushnell 1994 give detailed accounts of this battle and the retreat of the mission system southward).

As Worth (1995:47) has discussed, the retreat involved population relocation and aggregation. Santa Catalina had been conjoined with a more northern mission, Satuache, around 1663. Together, these peoples evacuated southward to Sapelo Island in 1680. The Spanish burned the mission buildings of Santa Catalina before they left the island. On Sapelo, the Sápala mission had been combined with the Tupiqui mission around 1674. There were four groups, then, on Sapelo Island by 1681, but they maintained separate identities if not separate residences (Worth 1995:30). There was no respite for the Guale, however. The barrier island settlement was repeatedly harassed by pirates and was also in danger of British attack. By 1684, all Spanish personnel and their Indian allies or converts were moved south of the St. Marys River. Santa Catalina and Satuache were relocated to the abandoned Yamassee mission of Santa María on Amelia Island (see Chapter 7).

The Spanish hold over their converts became increasingly tenuous in the face of their failure to protect the natives, and the danger of British attack grew increasingly ominous. The attack came in 1702, when men led by Governor James Moore of South Carolina systematically destroyed each coastal mission on a drive to St. Augustine (Arnade 1959). Although Moore failed in his ultimate objective of ousting the Spanish from Florida, he succeeding in obliterating the mission system along the Atlantic coast. A few missions were reestablished around St. Augustine, including a reincarnation of Santa Catalina (Hann 1996:318), but these were dispirited survivals. There is no mention of Santa Catalina after 1726, though fifteen Guale were attached to the settlement of Tolomato in 1752. No Guale were recorded in the 1759 census (Hann 1996:324).

Conversion: Cause and Effect

The acceptance of Spanish sovereignty by the Guale can be seen as a conscious gambit on the part of the leadership to regulate power relations within and between native and colonial polities.[11] Indeed, at first the natives of *La Florida* did not consider political submission to include religious obedience. A number of polities "rendered obedience" but refused missions (Worth 1992:35). However, the Spanish would not negotiate trade with natives outside of the mission system. Apparently, access to trade goods, and especially the role that these goods played in elite sanctification, was a powerful motivation for caciques to accept the missionaries (Milanich 1994:295).[12]

Conversion, as opposed to acceptance, involved different processes. Axtell (1988a:51–52), alluding to native groups along the eastern seaboard under English control, considered conversion to Christianity as a revitalization movement of sorts: "The more desperate the Indians' social-cultural situation (as in seaboard Massachusetts), the greater the possibility of physical annihilation of the group and thus the greater the efficacy of life-giving conversion and revitalization, which Anthony Wallace [1966:30] defines simply as 'any conscious, organized effort by members of a society to construct a more satisfying culture.'" However, Axtell (1988a:54) believed that conversion occurred only when other avenues of resistance had failed: "But those tribes who could still put a piece of forest between themselves and the long arm of the invaders, those who escaped the worst of the maladies of European contact, had little need of the full 'civilized' cure offered by the Christian doctors." This prescription undoubtedly applied to many Guale. "The real history of the seventeenth-century Guale is actually not to be found on the island missions but rather in the interior pine forests to which they fled and regrouped. This movement was part of that wider consolidation which led to the Yamassee revolt of 1715, the last major expression of coastal southeastern rebellion against the European presence" (Jones 1978:208).

Those Guale who did accept missions in their midst saw major changes in the organization of their culture and society. Marriage patterns were affected to the extent that polygyny was exterminated. In addition, potential marriage partners were wiped out in epidemics, and some Guale Indian women became the wives or concubines of Spanish soldiers (Deagan 1990b). Residence patterns also changed, especially as populations were reduced by disease and as different mission populations were combined to maintain adequate personnel for a single mission (Hann 1986a).

Whatever the nature of the prehistoric subsistence and settlement system, there is no doubt that the Spanish friars redirected the system into more intensive horticulture. With the exception of the use of metal tools for clearing, the techniques of cultivation probably remained the same as in late prehistory (Silver 1990). However, the Spanish demand for cultivars necessitated changes in the organization of labor. Prior to contact, male involvement in cultivation was restricted to the heaviest clearing (Silver 1990). After contact, according to Bishop Calderón (Wenhold 1936:13), "in April they commence to sow, and as the man goes along opening the trench, the woman follows sowing." Females would have more fields to tend than before contact. The introduction of double-cropping (Deagan 1985:302) would have upset seasonal schedules for the procurement of other foodstuffs.

Other postcontact labor demands on Guale males included sending workers to St. Augustine for construction projects, running ferrys between the barrier islands, and transporting goods from mission outposts such as Santa Catalina to St. Augustine. Additional demands on women are not as clear in the documentary record. However, Bushnell (1981:99; see also 1994:112) states that a supply of sixty brewings of *cassina* (a tea drink made from *Ilex vomitoria*) a month for the garrison at Santa María was part of the responsibilities of the Indians at San Juan del Puerto on Cumberland Island; women would have done that brewing. No doubt women worked in the mission kitchens. Whatever contribution children had made to the pre-Columbian food quest was usurped: "The children, both male and female, go to the church on work days, to a religious school where they are taught by a teacher" (Wenhold 1936:14).

Increased demands on Guale labor may have resulted in changes in pottery production. Hypothetically, it might have been necessary to exploit clay resources closer to settlements, to reduce the time invested in clay preparation such as cleaning, or to simplify the finishing process, perhaps, as indicated in other research, by eliminating burnishing. There are no documents that discuss how the Spanish routinely acquired Native American wares, either in traditional or in colono-ware forms, in *La Florida*. Bushnell (1994:115) and K. Hoffman (1994:26) allude to earthenwares for sale in the markets of St. Augustine, but at present this appears to have been an informal, opportunistic affair. Presumably, Native American women produced most wares for their own use in mission villages or in Spanish towns. Some part-time specialization in pottery production might have been necessary to meet the demand for cooking vessels and colono-wares for unmarried colonists, soldiers, and friars, but this has not been demonstrated to date.

Carbon-isotope evidence from contemporary missions in the Southwest indicate that, though the Pueblo Indians were producing corn for the missions, their own corn consumption fell below that of the preceding period (Larsen 1994; Spielmann et al. 1990). Evidence from Santa Catalina in Georgia indicates that this was not the case for the Guale. Corn consumption increased over the Savannah phase, and exploitation of marine resources decreased (Schoeninger et al. 1990). These changes in subsistence practices might be reflected in differences in food preparation and serving vessels. Changes in group size and definition might also have changed vessel forms. The pre-Columbian pattern of a continuously cooking pot of food available all day long might also have been affected.

One consequence of population aggregation and the intensification of horticulture was the depletion of wood resources. Even prior to contact, aboriginal clearing practices and exploitation of fallen branches for firewood resulted in a "parklike" environ around native villages (Silver 1990:61). With increased clearing and demand for wood for building and firewood, forest resources may have become scarce. When Dunlop (1929:131) visited St. Catherines Island in 1687, he saw "much clear ground for 7 or 8 miles together," probably most of the arable land on the fourteen-thousand-acre island. Further evidence for the increased value of wood products might be seen in the fact that to gain admission to a church, each Indian was required to bring a log of wood to the house of the priest (Wenhold 1936:14). By 1655, the forests nearest to St. Augustine were too far away for timber to be carried to the city by Indian laborers (Rebolledo 1655, in Hann 1988:177). One of the main reasons the Indians gave to the *visitador*[13] in 1702 for not finishing the required stockade at Santa María was the lack of wood in the area. If wood did become scarce, pottery firing might have been affected.

Contact and missionization brought about population decline and the nucleation of disparate groups. Both processes may have affected pottery design. Loss of maternal relatives may have disrupted the transmission of design information between generations. As discussed in Chapter 1, colonial influences may initially result in formal and stylistic diversity in colono-wares, but population nucleation might also have brought about design simplification. In addition, with increased labor demands, the Guale may have lacked the time to produce painstakingly carved paddles and to incise elaborate designs; in other words, rescheduling of labor organization also could result in design simplification. However, if designs were religious in nature and the Spanish missionaries did produce profound changes in the aboriginal worldview, we might look for an abrupt change in the designs themselves.

Bishop Calderón apparently believed in the true conversion of the 13,152 Christian Indians he counted in *La Florida* in 1675: "As to their religion, they are not idolaters, and they embrace with devotion the mysteries of our holy faith" (Wenhold 1936:14). Modern researchers have been more skeptical (see Axtell 1988b for a review). Axtell (1988b:118–119), however, believed that those who insist that conversion was only "protective coloration" are wrong: "This assumption is misleading in three ways: (1) it is unwarrantedly reductionist and belied by countless historical examples, (2) it confuses the *social* functions of conversion for *groups* with its *emotional* and *intellectual* meaning for *individuals,* and (3) it confuses the *explanation* of conversion with the *validity* or *quality* of the result" (emphasis in original). Conversion, according to Axtell, was real.

Nevertheless, the extent to which the southeastern Indians accepted Catholicism cannot be answered satisfactorily with reference to contemporary documents because each European chronicler was biased by his own agenda. Primary documents written by Native Americans are rare, but those that do exist suggest that some of these individuals possessed a deep understanding of the faith. Certainly the most visible expressions of pre-Columbian Guale religious principles, burial mounds, disappeared. These typically contained primary flexed and secondary urn burials, often accompanied by shell beads and other artifacts. In mission cemeteries, unadorned primary supine burials became the norm. However, Father Pareja's *Confessionario* (Milanich and Sturtevant 1972) indicated that the friars had to be vigilant against religious recidivism. Is something as intangible as faith accessible to archaeology?

Several researchers have suggested that it is. Drawing on the contextual methodology of Hodder (1982, 1986) and initial applications by Braithwaite (1982), David et al. (1988) proposed a "semiotic" approach to the understanding of decoration of pottery. Their analysis went beyond the information theory, in which designs are understood to reinforce group cohesiveness. Rather, their research delved into the meaning of individual motifs. "While pottery may be invested with explicit messages, the decorative techniques, motifs, and designs also embody a potent implicit component that realizes the society's 'ultimate concern, its religious substance' " (David et al. 1988:379). According to David et al. (1988:378), the repetition of a small number of motifs arranged in a limited and rigidly organized set of designs in many artifact classes and physical contexts indicates that the motifs are "condensed symbols" expressive of underlying cosmological principles.

Although I am not convinced of David et al.'s assertion that all societies "assimilate" pots to people because the former is transformed by fire and the latter by enculturation, the case for particular meanings among specific peoples is plausible. Pauketat and Emerson (1991) have made convincing arguments for the meaning of Ramey Incised designs in agricultural rites of intensification. Emerson (1989:45–46) defended the practice of extracting the cultural meanings of symbolism at Cahokia as follows:

> The central problem in performing such a study is to define and use units of analysis that will allow us to deal with the realm of mental constructs—cosmology—on the basis of its material manifestations. From this perspective the problems are identical to those that archaeologists have in interpreting the rest of the artifact assemblage. The difference between the two realms of interpretation comes from the fact that traditionally it has been acceptable to make the leap from artifact to chronology, function, or definition of specific cultures. Archaeologists have been trained to accept the ambiguities in such transitions as inevitable and unobjectionable in their research. This is not the case with the transition from artifact to symbolism, except at a very superficial level.

This argument is comparable to those of Kosso (1991) and Patrik (1985), both of whom argued that there is little methodological difference between Binford's middle range theory and Hodder's contextual hermeneutics (see also VanPool and VanPool 1999).

It might well be impossible to understand meanings in cases where ethnography or an "indirect historic approach" is lacking or inapplicable (cf. Smith 1987:7–8). This is not the case for the Southeast. Using the contextual approach, it is possible to demonstrate that the basic cosmology of the southeastern Indians was represented in pottery motifs and that these continued to exist at least until the end of the Mission period. Evidence for these motifs is discussed in the next chapter.

Summary

Change in subsistence practices, rescheduling of native labor, nucleation of disparate populations, environmental depletion, and reorganization of the

Guale worldview probably all affected pottery production to some extent. Whether that effect is visible in sherds is testable. Such research entails the consideration of the three pottery assemblages associated with the Guale, which are described in the next chapter.

3

The Pottery of the Guale Indians,
A.D. 1300–1702

On the basis of stylistic differences and geographic location, Guale Indian pottery has been subdivided into three broad types. The earliest, Irene, is found in late Prehistoric and early Mission period sites; the type is restricted to coastal Georgia and South Carolina. As will be seen, Irene becomes Altamaha during the early Mission period. The dating and impetus for this is the principal focus of this research. In general, Altamaha wares are limited to Georgia (though see below). For historical reasons, virtually the same pottery is called San Marcos in Florida. Below, I will outline the attributes of the three types and present some ideas about the symbolism of the fundamental motif, the filfot cross.

Irene Pottery

Irene wares appeared along the Guale coast sometime between A.D. 1300 and 1350, depending on which researcher's chronology one uses (see below). Irene pottery, an areal variant of the Lamar ceramic tradition, was defined in 1941 by Caldwell and McCann during their work at the Savannah and early Irene phase Irene Mound site in Chatham County, Georgia. Caldwell and McCann recognized three Irene types: Irene Plain, Irene Incised, and Irene Filfot Stamped. As the definition implied, all stamped designs were a variant of the filfot cross (Figure 3.1). Incised designs consisted of a band of repeating or alternating motifs, most commonly the scroll and pendant concentric half circles (Figure 3.1). Plain, incised, and stamped vessels could also be decorated with applique pellets or nodes, particularly during the early Irene phase. All three types shared the same method of construction (coiling); temper was "invariably" grit or gravel (Caldwell and McCann 1941:47). Vessel forms consisted of jars, unrestricted or carinated bowls, and, occasionally, bottles (Braley et al. 1986:75; Caldwell and McCann 1941; Pearson 1984).

More recently, investigators have noted additional motifs occurring in some Irene phase sites. On the basis of work done at the Pine Harbor site, Larson (1984:68) suggested that Savannah Check Stamped was produced along with early Irene wares: "The quantity of Savannah Check Stamped in the midden argues that it was a ware that was contemporary with the Irene types." Check stamping has not been reported from most other coastal Irene sites, including Meeting House Fields.[1]

DePratter (1991; personal communication, 1999) noted a number of different rectilinear and curvilinear stamped motifs in late contexts along the Georgia coast. These included concentric circles, figure nines, crosses, line blocks, and others. This late profusion of other rectilinear and curvilinear stamped patterns is clearly postcontact, possibly dating to as late as circa 1600, and occurs with incised wares with Southeastern Ceremonial Complex symbolism.

After Irene was defined in 1941, there remained some confusion over whether Irene pottery was a Mission period or pre-Columbian phenomenon. Braley (1990) and Braley et al. (1986) give a synopsis of the argument. Even before the belated appearance of radiocarbon dates for the Irene phase (Braley 1990; Braley et al. 1986; DePratter 1984; Pearson 1984; Saunders and Russo 1988), however, the consensus was that Irene pottery originated before contact, developing out of the Savannah phase by about A.D. 1350 and terminating in the Altamaha phase by around A.D. 1550 (e.g., DePratter 1979; cf. Crook 1986:38, 1990:36). South and DePratter (1996:47), however, suggested that Irene filfot stamping possibly continued into their Altamaha phase (1575–1715) and was in use at the same time as more familiar Altamaha Simple Stamping and Line Block.

The Irene phase has usually been divided into an early (A.D. 1350–1450) and late (A.D. 1450–1550) component by the appearance of incising around A.D. 1450. Braley (1990) has refined the definition of the Irene phase, subsuming the Pine Harbor "complex" (discriminated by Larson 1955; 1978) into the Irene phase and subdividing Irene into three phases: Irene I (A.D. 1300–1350), Irene II (Pipemaker's Creek, A.D. 1350–1450), and Pine Harbor (A.D. 1450–1580). In this chronology, the first incising, which tended to be bold, appeared at the beginning of the Irene II phase. The Pine Harbor phase is contemporaneous with the relocation of the majority of the prehistoric Guale population south, away from the Savannah River to the Altamaha. The phase is discriminated on the basis of the appearance of the

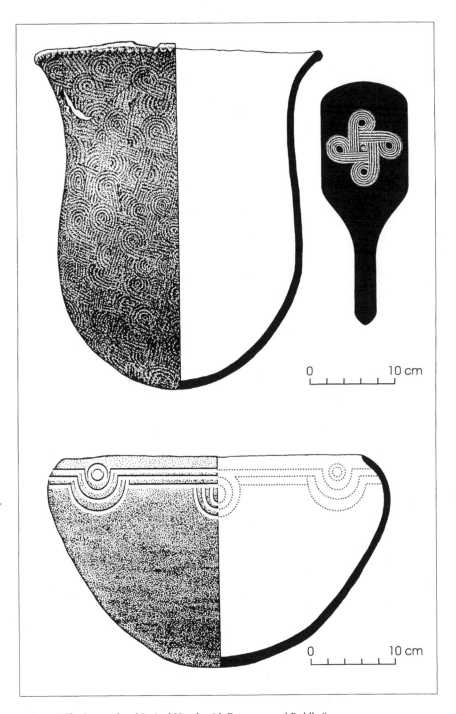

3.1. Irene Filfot Stamped and Incised Vessels with Reconstructed Paddle Stamp.

type McIntosh Incised after A.D. 1450. McIntosh Incised is fine-line incising of Southeastern Ceremonial Complex symbolism. In his chronology, then, Braley put the origin of the Irene phase somewhat earlier than other researchers and placed the incipience of incising one hundred years earlier.

The coastal ceramic sequence is usually seen as derived from interior Georgia, where incising is said to begin around A.D. 1450 (DePratter 1984; Hally and Rudolph 1986:63). According to Anderson and Joseph (1988:250), however, incising was present in very small amounts somewhat earlier, around A.D. 1350. These data suggest that incising could have begun earlier than A.D. 1450 on the coast. Pipemaker's Creek phase incising, then, should be associated with early rim treatments (described below), and indeed it was at the Irene site.

In addition to the appearance of incising, and the trend toward finer-lined incising, several other pottery attributes appear to be temporally sensitive. On the basis of materials from the Kent Mound on St. Simon's Island, Georgia, the Pine Harbor site, and the Irene Mound site, Cook (1980b:163) documented an increase in plain and incised wares through time at the expense of complicated stamping. Because this same trend was observed in the comparison of the pre-Columbian and Colonial period materials at Harris Neck (Braley et al. 1986), it appears as though it continues well into the Mission period.

Rim treatments also changed through time; the sequence on the coast is quite similar to that in the Lamar interior. Plain rims were the most prevalent type throughout the Irene phase. In addition to plain, the earliest rim treatments, also present on late Savannah wares, were composed of nodes—relatively large, circular to oval applique; rosettes—smaller circular applique pellets with cane punctations; and plain applique rim strips (Figure 3.2). Somewhat later, nodes, pellets, and plain rim strips disappeared, and segmented rim strips became the most popular treatment after unmodified rims. In addition, there were a variety of experimental treatments such as segmented and cane punctated rim strips. During the very late Irene phase, rim strips were most commonly segmented or cane punctated, and punctation directly on the vessel wall became common.

This progression has been demonstrated, with minor variations, in several studies. Pearson (1984) compared "incidental rim treatments" from three coastal Irene sites: the Irene Mound site (late Savannah–very early Irene; the Red Bird Creek site in Bryan County, Georgia (early Irene); and the Kent Mound site on St. Simon's Island (mid to late Irene). Pearson (1984:22) found that "plain rims occur in high frequency at all three sites

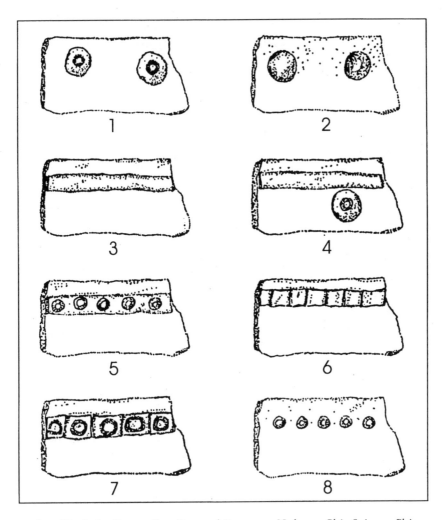

3.2. Irene Rim Styles. Key: 1 = Cane Punctated Rosette; 2 = Nodes; 3 = Plain Strip; 4 = Plain Strip with Cane Punctated Rosette; 5 = Cane Punctated Strip; 6 = Segmented Strip; 7 = Cane Punctated, Segmented Strip; 8 = Cane Decorated (from Pearson 1984; by permission).

and apparently were a popular treatment throughout the Irene phase. There is an increase in the use of appliqued rim strips, especially of segmented [punctated with a wide, blunt instrument] rim strips. The use of nodes as a rim decoration appears to decline through time."

On the basis of the data from the Kent Mound, Pearson believed the segmented strip was associated with an early to middle Irene phase occupation and that the cane punctated rim strip and cane punctations directly on the vessel wall were "associated with the very late part of the Irene phase, just before and up to historic contact" (Pearson 1984:22). However, Pearson's (1984:21, Figure 7) data indicated that the segmented rim strip continued to increase through time, becoming most common during the middle to late Irene when it constituted nearly 40 percent of the rim types, and that the cane punctated vessel was the second most common treatment at the Irene Mound site (early Irene). Pearson (1984:21, Figure 7) also indicated more standardization in rim treatment through time, with fewer kinds of treatments at the later Kent Mound than elsewhere.

At Kent Mound, an early through late Irene phase mound on St. Simons Island, Cook (1986:17; 1980b:165) found a progression of rim styles somewhat different from those described by Pearson. Cook noted an increase in the frequency of cane punctations that occurred during the middle Irene, with a concomitant decrease in segmentation of the strip, and an increase in the frequency of plain rims over time. Cook's (1986) comparison of the Kent Mound materials to those of the Seven Mile Bend Site in Bryan County, Georgia, confirmed this progression. Cook also noted (1986:19) that rim pellets or nodes have been recovered from contexts dating up to the last quarter of the sixteenth century, though they are rare.

It should be noted that both of these results are predicated on the assumption that there is no significant spatial variation in rim treatments at contemporaneous Irene sites. However, only the early Irene Red Bird Creek site has been radiocarbon dated (to the late Savannah phase), and relative chronologies have been based on rim treatments, so the question of spatial variation cannot be addressed with the data at hand.

Finally, on the basis of these studies, folded rims appeared some years after contact. Cook found no folded rims in the Kent Mound, but noted their presence in very late Pine Harbor site village and burial mound contexts. Cook (1986:19, 1980b:165) correlated their appearance with the Mission period[2] (cf. DePratter 1984). Folded rims do appear earlier in some interior Lamar tradition phases; most important for this discussion are those in the Duval (A.D. 1375–1450), Iron Horse (A.D. 1450–1520), and Dyar (1520–1580) phases along the Piedmont Oconee River (Smith and Williams 1990). In this area, rim folds progress from narrow to thicker folds through time. Because these are some of the phases out of which the traditional coastal sequence is believed to be derived, it might be expected that folded rims would occur as early as 1400 along the coast. All the evidence argues against this conclusion, however.

Irene pottery continued to be produced after contact. Terminal dates for the complex have been put at A.D. 1550 (DePratter 1984) and A.D. 1580 (Braley 1990). However, several dates from the Meeting House Fields site (Saunders and Russo 1988:Chapter 5) suggested that Irene pottery continued to be made with little modification into the seventeenth century (see also Caldwell and McCann 1941:73; Crook 1986:38; South and DePratter 1996). Indeed, some interior sites containing Irene pottery could represent the habitations of Guale fleeing colonial control and may also date to the seventeenth century. More research is needed to establish firm terminal dates for Irene wares. These dates ultimately may be shown to depend more on local histories than on regional events.

Altamaha Pottery

Altamaha pottery was originally described by Larson (1953). The temporal and typological relationship to Irene phase wares was acknowledged at the time the type was defined (Larson 1953, 1978:136). Braley et al. (1986) studied Altamaha phase pottery associated with Spanish artifacts at the Harris Neck Wildlife Refuge on Harris Neck Island. They stated (Braley et al. 1986:14): "The archaeological complex dating to the protohistoric period (ca. A.D. 1550–1680) shows the direct outgrowth from the prehistoric Irene/Pine Harbor culture. Altamaha . . . ceramics are very similar to the earlier Irene . . . wares but the design elements of the complicated stamping became more simplified, and fine-line incising became more widespread (Snow 1977; Cook 1980). Curvilinear complicated stamping was replaced by line-block stamping, check stamping returned, and some vessels were painted with red slip." In addition, paddle designs were carved with bolder and deeper lands and grooves (see Chapter 6). There was also a shift from the use of cane decorated vessels, segmented strips, and cane punctated strips in the late pre-Columbian period to an emphasis on cane punctated folded rims in the Colonial period (Braley et al. 1986:137).

Despite the changes in design execution, the principal motif remained the same as in the Irene phase. Brewer (1985:24) determined that all identifiable complicated stamped designs at the Wamassee Head site on St. Catherines Island (the aboriginal component of the Mission Santa Catalina) consisted of "four blocks of parallel lines arranged at right angles to one another around a central node" (Figure 3.3). This design was essentially a filfot cross composed of straight lines rather than scrolls.[3] Brewer termed the motif "San Marcos Complicated Stamped." The motif is also visible on sherds from colonial contexts at Harris Neck (Braley et al.

1986:82, Figure 30) and on sherds from St. Augustine (e.g., Otto and Lewis 1974:100, Plate 1).

Vessel forms from Wamassee Head consisted of small and large globular jars, unrestricted bowls, and several new forms: inverted bell-shaped bowls, and plates and bowls with broad, flattened rims (called brims or marleys) like modern dinner plates (Figure 3.4) (Brewer 1985:20). Other reported Altamaha colono-ware forms include pitchers and *ollas* (a globular cooking

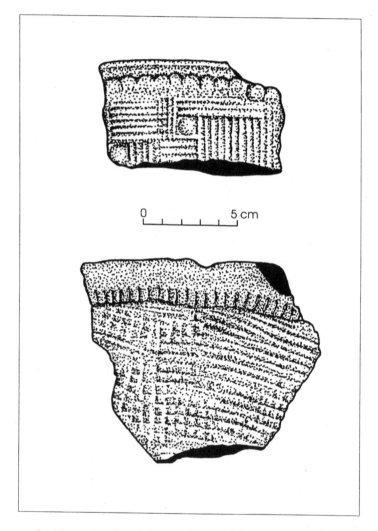

3.3. San Marcos Complicated Stamped: Motif and Overstamped Motif (from Brewer 1985; by permission).

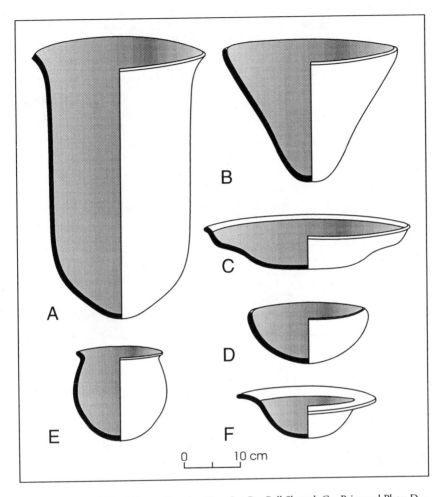

3.4. Mission Period Vessel Forms. Key: A = Deep Jar; B = Bell Shaped; C = Brimmed Plate; D = Restricted Bowl; E = Globular Pot; F = Brimmed Bowl (from Brewer 1985; by permission).

pot), both with strap handles and *escudilla* or *taza* (small cups) forms. At Wamassee Head, the *taza* and deep brimmed plates tended to be red filmed. The frequency of colono-wares and red filming appears to vary depending on temporal factors as well as on site function. Colono-wares were rare in urban St. Augustine but seemed to be common at mission sites and associated pueblos. They were, nevertheless, quite rare at Harris Neck (Braley et al. 1986:84, Table 11), which may have been the site of Tolomato (Worth, personal communication, 1999). A mission was established at that site, but it was destroyed in the Juanillo rebellion and not rebuilt. Occupation may have been too early, too short, too contentious, or all of the above, to foster the development of colono-wares. Similarly, South and DePratter (1996:52) note that red filming was absent from Santa Elena and so believe it to have been developed or adopted after 1587. The Orista and Escamacu in the area were in constant rebellion against that short-lived colonial town; it is not surprising that red filming does not appear in this context.

San Marcos Pottery

Smith (1948, 1949) originally described San Marcos Stamped as a type and explicitly subsumed previously defined Ft. King George types found on the Georgia coast (Caldwell 1943; Larson 1958:14) into San Marcos. He initially defined only the stamped wares, leaving red filmed, incised, and plain wares unnamed. Smith recognized at the time that San Marcos represented an extension of Late Lamar culture into Florida and that there was a close relationship between San Marcos, "red filmed ware" types and Spanish colonial occupations (Smith 1948:315–316). Paste temper was defined as usually grit, sometimes crushed limestone, and, rarely, grog. Vessel forms included small to large globular jars and shallow bowls, with rims straight or slightly flaring and sometimes folded (Smith 1948:315).

On the basis of his excavations in the moat of the Castillo de San Marcos in St. Augustine, Smith identified a number of different curvilinear/rectilinear motifs for San Marcos (Smith 1948:320, Plate XXXI). Most of these reportedly disappeared after 1680, to be replaced by cross simple stamping (Smith 1948:314, 315). More recent analysis of the aboriginal pottery in St. Augustine (Piatek 1985) has indicated a wide variety of nonlocal aboriginal wares; some of the motifs depicted in Smith (1948:320) should not be classed as San Marcos.

Otto and Lewis (1974:106) offered a refinement of the San Marcos type: "The San Marcos type embraces three Stamped (simple, check, and rectilinear or curvilinear complicated stamped) and Plain surface subtypes. The Plain surface examples can be further subdivided into two varieties: Plain and Plain Burnished. Also, there is the Red-Filmed sub-type which is generally plain though at least one stamped red-filmed example was recovered. . . . We hypothesize that the stamped examples probably functioned as cooking vessels while the plain vessels served primarily as tableware."

The types Altamaha and San Marcos have become badly conflated in the literature. Many researchers see nothing but an areal distinction between the two: if the archaeologist is in Georgia the type is Altamaha;

in Florida the type is San Marcos (e.g., Brewer 1985:19; DePratter 1984:48; Thomas 1987:14; Walker 1985:64). However, there are temporal and historical reasons to hypothesize some attribute differences between the types. San Marcos is later, and the bulk of it entered St. Augustine and other environs after 1650, that is, after population loss and nucleation. Braley (1990:100) distinguished Altamaha *assemblages* (as opposed to sherds) from San Marcos assemblages—he wrote that the cross simple stamping reportedly characteristic of San Marcos was rare at Harris Neck. Deagan (personal communication, 1991, 1999) also differentiates Altamaha from San Marcos pottery in St. Augustine. According to Deagan, Altamaha is characterized by stamping and incising on the same vessel, by the lack of folded rims, and by whole cane as opposed to half cane punctations under the rim. She has observed that pottery with these Altamaha-like characteristics comes only from earlier contexts in St. Augustine.

At present, any differences between Altamaha and San Marcos pottery remain to be formally demonstrated. A comparison of the assemblages from the two Santa Catalinas can be used to address the reality of the distinction (see Chapter 7). Furthermore, with good contextual control and careful observation, it may be demonstrated that the Guale continued to produce San Marcos Complicated Stamped (*sensu* Brewer) at least until the removal of the missions to Florida. The progression from the "invariant" use of the filfot cross in the Irene phase to the production of only San Marcos Complicated Stamped at Wamassee Head would suggest that this is so. If true, it must be recognized that many San Marcos Simple Stamped or Cross Simple Stamped sherds in Florida are just incomplete, overstamped portions of the rectilinear filfot cross motif. Furthermore, that pervasive motif, like many other pottery motifs in the Lamar tradition, may have functioned as a "condensed symbol" (David et al. 1988), reflecting bedrock cosmological principals of the Guale and their interior relatives.

The Filfot Cross as a Cosmological Symbol

Variations on four-field filfot cross motif characterize many Lamar-related types in the late Mississippian period in the Southeast (e.g., Snow 1990). The prevalence and longevity of the filfot cross and related motifs derive from the fact that the design is a representation of southeastern Indian cosmology. Hudson (1976:122) described the basis of that cosmology:

> The southeastern Indians conceived of This World as a great, flat island resting on the surface of the waters, suspended from the vault of the sky by four cords attached at each of the cardinal directions.

Most of them evidently thought that the island was circular in shape, but that it was crosscut by the four cardinal directions, and it is reasonable to assume that each southeastern society conceived of itself as occupying the center of the circle. It is also reasonable to assume that the circle and cross motif of the Southeastern Ceremonial Complex represents This World, the four directions, and the center.

Fundaburk and Foreman (1957:58; see also Waring and Holder 1968; Waring 1968) referred to this motif as the "Cosmic or World Symbol" and interpreted it essentially the same way as Hudson did, though they believed the central circular element represented the sun at its zenith, the period of its greatest power. Willoughby (1897:10) also considered this design a "cosmic symbol" and observed: "When a man desired to represent symbolically the world as known to him, he drew a circle representing the horizon, in the center of which he placed a smaller circle symbolic of the sun in the zenith. From the central sun symbol four lines were drawn to the outer circle, dividing it into four equal parts, these lines representing the four world-quarters and the four winds."

The sun, the source of all warmth, light, and life, was one of the principal Southeastern deities; some groups conceived of the sun as female and others as male. The earthly representative and ally of the sun was sacred fire, the principal symbol of purity. Many Southeastern groups built their sacred fire in the shape of a cross so that the fire burned in the center. According to Howard (1968:19), the concept of the sacred fire, associated with the sun and fed by four logs oriented with the cardinal directions, was "the most widespread and basic ceremonial concept in the Southeast." Fires are still built according to these concepts in modern Green Corn ceremonies in Oklahoma (Howard 1968).

The world symbol was replicated in a number of media. It occurred, alone or with other mythological symbols, on shell gorgets, pottery, banners (Fundaburk and Foreman 1957:58), gaming stones (Fundaburk and Foreman 1957:Plate 96), and copper (Fundaburk and Foreman 1957:Plates 109, 110), and it was and is represented in the sacred fire and perhaps in the plan of the square ground itself. Although it was embedded in Southeastern Ceremonial Complex iconography, the symbol had great antiquity in the Southeast, appearing at least by the beginning of the Woodland period in the interior (Hudson 1984:8). By A.D. 1300–1350, the world symbol was the only motif carved on the wooden paddles used to stamp Irene pottery—surface treatments from the preceding coastal Savannah period, including cord marking and check stamping, completely disappeared. The representation of this single motif in many media and physical contexts would seem to justify the consideration of the filfot cross and its later variants as "condensed symbols."

4

Methods

The research questions and pottery characteristics discussed in the previous chapters dictated the attributes recorded for each of the five contexts studied. The database involved two (or three if Altamaha and San Marcos are considered distinct types) pottery types spanning 400 years of production; however, attributes recorded were held constant for each type so that they could be directly compared. The evolutionary relationship of the types made this program possible. The following discussion deals with the attributes selected and the analysis techniques.

Attribute Selection, Measurement, and Recording

The operationalization of an attribute analysis for pottery has been well explicated by Redman (1978, especially Figures 8.4 and 8.5), whose original hierarchical approach has since been greatly elaborated by Carr (1995). Analysis for this study was begun in the late 1980s and completed in the early 1990s, so Redman's work influenced the research design. Redman's hierarchical approach allows for the examination of both subtypical and typological variation within "tentative interpretive frameworks" (Redman 1978:170) that explicitly recognize the influence of the technology of production and the function of ceramics within a society.

Technological Attributes

As suggested by Redman, initial attribute selection for this study was based on review of the available ethnographic, historical, and archaeological evidence, much of which was presented in the previous chapters. Attributes traditionally considered both technological and stylistic were recorded. However, during analysis the lines between technology and style began to blur (see, for instance, Chapter 6). The list of attributes that follows is organized roughly along those lines, but it is acknowledged that the two categories are inextricably intertwined. Unless noted, attributes were recorded for all sherds used in the study.

Temper

Probably a better term for this attribute would be *inclusions* because *temper* implies an intentional additive to the clay paste by the potter. Most of the inclusions recognized were added, although sand may be an exception. No attempt was made to discriminate intentionally added sand from sand inclusions by grain size or shape. That level of paste analysis was beyond the scope of these investigations. The term *temper* is used here in recognition of the majority of additives to the pastes.

Major temper categories included quartz sand-size grains and grit-sized grains; tempering with grit and grog, limestone, and shell was also observed. Sand and grit were distinguished following the Wentworth scale (Shepard 1980:118). Quartz inclusions were considered *sand* if the particles were less than .25 millimeter, and the term *grit* was used for all particles over this size. When in doubt, grain size was verified using a binocular microscope with a micrometer. All sherds coded as tempered with limestone or shell tested positive for calcium by reacting with a 5 percent solution of hydrochloric acid. A *grog* designation indicates that there were inclusions of fired clay distinct from the paste. However, no attempt was made to determine whether the grog represented ground-up sherds.

Burnishing

Interior burnishing was considered a technological trait because interior burnishing reduces vessel porosity and increases surface hardness. Burnishing was determined by paste compaction rather than luster because luster can be destroyed by further drying of the vessel after burnishing (Rice 1987:138), by firing (Shepard 1980:124), by use-wear, and by postdepositional processes. Exterior burnishing was considered a stylistic trait; this is reflected in the recognition of interior and exterior burnished sherds as a different type from plain (exterior unburnished) sherds.

Slipping

Two types of "films" or "slips," red and black, were used on Mission period pottery. These were probably pigmented slips (fine clay suspended in water and applied in a thin coat before firing), but they could have been paints (Ann Cordell, Florida Museum of Natural History Ceramic Laboratory, personal communication, 1991). Some sherds did have the substance painted in bold designs along the marley. However, complete coverage of either the marley or the entire vessel interior was more common. A red slip was by far the most prevalent kind, but there were rare instances of black or red and black filmed sherds. With only a handful of exceptions (which may have been eroded), all slipped sherds were burnished. In this as in other instances, burnishing was functional as well as decorative. Burnishing promotes adhesion of the slip to the vessel (Rice 1987:150) and, as noted above, would reduce vessel porosity.

Firing

Subsamples of sherds from all three sites were analyzed for fired color. Subsamples were used because of the size of the assemblages and the expected redundancy of the information. To control for variation in core color due to the location of the sherd on the pot, firing colors were read on rim sherds only. For the Meeting House Fields site, the sample consisted of all rims of adequate size from the 1988 excavations. For the St. Catherines Island sample, a set of proveniences was randomly selected from all structures, and color characteristics of the rims in those proveniences were recorded. For the Amelia Island sample, sherds were studied from a systematically unaligned series of pits in each structure. Interior, exterior, and core colors were recorded under fluorescent light with reference to the Munsell color chart.

Form

Where possible, vessel form was recorded. In many cases, however, only lip orientation was recovered because both Altamaha and San Marcos vessels tended to break at the base of the rim fold. This phenomenon was so prevalent that a special code was created for the unidentifiable surface decoration of the vessels from which these rim sherds came to distinguish them from sherds for which the surface decoration was merely illegible. An analogous situation occurred with the colono-ware brimmed vessels, by far the largest category of colono-wares. These vessels commonly broke at the point of inflection between the marley and the body of the plate. A code for "unidentified brimmed vessel" was used for those marleys.

Vessel diameter was taken where possible, but few sherds were large enough to provide reliable diameters. A comprehensive program of cross-mending might yield enough data to analyze vessel diameters. However, this was not undertaken for this study.

Stylistic Attributes

Theoretically, pottery decoration is infinitely variable. Nevertheless, the traditional uses of style, with or without symbolic meaning, tend to limit the choices of the potter. That styles evolve with little cultural change is attributable to drift (Binford 1963). The few studies on the diachronic changes in Irene and Altamaha wares have emphasized variables such as rim treatments and rim depth *apparently* affected by drift. This study includes those variables as well as design motif and other attributes that might be under more conscious control.

The following stylistic attributes were selected: surface decoration/design motif, rim style, and depth of the rim fold. Land and groove width was also recorded for a subsample of sherds. Each of these was recorded as follows.

Surface decoration

The bulk of all the collections studied consisted of heavily overstamped sherds. It was, therefore, impossible to code at the level of design motif for most sherds. What was coded for each sherd was the highest level of the motif visible. When only simple stamping (parallel lines) was visible, one code number (396) was used. If perpendicular lines were visible (in other words, two of the cardinal directions represented in the world symbol), a different code was used. Sometimes checks were incorporated into the parallel lines; if so, a different number was applied. Sherds with a central element—inelegantly called "dots" during the analysis—were given a different code number, as were different executions of the "sun." These usually were circular but occasionally were square or rectangular. Where partial or total motifs were visible, they were recorded with reference to a series of drawings associated with code numbers. Overstamping was recorded only for the various combinations of simple stamping.

There is a great deal of information, then, on motifs in this study. In general, however, code numbers for all designs were collapsed into a set of "master codes" (rectilinear, curvilinear, dot, check, obliterated stamped, plain, burnished plain, incised, and incised and stamped). Dots were combined with either rectilinear or curvilinear stamped when not the focus of the question at hand.

Incised designs were recorded similarly. No attempt was made to assign the incised designs to type. Unlike the situation in the Apalachee area, East Coast incising has not been systematically studied. Terms such as Lamar Bold Incised and Altamaha Incised, for example, are rather loosely applied, and sometimes geographical location and characteristics of execution are conflated. In addition, for the Amelia Island material, the use of these type names might imply that the material was extra-local, which is probably not true, at least for late Spanish mission sites. As for the stamped sherds, elements or motifs were recorded with reference to a series of drawings. The presence of stamping below incising was noted, and, for a subsample, land and groove widths were measured.

Rim style

Rim "style" was conceived as the combination of two attributes called rim treatment and rim elaboration. The former defined whether a vessel had a plain rim, a punctation directly on the vessel wall, an applique rim strip, an applique node or pellet, or a folded rim. The latter consisted of the more decorative elements, the "elaborations" of the basic rim treatments defined in the first category. Rim elaborations included incising and the variety of punctation styluses used to impress applique strips, vessel walls (these punctated, plain rimmed vessels are referred to as "decorated" vessels throughout this volume), or folded rims.

In some instances it was difficult to determine whether or not a rim was folded. This was particularly true for the Meeting House Fields site pottery assemblage. Several rims were identified as folded but were later interpreted to be applique strips applied flush with the lip and then smoothed. In all but two of these cases, closer inspection revealed those smoothing marks, as well as areas that were not well smoothed.

Depth of rim fold

Folded rims were measured from the base of the rim to the center of the lip. Rim strips were measured similarly; strip width was also measured for the Meeting House Fields site but is not discussed in this volume.

Land and groove width

Land and groove widths were recorded for a subsample of the complicated stamped sherds from each site. The subsample consisted of all sherds with central dots. The main purpose for selecting these sherds was to reduce the sample size of eligible sherds to a manageable level with some criterion that could be easily applied during the main analysis. In addition, it helped to avoid repeated measurements of the characteristics of the same paddle because many of these were recognizable by unique executions of the central dot. Some duplication, though, is doubtless present.

Analysis Techniques

The coding system used for this study was developed by archaeologists with the Florida Bureau of Archaeological Research and Florida State University for use in mission excavations throughout *La Florida*. However, that system was not designed for a rigorous ceramic analysis, and major changes were made to adapt the system to this study. Nevertheless, terminology and definitions that already existed in that code system were used. For instance, vessel form descriptions in this study are as defined therein; all attributes defined in the preexisting codebook were coded with the same numbers (and definitions) as described in Shapiro (1987).

Data are presented in two formats, by sherd (count and weight for most attributes) and by minimum number of vessels (MNV). In general, information on the assemblage as a whole is presented by sherd. Information that could be reduced to data by vessel (e.g., rim style and vessel form) are displayed by MNV. Often specific attributes were missing or unidentifiable on some sherds. Those sherds or vessels were deleted for specific tests and table results. Thus sherd or MNV totals will not match in every table. Count totals are given at the beginning of each analysis section; where tables do not match those values, there were missing data.

The MNV was established similarly for all sites. With the use of computer printouts with all attributes sorted, rim sherds were combined into single vessels if they shared vessel form and rim style, temper, and master code surface treatment or unique motif code and if measurements such as rim fold depth were close (these tend to be variable even on single sherds; deviations of less than 1 cm were accepted). Other measurements included punctation size, brim width, land and groove widths, diameter of dot, and vessel diameter. For the Meeting House Fields site sample, it was assumed that there was no crossmending between house middens; pottery from each midden was treated as a separate assemblage. A similar assumption was made for structures at the missions.

The MNV approach is intended to remove the bias present in the differential recovery of vessels. The technique used here, and the MNV approach in general, may depress the frequency of common forms of plain and some stamped vessels because they lack attributes that record individual variation. This can be seen in the data presented in the following chapters, particularly in the differences in percentage totals between sherd and MNV for some attributes such as incising and sand tempering.

5

The Meeting House Fields Site

In this chapter, the Meeting House Fields site is described, previous research is detailed, and the 1988 field season, designed to ensure the adequacy of the site for this research, is discussed. Radiocarbon data and ceramic analyses are applied to the question of intrasite contemporaneity. Finally, the technological and stylistic attributes of the pottery of this late pre-Columbian to Mission period site are presented as baseline data for the study of pottery change in subsequent chapters.

Site Background

The Meeting House Field site is one of fifty-four Irene phase (A.D. 1300–1580) sites known on St. Catherine's Island, Georgia. The site occupies a .5-kilometer-wide peninsula, 1.5 to 3 meters above sea level, on the estuarine (west) side of the island (Figure 5.1). The westernmost portion of the site is undisturbed and is covered in a climax forest of magnolia with little understory (Figure 5.2). This undisturbed area is a maximum of 50 meters wide and is bordered on the east side by a field ditch. East of the ditch is an old field, and this portion of the site has been extensively plowed. Currently, however, this area is being returned to a more pristine state and is in successional pine.

Meeting House Fields is a typical Irene phase site in several respects. Both on barrier islands and on the mainland, the bulk of Irene phase sites are situated adjacent to or within 100 meters of the salt marsh edge (Pearson 1979:70). The presence of archaeologically recovered burned corncobs from Meeting House Fields and other Irene phase sites notwithstanding, this environmental situation reflects the society's reliance on estuarine resources.

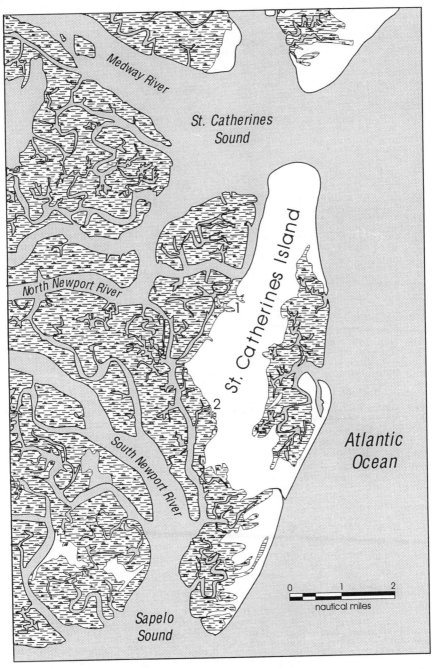

5.1. Meeting House Fields, Site Context. Key: 1 = Meeting House Fields; 2 = Santa Catalina de Guale.

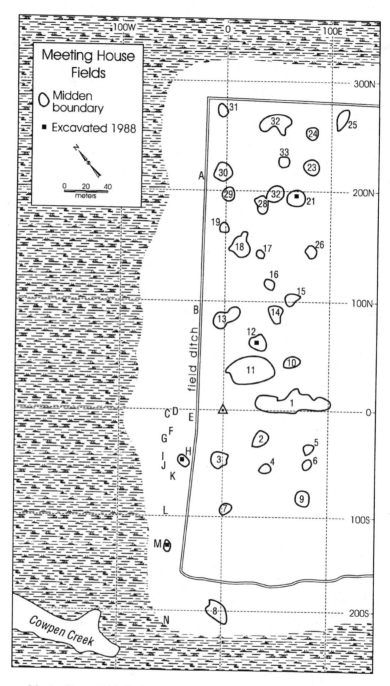

5.2. Meeting House Fields Site Map.

The typical Irene phase site structure, also present at Meeting House Fields, consists of numerous discrete shell midden deposits, presumably reflecting the refuse of adjacent dwellings scattered (apparently) randomly over the site.[1]

Joseph Caldwell was the first to excavate at the site. In 1969, he dug a unit in the northern portion of what has subsequently been labeled Midden E. Although the materials from his expedition were analyzed, they were not included in the analysis. This was because there were few records of his excavations and because, even without Caldwell's materials, the sample size of pottery from Midden E was much larger than that from the other middens.

Meeting House Fields was tested again in 1975 by the American Museum of Natural History. During that season, a field map locating the visible middens in the undisturbed western portion of the site was made using a compass. Middens were given letter designations (Figure 5.2). Excavation units were placed in five of the fourteen middens located, and a vertical series of 14C samples were obtained from Midden E, one of the largest. Ceramics from the five units were analyzed. Although there were discrepancies between the absolute results of the radiocarbon tests and relative dating on the ceramics (see below), this preliminary analysis indicated that Meeting House Fields might be useful in a research project designed to study pottery change during the Mission period.

As discussed in Chapter 1, the ceramic assemblage from a late Irene phase site would provide the necessary baseline data from which to study change during the subsequent Mission period. The site needed to be a single component site to avoid confounding the study with transitional attributes. In addition, the site could not be a seasonal or special purpose site that might not contain a full range of pottery forms or decorative attributes (e.g., Plog 1980). Finally, the location of the site on the same island as the next contexts considered, those from the Mission Santa Catalina, helped to control for the variability in stylistic attributes between major river drainages observed by Caldwell (1971) along the Georgia coast.

Site Mapping

A three-week field season (November–December 1988) was undertaken to gather additional data about the site, information necessary to answer explicit questions crucial to the aforementioned research program. Specifically, we needed basic information about absolute and relative chronology, site size, and internal settlement organization to assess site function. A site survey was proposed, employing extensive subsurface probing at approximately 1-meter intervals for plowed-over shell middens in the old field (Saunders and Russo 1988). When shell was located, middens were defined by probing at smaller intervals. Identified middens were designated with numbers to distinguish them from those located during the earlier survey. Midden boundaries were flagged and mapped using a transit. In some cases, particularly for Midden 1 and Midden 24, boundaries were difficult to establish. It is probable that these represent several smaller middens blurred together as they were repeatedly plowed.

During the three weeks, a 500 (gNS) × 100 meter area was mapped (Figure 5.2). Another 250 (gEW) × 70 meter area was covered less intensively; middens located during this phase of the testing were not further defined and are not plotted on Figure 5.2. This more informal testing did establish that shell middens were present up to 370 meters east of the field ditch. Physiographic features suggested the site could extend twice as far. It was apparent, then, that the site was quite large. With respect to Pearson's Ossabaw Island study, Meeting House Fields would be a Class II site—situated in a favorable environmental zone and extensive, but with no associated mounds.

Radiocarbon Dates

Radiocarbon dates were obtained to determine whether the middens at the site were contemporaneous with one another. Of course, ^{14}C dates can provide only the broad boundaries of site occupation; it was hoped that ceramic seriation would provide a finer relative chronology (see below). For the following discussion it is important to note that $^{13}C/^{12}C$ was not run for this series of samples. Therefore, the raw shell date was aged 420 years to compensate for stable isotope fractionation along the southeastern Atlantic coast (M. Tamers, Beta Analytic, personal communication, 1991). A local reservoir correction (-5 ± 20; Stuiver et al. 1986) was also added to the dates run on shell. Recalibration of both carbon and shell dates was obtained using the CALIB v.3 program (Stuiver and Reimer 1986). Whether these corrections and calibrations produce a more accurate shell date than the raw count is still open to question (Murray Tamers, Beta Analytic, personal communication, 1991).

Laboratory numbers, source materials, proveniences, and uncorrected and corrected/calibrated date ranges are shown in Table 5.1. Figure 5.3 presents the calibrated date range taken to one and two sigma, or within a 68 percent and 95 percent probability that the actual date falls within the range, respectively. The uncorrected/uncalibrated date is indicated within that range by an asterisk.

The results of the Midden E assays indicate an occupation between circa A.D. 1260 and A.D. 1420 for the deposition of Levels 3–8. Two dates from Levels 2 and 3, Beta 21972 and Beta 21973, suggest a later occupation, perhaps extending into the Mission period. However, these contradict a fully prehistoric date from Level 2. No notes on the removal of the samples for these dates are available to help explain these discrepancies. At present it seems prudent to ignore the upper-level dates.

Aspects of the ceramic assemblage indicated that the radiocarbon dates from the lower levels should be interpreted toward the more recent end of the range. Surface decoration on the pottery of Midden E was predominantly plain (33.7 percent) and complicated stamped (57.7 percent). Incising, though a minority treatment, was consistently present (Table 5.2; complete inventories of midden assemblages by level are presented in Table A.1). Most of the incising was characterized as fine ($\leq$1 millimeter), but designs were simple and composed of relatively few lines. The fact that rim treatments throughout Midden E consisted primarily of plain, applique strips with segmentations or cane punctations and cane decorated vessels (Table A.2) may indicate that Midden E was deposited in the Pine Harbor phase.

Additional radiocarbon samples were taken from each midden excavated during the 1988 season and from all previously excavated contexts. Samples selected for dating were chosen on the basis of the results of the ceramic analysis. Those results indicated that Middens 12 and 21 might be earlier than the other middens; samples were processed from both these middens. A single sample was run from Midden 12; one oyster, one clam, and one charcoal sample were processed from Level 3 of Midden 21. A similar series was processed from Level 3 of Midden M, which contained fragments of a pipe with Southeastern Ceremonial Complex designs (Figure 5.4). Other samples were processed from the top and bottom of Midden H to determine dates of initial deposition and abandonment of this deepest midden excavated. A sample was also processed from Midden N, which had ceramics that appeared earlier than Irene wares.

The results of the processing are presented in Figure 5.3 and Table 5.1 (Midden N appears only in Table 5.1). Midden N was indeed earlier than the other middens tested, probably dating to the Wilmington II phase (DePratter 1979:111). Most of the other dates fell within the late Irene phase. Furthermore, if two sigmas are considered, all middens could

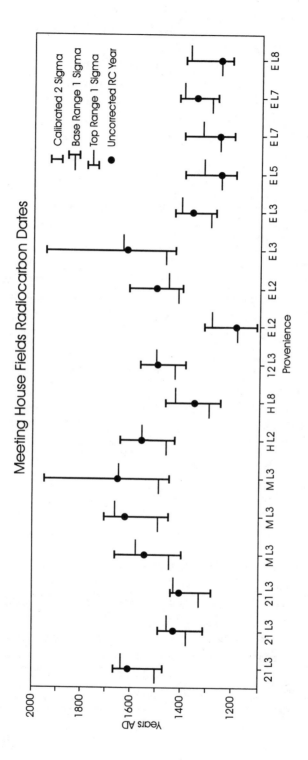

5.3. Radiocarbon Dates from Meeting House Fields.

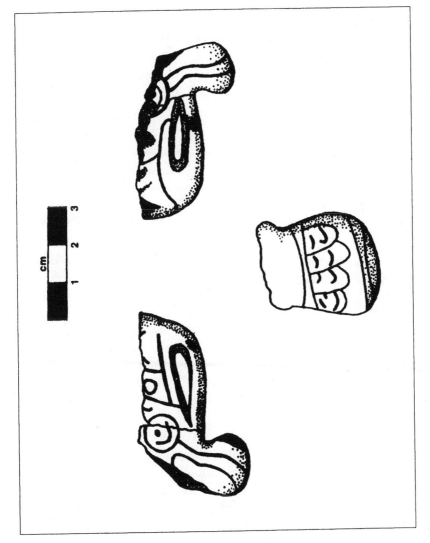

5.4. Pottery Pipes with Southeastern Ceremonial Complex Motifs.

have been deposited contemporaneously, though attribute analysis argued for a different conclusion (see below). Midden H appeared to have been deposited over a period of around one hundred years.

Somewhat surprising was the number of dates that extended into the seventeenth century. Two dates from Midden M can be considered Altamaha phase; the presence of the pipe with Southeastern Ceremonial Complex designs is also suggestive of a late date. Sigmas extended the deposition of the upper levels of Midden H into that phase, but there was no independent evidence to suggest anything later than the Pine Harbor phase. An oyster date from Midden 21 also extends into the seventeenth century. However, two other dates from the same level fall in the early fifteenth century, or late Pipemaker's Creek phase. These dates are supported by ceramic attributes. All pottery recovered from the site, even from Midden M, displayed the light stamping and thin lands and grooves characteristic of Irene phase designs. No bolder Altamaha-like stamping was observed. There was no red filming, and no colono-ware forms or European artifacts were recovered. Two rims were classified as folded (one of these was amended to "possibly folded"). However, these came not from middens with later radiocarbon dates nor from the upper levels of deep middens. They were from the basal levels of Midden H (Levels 7 and 8). Both rims were plain and rounded and had irregular, thinned bases (see Figure 5.5). Folds were relatively deep, 18.8 and 17.4 millimeters. With the thinned bases, the lack of rim elaboration, and the rounding of the lips, these rims bore more resemblance to Late Woodland period rims than to Altamaha folded rims.

Comparable Irene ceramic studies with accompanying radiocarbon data were scarce. Irene phase radiocarbon dates existed from only two other sites.[2] Pearson (1984) reported one date from the Red Bird Creek site in Bryan County, Georgia. The single sample, consisting of charred wood from a burned wattle and daub structure at the site, dated to A.D. 1145 ± 60. Pearson (1984:8) considered this date "too early." A calibrated date extended two sigmas yielded a range of A.D. 1039–1280—still short of the beginning of the early Irene phase as presently defined. With incising present at .5 percent, the ceramic assemblage from Red Bird Creek suggested a Pipemaker's Creek occupation. Braley (1990; see also Braley et al. 1986) published two Irene phase dates on charcoal from features at the Harris Neck National Wildlife Refuge (9MCI41) site, A.D. 1430 ± 60 and A.D. 1400 ± 70, yielding an uncorrected/uncalibrated range of A.D. 1330–1490 (2σ cal A.D. 1310 [1420] 1470 and 1290 [1410] 1470, respectively). On the basis

5.5. Representative Sherds from Meeting House Fields. Scale in centimeters.

of the absence of nodes or rosettes and the presence of "busier" incising, Braley et al. (1986:133) favored the latter part of the range.

Site Seasonality and Function

Shell samples were taken to address the issue of seasonality and, less directly, site function. Growth rings on sectioned clams *(Mercenaria mercenaria)* and size of the parasitic oyster drill *(Boonea impressa)* were analyzed to ascertain the principal seasons of oyster and clam exploitation at the site and, by extension, some of the seasons of site occupation (Russo 1991; Saunders and Russo 1988). Column samples were taken from every midden excavated in either 1975 or 1988. Selected subsamples, based on mercenaria abundance, were analyzed from Middens E, H, M, 12, and 21. Results indicated that the site was occupied, or at least exploited, year round. On the basis of these data, in addition to faunal and artifact diversity (Saunders and Russo 1988), Meeting House Fields is believed to have been a permanently occupied, probable village site.

One midden, however, Midden M, had a distinctly different seasonality profile. Although evidence from other samples indicated exploitation of molluscs throughout the year, only fall, winter, and spring exploitation was identified at Midden M. Whether these data reflect a change in seasonal subsistence patterns that could be correlated with the late radiocarbon dates from that midden must await the analysis of the vertebrate fauna.

Detailed results of this facet of the study are reported elsewhere (Saunders and Russo 1988; Russo 1991), but a comment is in order. There was a marked seasonality in the exploitation of the species studied. In general, oysters were exploited from the spring through the summer months and into the fall; clams were collected in the winter (Russo 1991:218; Saunders and Russo 1988:73). In several instances, a single sample from a midden was strongly seasonal, but the series of vertical samples indicated more prolonged use of the site. These results have implications for sample selection by other researchers.

Pottery Analysis

The Meeting House Fields pottery assemblage included all sherds from midden contexts recovered during the 1975 and 1988 excavations.[3] Middens were screened through ¼-inch mesh, but pottery less than 1 centimeter square was only counted and weighed and is not considered further in this analysis. Total count for Irene phase sherds used in this part of the study was 2,453. As discussed in the Methods section, total count is the basis for the discussions. Minimum number of vessels calculations were used for vessel form analysis and for rim treatment and rim elaboration. However, because all studies of temporal changes in rim attributes in Irene phase assemblages have been based on count, the cluster analysis and the discussion of attributes in Table 5.4 are also based on count.

Analysis of the pottery was conducted in three stages (Saunders and Russo 1988). The first two stages tested the hypothesis that the Meeting House Fields site was a single component, late Irene phase site. In the first stage, intramidden analysis, the incidence of plain, burnished plain, incised, and stamped pottery was examined by each 10-centimeter level to determine whether there was enough time depth in midden deposition to observe changes in the frequency of these attributes through time. Levels that contained pottery attributes determined to be earlier than the late Irene phase would be segregated and the pottery described separately from latter materials.

The second stage of analysis involved the determination of contemporaneity between middens—at a finer scale than is possible with radiocarbon dates. Intermidden assemblages were examined using both surface decoration and rim style. If different areas of the site were occupied at different times, intermidden assemblages should vary regularly along a number of different attributes; the middens could be clustered to produce a chronology of spatial use for the site. Ceramics from middens earlier than the late Irene phase would be discussed separately.

The initial results from that earlier analysis suggested that the middens were contemporaneous (Saunders and Russo 1988); values of attributes for the site as a whole were discussed. However, reanalysis for this book, and an appreciation of Braley's division of the late Irene into Pipemaker's Creek and Pine Harbor phases, has made it possible to divide site occupation into two components.

Intramidden Analysis

Intramidden analysis yielded mostly negative results (Appendix A) in that temporally sensitive pottery attributes did not covary through time within most middens. Several middens (12, B, D, J) showed no convincing evidence of regular change in attributes of surface treatment. This was attributed to the lack of time depth in midden deposition and also, in the cases of middens B, D, and J, small sample sizes. The relative frequency of plain wares did appear to increase toward the surface of Midden 21. However, so few sherds were recovered from Level 1 that it was impossible to determine whether this was a trend. In any event, surface treatment percentages indicated a deposition within the same phase. In Midden E, the high incidence of incised wares in Levels 1 and 2 represented sherds of a single vessel, so a dramatic rise in the frequency of incising near the end of the deposition of the midden was discounted.

Indeed, the frequencies of other treatments did not change in any regular manner. Incising did not appear in Midden H until Level 4, and some time depth in midden deposition is indicated by the radiocarbon dates. As in Midden E, however, other surface decorations did not show regular change. For example, the frequencies of stamped and plain wares between Levels 7 and 1 in Midden H were almost identical. These somewhat ambiguous data were interpreted to mean that middens could be treated as wholes for the subsequent analysis.

Intermidden Analysis

Cluster analysis using surface treatment and rim treatment of the midden assemblages produced a bipartite division of the middens on the site (Figures 5.6–5.8). Distance measures and clustering routines included in MINITAB Release 10 were used in the analyses of the percentage total (count) of body sherds in each surface treatment and percentage total

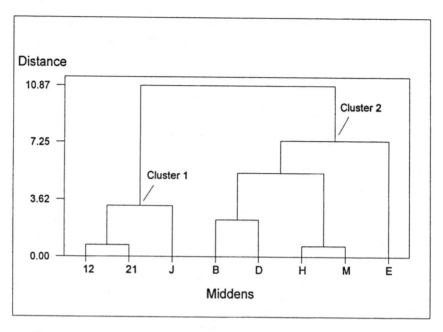

5.6. Cluster Analysis of Surface Treatment.

(count) rims for style (the combination of rim treatment and rim elaboration). The procedure was run for several different distance measures and clustering methods. Results using the average linkage clustering method based on a squared Euclidean distance matrix are presented here except where noted. In most cases, other clustering routines produced results very similar to the average linkage method.

For surface treatment (Figure 5.6), Middens 12, 21, and J formed one major cluster (Cluster 1), and B, E, D, H, and M formed the other (Cluster 2).[4] In Cluster 1, plain sherds constituted 20 percent or lower of midden totals, and stamped sherds comprised 72 percent of the total (Table 5.3). In Cluster 2, plain sherds ranged between 30 percent and 40 percent of the midden totals, and stamped sherds amounted to less than 60 percent in each midden. In addition, in the first group, only Midden J had incising (n = 1). Overall, Cluster 1 had more burnished plain wares, though the average for Cluster 2 would have been higher had Midden E not been included.

The rim style clusters were less successful. Standardized data subjected to average and Ward's method clustering routines chained; in other words, each midden rim assemblage was joined to the previous assemblage in a long string rather than clusters because there was no strong patterning in

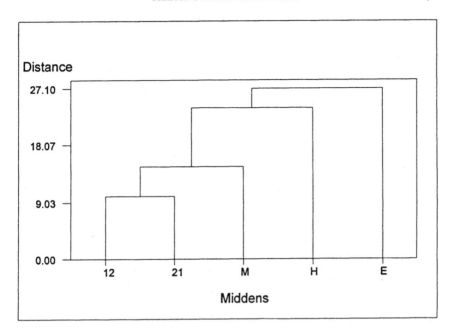

5.7. Cluster Analysis of Rim Style Showing Chaining.

the data (Figure 5.7; Middens B, D, and J were not included because they had only three, five, and six rims, respectively). Curiously, unstandardized data did form clusters (Figure 5.8) with intuitively pleasing results—that is, the clusters essentially mirrored the results from the surface treatment analysis. In the unstandardized average linkage, Middens 12 and 21 formed one cluster, and Middens E, H, and M formed the other. Middens 12 and 21 were the only middens in this subsample with pellets or nodes, segmented applique strips with cane punctations, and no incised rims; they had, *in general,* fewer decorated cane vessels and far fewer plain rims than the second cluster (Table 5.4, Appendix A). These results should be viewed with caution however, for three reasons. First, data should be standardized; second, even though percentages were used, there was a large difference in sample size between Cluster 1 and Cluster 2 that could have affected the data; and three, results were not the same using a different clustering method. In the Ward's method result, Midden M clustered with Middens 12 and 21. All other data argue that Midden M is much later than Middens 12 and 21.

On the basis of surface treatment, then, and, to a lesser extent, rim style, Middens 12, 21, and J (Cluster 1) were hypothesized to have been deposited earlier than the other middens. Surface treatments for Clusters 1 and 2 were

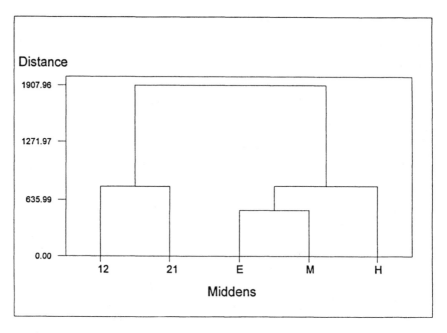

5.8. Cluster Analysis of Rim Style, Data Not Standardized.

compared to similar data from other Irene sites with radiocarbon dates
(Table 5.5) to see how the data might seriate. For Meeting House Fields
Cluster 1, percentages of all surface treatments except incising suggested
that it was later than the Harris Neck pre-Columbian period component
(circa A.D. 1415 ± 65). Similarly, Cluster 2 appeared even later than the
Harris Neck Colonial period component (A.D. 1650 ± 70) except for the
values on incising, which were, nevertheless, significantly higher than the
values on this attribute in the pre-Columbian component at Harris Neck.[5]
Other data from Middens E and H also suggested a late deposition date.
Evidence for the inclusion of basal levels of Midden E in the Pine Harbor
phase was given above; radiocarbon dates from Level 3 and fine-line incising
on some of the incised sherds from Level 6 in Midden M indicated a Pine
Harbor phase or later deposition for that midden. As noted above, Levels
3 and 4 of Midden M contained pieces of pipes incised with Southeastern
Ceremonial Complex designs (Figure 5.4), which are indicative of a very late
Irene phase or postcontact period deposit (Cook and Pearson 1989:155, 163;
Larson 1958). Midden H had no incised material until the upper levels, but
the lower levels had relative frequencies of plain to stamped wares similar
to those from Midden M—the cluster analysis of surface treatment joined

these to middens at a very low distance level (Figure 5.6). Together with the radiocarbon dates and rim style information, these data could be interpreted to support a middle Irene (Pipemaker's Creek except for the virtual absence of incising) deposition for Cluster 1 middens. A terminal Pine Harbor phase deposition was indicated for the Cluster 2 middens, though the terminal date for this phase may have to be extended to accommodate the radiocarbon dates and ceramic data from Midden M. In fact, given the radiocarbon, ceramic (not including the cluster analysis), and faunal data, Midden M may be significantly later than the other Cluster 2 middens. However, there is insufficient information on functional versus temporal differences in Irene phase middens to ascertain this with the data at hand.

Vessel Form Analysis

One hundred and twenty-seven vessels could be defined in the rim assemblage of 211 sherds (Appendix A). Only a few distinct forms were recovered from Meeting House Fields (Table A.3 shows the distribution of all recognized vessel forms in all middens). These included excurvate restricted, excurvate unrestricted, and, more often, excurvate unidentified rims presumably belonging to jars (Figure 3.1). There were a few instances of a widely flaring, restricted, long-necked jar, called a "bottle" in the analysis shorthand. Simple, slightly incurved, and straight-sided bowls were numerous. The straight-sided bowls may actually be carinated, unrestricted or carinated, restricted bowls. No points of inflection were recovered to discriminate between these three alternatives. However, the presence of one beaker handle in Midden M indicated that at least some of these straight-sided rims may come from beakers, also called "bean pots" (e.g., Harn 1980:108), a late Mississippian vessel form not usually described for coastal sites. Others may represent "water bottles" (Caldwell and McCann 1941:49, Figure 22).

For comparison between clusters, the seven recognized vessel form categories were collapsed into four categories: simple bowls, straight-rimmed vessels, jars, and bottles. The comparison of the relative frequency of these forms by cluster is presented in Table 5.6. There appeared to be no significant difference between the clusters except that bottles occurred only in Cluster 2. This would seem to be another piece of data supporting a later deposition for Cluster 2 middens. However, preservation factors may also be responsible for this difference. Large sherds were required for the determination of this form, and larger sherds were recovered from the undisturbed portion of the site where all Cluster 2 middens were located.

Bowls were more commonly plain or incised, and jars were more commonly stamped. However, the statistical association between vessel form and surface treatment at Meeting House Fields was weak at best (Tables 5.7 and 5.8; sample sizes were too small to analyze vessel form by surface treatment by cluster). Stamped, incised, and plain surfaces occurred on all forms, just as Caldwell and McCann indicated in their 1941 type definitions from the (early Irene) Irene site.

Vessel form was also associated with rim treatment (Tables 5.9 and 5.10). The high probability of association was derived from the large percentage of bowls with plain rims and the corresponding lack of applique rims on bowls.

Other Indices of Change

As discussed in Chapter 3, there were attributes other than those commonly reported that might be sensitive to either temporal change or changes in social groups. Data from the Meeting House Fields site was to provide baseline information for the relative frequency of curvilinear to rectilinear stamping; the frequency of sherds with central dots as opposed to sherds on which the dot was not visible; the popularity of various punctation tools used to decorate applique strips and vessels; the depth of the rim strips; the frequency of burnishing; temper types; and sooting for comparison to later Guale contexts. For the Meeting House Fields site, these variables were analyzed by cluster, unless too few sherds with adequate attribute information were available, in which case clusters were combined. Tables displaying this information are included in Appendix A.

Temper

Irene phase ceramics are defined as having a grit- or gravel-tempered paste (Caldwell and McCann 1941:46–48). However, a little over 20 percent of the sherds at Meeting House Fields were sand tempered; grog tempering was apparent in a very few sherds with Irene filfot stamped motifs (Table A.4). Sand tempering apparently increased in the Pine Harbor phase. Whereas only 8 percent of the sherds in Cluster 1 were sand tempered, 28 percent of the Cluster 2 sherds were sand tempered. An analysis of temper by vessel form (Table A.5) indicated no concrete association between a vessel form and temper, though the ratio of sand-tempered to grit-tempered bowls was more even than the ratio of other forms to temper.

Why there was a spate of sand tempering in the late Irene phase is unknown. One possible explanation can be derived from the fact that grit (quartz grains larger than .25 millimeters) is not available on St. Catherines

Island and must be collected from sand (grit) bars in the adjacent salt marsh (Royce Hayes, personal communication, 1988). For environmental or social reasons, these bars may have become less available during the late occupation of Meeting House Fields. Another intriguing possibility is that vessel size may have decreased in the late Pine Harbor or early Altamaha phase. Braley et al. (1986:137) found that at Harris Neck small vessels tended to be sand tempered and larger vessels grit tempered. They attributed this correlation to differences in manufacturing techniques for vessels of different sizes. A decrease in vessel size might suggest some demographic changes (Shapiro 1984), but could also relate to site function and/or site seasonality.

Burnishing

The frequency of burnishing for all sherds not classified as Burnished Plain is displayed in Table A.6. Roughly 75 percent of all sherds had burnished interiors. There appeared to be slightly less interior burnishing in the Cluster 2 assemblage. Not shown are those few sherds (comprising less than 1 percent of the total) in Cluster 2 that had burnished exteriors and unburnished interiors.

Sooting

Sooting was rare in the Meeting House Fields assemblage and therefore cannot be meaningfully analyzed by cluster. Overall, a little over 7 percent of the sherds had sooted exteriors. Exterior sooting was most common on stamped sherds, uncommon on plain sherds, and rare on burnished plain and incised sherds. No burnished plain or incised sherds had sooted interiors.

Rectilinear versus curvilinear stamping

Table A.7 gives the relative frequencies of rectilinear versus curvilinear stamping by cluster. The analysis based on sherd count indicated that there was virtually no difference between the two clusters. Analysis by sherd weight, however, suggested a slight increase in the incidence of rectilinear stamping in Cluster 2.

Central dots

The ability to discriminate the central dot of the filfot cross in the heavily overstamped sherds was poor (Table A.8). Of all stamped sherds (surface roughened not included), central dots could be seen on only 6 percent to 8 percent of the sherds (or 8 to 10 percent if weight was used).

Rim elaboration

Cluster totals for the analysis of rim style were given above. Table A.9 gives values for rim elaboration only. Segmentation of the rim (including all varieties of stick and fingernail impressions) increased in Cluster 2. There was a slight increase in the incidence of fingernail punctation in Cluster 2 over Cluster 1 and, surprisingly, a decrease in the use of cane punctation.

Rim depth

There was no difference between Cluster 1 and 2 in the depth of the rim strip below the lip. Mean depth for both clusters was 10 millimeters (Table A.10). An idea that the rim strip might have moved upward toward the rim through time, "drifting" toward and eventually developing into the folded rim, was not supported by these data.

Land and groove width

For Cluster 1, mean land and groove width on stamped sherds was 1.4 and 1.8 millimeters, respectively (Table A.11). Mean land size in Cluster 2 was virtually identical; mean groove size was slightly smaller. In the later motifs, land and grooves were more equal in width—a trait shared with historic Guale motifs. However, both lands and grooves were still quite small compared with later sherds. These results confirmed the lack of Altamaha-like stamping at the site.

Motifs

Every attempt was made to discriminate different motifs (with different code numbers) during the analysis. More often than not, the characteristic overstamping made this difficult. Nevertheless, a number of different variations in the execution of the filfot cross were recorded. For instance, the center of the scroll could be a simple groove (a circular land on the paddle) or contain a discrete circle or a square. In one instance, a spiral was used for the cardinal elements instead of a scroll. There was only one sherd in the assemblage that was distinct enough to be considered a trade ware (Figure 5.5). The design appeared to be yet another variation on the filfot cross, but the crossbar through the circular element suggested a more elaborate treatment than was usually found at the site. That sherd, from Level 3 of Midden 12, also had an uncharacteristic buff to pink exterior and a sandy paste.

Incised designs were classified as either bold or fine; both styles occurred in each midden with incising. Although the total design was not usually recoverable, no incising (except that on the pipes) was found that could not be interpreted as part of either a scroll, concentric semicircles, or rounded chevrons. In contrast to what was found in the succeeding sites, punctation was not used either immediately below the rim or as filler in the incised designs.

Summary

Radiocarbon samples and the ceramic assemblage from the Meeting House Fields site indicated that the site was occupied principally during the late Irene phase. Discounting the oyster date from Midden 21, radiocarbon dates indicated that the middens in Cluster 1 were deposited between A.D. 1310 and 1570 (corrected/calibrated; Beta 30265 not included). Despite the lack of incising in this cluster, the surface decoration and rim attribute data (principally in the preponderance of cane punctate rim strips) seemed to indicate that deposition occurred in the middle of this range, or in the late Pipemaker's Creek phase. Small sample sizes may be the reason for the absence of incising in these units.

Pottery in Cluster 2 appeared later than that of Cluster 1. Pottery attributes and most radiocarbon dates suggested a late Pine Harbor phase occupation. Despite the relatively early radiocarbon dates from Midden E, it was included in this cluster on the basis of ceramic attributes. The presence of Southeastern Ceremonial Complex incised designs, the results of the zooarchaeological study, and the radiocarbon dates from Midden M might suggest that this midden was deposited later than the rest. Cluster analysis of surface decoration, however, joined M with the other middens of the cluster, particularly Midden H, at high R-squared values.

Applying the sigmas did extend the possible deposition date of some middens in Cluster 2 to a time coeval with the occupation of the earlier and later Santa Catalina missions. The possibility that portions of the Meeting House Fields were contemporaneous with the mission was considered. In this scenario, the Guale at Meeting House Fields were not won over by the Spanish. The presence of Southeastern Ceremonial Complex materials in Midden M might indicate participation in a native revitalization movement. If this were true, then it might also be reasonable to propose that Guale living outside the mission system or other venues of directed change continued to make traditional paddles and pots after Altamaha ware were well established elsewhere (Saunders and Russo 1988). However, the proximity of the Meeting House Fields site to the mission (they were just under 2 kilometers apart); the absence of any preserved

European materials, whether acquired through trade or other means[6]; and the lack of any transitional attributes in the pottery assemblage weaken this hypothesis. However, in a revitalization context, these absences do not render it completely untenable. Here it can only be conceded that, at present, coastal archaeologists lack the ability to discriminate among late pre-Columbian, Contact, and even Mission period nonmission sites except by the presence or absence of European artifacts, the frequency of which, in any given site, is determined by various historical and preservational factors. Although this fact is recognized, at present the Cluster 2 materials are considered to date to the middle to late sixteenth century; Midden M may be functionally rather than temporally distinct.

There were few surprises in the descriptive data amassed here. Surface decorations and rim treatments were similar to those described elsewhere. There were a few exceptions. Nodes, often considered an attribute of the early Irene phase, were recovered from the relatively late contexts in Cluster 1. However, as discussed previously, this treatment is found as a rare occurrence in later contexts. Although two folded rims were identified, none were found that could be considered transitional to Altamaha wares, even in quite late Pine Harbor phase deposits. Vessel forms were consistent with the late Irene phase, with the exception of the recovery of a possible "bean pot" handle and the lack of carinated bowls. Sand tempering appeared to increase late in the phase, but whether this could be attributed to vessel size or to other factors could not be determined.

Other attributes, such as the relative percentages of rectilinear versus curvilinear stamping or the percentage of stamped sherds in which the hub of the filfot cross is visible, are not generally reported. Those data were prepared to answer specific questions concerning microchange in design motifs from the Irene phase to the Mission-period Guale. The peoples of the terminal occupation at Meeting House Fields *could* have been directly antecedent to those at the mission of Santa Catalina or separated from them by a single generation. In any event, data from Meeting House Fields, especially with Pipemaker's Creek and Pine Harbor occupations segregated and the analysis done by cluster, provide excellent baseline information for research into ceramic change in the Mission period. The question to be explored next is to what extent pottery assemblages changed at the late sixteenth century manifestation of Mission Santa Catalina.

Table 5.1. Radiocarbon Dates from Meeting House Fields.

SAMPLE NO.	SOURCE	PROV.	C-14 AGE	CALIBRATED 1 sigma	CALIBRATED 2 sigma
Beta-20806	Oyster	E L2	1190 ± 60	1190 (1250) 1300	1100 (1250) 1330
Beta-21972	Charcoal	E L2	1510 ± 50	1430 (1450) 1480	1410 (1450) 1630
Beta-21973	Charcoal	E L3	1630 ± 60	1480 (1530, 1540, 1630) 1650	1450 (1530, 1540, 1630) 1950*
UGA-1009	Charcoal	E L3	1370 ± 60	1310 (1400) 1420	1290 (1400) 1440
Beta-20807	Oyster	E L5	1260 ± 60	1260 (1300) 1330	1200 (1300) 1410
Beta-20808	Oyster	E L7	1270 ± 60	1270 (1300) 1340	1210 (1300) 1410
Beta-21974	Charcoal	E L7	1360 ± 50	1310 (1400) 1410	1290 (1400) 1430
UGA-1010	Charcoal	E L8	1265 ± 60	1280 (1300) 1390	1240 (1300) 1400
Beta-30265	Oyster	21 L3	1610 ± 50	1500 (1540) 1640	1460 (1540) 1670
Beta-30263	Clam	21 L3	1420 ± 60	1380 (1420) 1460	1310 (1420) 1490
Beta-30264	Charcoal	21 L3	1410 ± 60	1330 (1410) 1440	1300 (1410) 1460
Beta-30270	Oyster	M L3	1550 ± 80	1450 (1500) 1590	1400 (1500) 1670
Beta-30268	Clam	M L3	1630 ± 80	1490 (1580) 1670	1440 (1580) 1710
Beta-30269	Charcoal	M L3	1660 ± 60	1520 (1640) 1660	1460 (1640) 1950*
Beta-30266	Clam	H L2	1560 ± 60	1460 (1500) 1560	1430 (1500) 1660
Beta-30267	Clam	H L8	1350 ± 80	1300 (1370) 1430	1250 (1370) 1470
Beta-30262	Clam	12 L3	1500 ± 60	1430 (1460) 1510	1400 (1460) 1570
Beta-30271	Clam	N L3	890 ± 70	870 (950) 1020	780 (950) 1060

* Denotes influences of bomb C-14

Note: Asymmetrical dates result from the non-linearity of the logarithmic relationship between sample C-14 activity and age (Long and Rippeteau 1974:207).

Table 5.2 Midden E, Surface Treatment by Level.

	Stamped				Plain				Burnished Plain				Incised				All			
	Count		Weight		Count		Weight		Count		Weight		Count		Weight		Count		Weight	
LEVEL	N	Pct	N	Pct	N	Pct	N	Pct	N	Pct	N	Pct	N	Pct	N	Pct	N	Pct	N	Pct
1	46	55.4	430.7	70.1	26	31.3	414.4	23.0	.	.	.	.	11	13.3	42.6	6.9	83	100	614.7	100
2	34	33.0	468.8	45.1	49	47.6	430.1	41.4	3	2.9	28.4	2.7	17	16.5	112.0	10.8	103	100	1039.3	100
3	46	73.0	577.1	71.6	10	15.9	85.4	10.6	3	4.8	76.2	9.5	4	6.3	67.0	8.3	63	100	805.7	100
4	50	72.5	678.0	85.1	17	24.6	108.8	13.7	1	1.4	6.2	0.8	1	1.4	3.9	0.5	69	100	796.9	100
5	38	58.5	468.0	64.5	23	35.4	242.1	33.4	2	3.1	11.7	1.6	2	3.1	3.6	0.5	65	100	725.4	100
6	71	64.5	893.8	73.4	28	25.5	240.0	19.7	1	0.9	4.2	0.3	10	9.1	78.9	6.5	110	100	1216.9	100
7	66	49.3	944.2	61.5	58	43.3	508.0	33.1	2	1.5	19.2	1.3	8	6.0	64.4	4.2	134	100	1535.8	100
8	115	61.2	1237.9	67.8	66	35.1	528.1	28.9	1	0.5	12.7	0.7	6	3.2	47.9	2.6	188	100	1826.6	100
9	31	66.0	266.1	74.8	14	29.8	79.6	22.4	.	.	.	.	2	4.3	10.0	2.8	47	100	355.7	100
10	3	60.0	17.2	61.0	1	20.0	7.5	26.6	.	.	.	.	1	20.0	3.5	12.4	5	100	28.2	100
All	500	57.7	5981.8	66.9	292	33.7	2371.0	26.5	13	1.5	158.6	1.8	62	7.2	433.8	4.8	867	100	8945.2	100

Note: Uid/Other not included. Stamped = total of rectilinear, curvilinear, dot, and surface roughened.

Table 5.3. Surface Decoration by Cluster.[1]

CLUSTER	Stamped				Plain				Burnished Plain				Incised				All			
	Count		Weight		Count		Weight		Count		Weight		Count		Weight		Count		Weight	
	N	Pct	N	Pct	N	Pct	N	Pct	N	Pct	N	Pct	N	Pct	N	Pct	N	Pct	N	Pct
1	514	71.7	5096.4	76.6	138	19.2	1041.6	15.7	64	8.9	508.3	7.6	1	0.1	5.3	0.1	717	100	6651.6	100
2	870	52.4	10841	61.4	588	35.4	4908.1	27.8	92	5.5	1095.4	6.2	110	6.6	800.8	4.5	1660	100	17646	100
All	1384	58.2	15938	65.6	726	30.5	5949.7	24.5	156	6.6	1603.7	6.6	111	4.7	806.1	3.3	2377	100	24297	100

1. Uid/Other not included.

Table 5.4. Rim Style by Cluster (Count).

	Rim Style											
	Treatment											
	Plain				Decorated							
	Elaboration				Elaboration						Elaboration	
	Plain		Incised		Dec Cane		Dec Finger		Dec Stamped		Pellet/Node	
	Count		Count		Count		Count		Count		Count	
Cluster	Sum	Pct	Sum	Pct	Sum	Pct	Sum	Pct	Sum	Pct	Sum	Pct
1	8	21.6	0	0	2	5.4	0	0	0	0	6	16.2
2	69	43.1	23	14.3	17	10.6	2	1.3	2	1.3	0.	0
All	77	40.1	23	11.7	19	9.6	2	1.0	2	1.0	6	3.0

Table 5.4. (cont).

	Rim Style											
	Treatment											
	Applique Strip								Folded		All	
	Elaboration								Elaboration			
	Strip Segmented		Strip Cane		Strip Segment/Cane		Strip Pinch		Fold Plain			
	Count		Count		Count		Count		Count		Count	
Cluster	Sum	Pct	Sum	Pct	Sum	Pct	Sum	Pct	Sum	Pct	Sum	Pct
1	6	16.2	9	24.3	5	13.5	1	2.7	0	0	37	100
2	25	15.6	17	10.6	0	0	3	1.9	2	1.3	160	100
All	31	15.7	26	13.2	5	2.5	4	2.0	2	1.0	197	100

Table 5.5. Surface Treatments: Percentages Compared from Radiocarbon Dated Sites.

	Red Bird Creek	Meeting House Fields, CL 1	Meeting House Fields, CL 2	Harris Neck Prehistoric	Harris Neck Mission Period
Plain	2.8	19.4	35.4	11.0	15.1
Burnished Plain	18.1	8.9	5.6	.1	4.8
Stamped	78.5	71.4	52.4	84.5	65.1
Incised	.6	.1	6.6	3.6	15.0

Notes:

Red Bird Creek percentages (Pearson 1984) have been refigured without earlier and unidentified sherds.

Harris Neck Prehistoric Component, feature data only (Braley et al. 1986:53, Table 3); percentages refigured without unidentified and rims.

Harris Neck Protohistoric Component (Braley et al. 1986:74, Table 7) XU1 and non-Irene phase material excluded).

Table 5.6. Vessel Form by Cluster.

Frequency Percent Row Pct Col Pct	Vessel Form				
	Bowl	Straight	Jar	Bottle	Total
Cluster 1	4 3.15 13.33 17.39	12 9.45 40.00 30.00	14 11.02 46.67 24.14	0 0.00 0.00 0.00	30 23.62
Cluster 2	19 14.96 19.59 82.61	28 22.05 28.87 70.00	44 34.65 45.36 75.86	6 4.72 6.19 100.00	97 76.38
Total	23 18.11	40 31.50	58 45.67	6 4.72	127 100.00

Table 5.7. Vessel Form by Surface Decoration.

Frequency Percent Row Pct Col Pct	Surface Decoration				
	Stamped	Plain	Burnished Plain	Incised	Total
Bowl	5 4.00 21.74 8.93	9 7.20 39.13 17.65	4 3.20 17.39 44.44	5 4.00 21.74 55.56	23 18.40
Straight	17 13.60 43.59 30.36	19 15.20 48.72 37.25	0 0.00 0.00 0.00	3 2.40 7.69 33.33	39 31.20
Jar	32 25.60 56.14 57.14	21 16.80 36.84 41.18	3 2.40 5.26 33.33	1 0.80 1.74 11.11	57 45.60
Bottle	2 1.60 33.33 3.57	2 1.60 33.33 3.92	2 1.60 33.33 22.22	0 0.00 0.00 0.00	6 4.80
Total	56 44.80	51 40.80	9 7.20	9 7.20	125 100.00

Note: 2 Unidentified deleted.

Table 5.8. Chi-Square Test, Vessel Form by Surface Decoration.

Frequency Frequency Expected Deviation Cell Chi-Square	Surface Decoration[1]		
	Stamped	Plain	Total
Bowl	5 8.8364 -3.836 1.6656	13 9.1636 3.8364 1.6061	18
Straight	17 17.673 -0.673 0.0256	19 18.327 0.6727 0.0247	36
Jar	32 27.491 4.5091 0.7396	24 28.509 -4.509 0.7132	56
Total	54	56	110

[1] Incised and Burnished Plain removed to obtain adequate cell size.

Statistics For Table Vessel Form by Surface Decoration

Statistic	DF	Value	Prob
Chi-Square	2	4.775	0.092

Table 5.9. Vessel Form by Rim Treatment.

Frequency Percent Row Pct Col Pct	Rim Treatment					
	Plain	Decorated	Pellet/ Node	Applique	Folded	Total
Bowl	17 13.82 77.27 29.31	2 1.63 9.09 11.76	2 1.63 9.09 50.00	1 0.81 4.55 2.38	0 0.00 0.00 0.00	22 17.89
Straight	17 13.82 42.50 29.31	5 4.07 12.50 29.41	0 0.00 0.00 0.00	17 13.82 42.50 40.48	1 0.81 2.50 50.00	40 32.52
Jar	21 17.07 36.84 36.21	9 7.32 15.79 52.94	2 1.63 3.51 50.00	24 19.51 42.11 57.14	1 0.81 1.75 50.00	57 46.34
Bottle	3 2.44 75.00 5.17	1 0.81 25.00 5.88	0 0.00 0.00 0.00	0 0.00 0.00 0.00	0 0.00 0.00 0.00	4 3.25
Total	58 47.15	17 13.82	4 3.25	42 34.15	2 1.63	123 100.00

Frequency Missing = 4

Table 5.10. Chi-Square Test, Vessel Form by Rim Treatment.[1]

Frequency Expected Deviation Cell Chi-Square	Rim Treatment			
	Plain	Decorated	Applique	Total
Bowl	17 9.7345 7.2655 5.4227	2 2.8319 -0.832 0.2444	1 7.4336 -6.434 5.5682	20
Straight	17 18.982 -1.982 0.207	5 5.5221 -0.522 0.0494	17 14.496 2.5044 0.4327	39
Jar	21 26.283 -5.283 1.062	9 7.646 1.354 0.2398	24 20.071 3.9292 0.7692	54
Total	55	16	42	113

[1] Unusual rims and rare vessel forms deleted to ensure adequate cell size.
Frequency Missing = 2

Statistics For Table Vessel Form by Rim Treatment

Statistic	DF	Value	Prob.
Chi-Square	4	13.9995	0.007

6

Mission Santa Catalina de Guale, St. Catherines Island, Georgia

The Guale coast was targeted early in the European colonial effort. The Spanish struggle to secure the area against first French, and then British, encroachment attests to the importance, justified or not, that the European powers attributed to the area (see P. Hoffman 1990). Pedro Menéndez de Avilés, founder of St. Augustine, sailed north to Guale in 1566, partly to establish northern outposts but also to remove a number of Frenchmen, remainders of the garrison at Charlesfort, known to be living among the Guale. Most of the French escaped, but one remained to argue the logic of French control of the area on the basis of the similarity of the words "Gallia" and "Guale." Menéndez was not persuaded, and the Guale, recognizing the superiority of the Spanish forces, turned this last Frenchman over to the Spaniards (Bushnell 1994:37).

On this same excursion, Menéndez met with the chiefs of Guale and Orista and left five or six soldiers in Guale to serve as catechists; this might be considered the first Mission Santa Catalina. On a second visit that year, he established a garrison of thirty men in the town of Guale (Hann 1990b:13). The location of this garrisoned town is disputed. It may have been on the inland side of Ossabow or Skidaway Island as Jones (1978:181) believed, or it may have been on St. Catherines Island (Bushnell 1994:38; Hann 1990b:13). The first missionaries, Jesuits, arrived in Guale in 1568 full of optimism. One of these, Fray Rogel, wrote that the Guale were "good workers, tillers of the soil. There are twenty-three friendly chieftains there and it would be easy to preach to them for almost all the Spaniards living there know the language. . . . I am sure they would make good Christians" (Rogel 1568:85, quoted in Bushnell 1994:40). By 1570, another Jesuit, Antonio Sedeño, described Guale territory as "the most miserable thing ever discovered" (Jones 1978:190; Zubillaga 1946:424) and the Guale, as well as their northern neighbors, as obdurately heathen. No doubt contributing to an already difficult situation, an epidemic struck Guale in 1569–1570, and the area was experiencing a severe drought (Jones 1978:190; Stahle et al. 1998:565). In 1570, having failed to make a single lasting convert, the Jesuits abandoned their missionary efforts in *La Florida*.

The first Franciscan missionaries arrived in Guale in 1573. One of this group baptized the chief of Guale and his wife in 1575 (Bushnell 1994:42; Jones 1978:182), just before the rebellion of 1576. That rebellion resulted in the burning of Santa Elena, the capital of *La Florida* and the home of Menéndez. The town was rebuilt, but it seems that no missionary activity was resumed. Although a Santa Catalina appears on the 1587 mission list, it does not seem to have had friars (Hann 1990b:24); most authorities date the second apparition of Santa Catalina to 1595. Thus, after the 1576 rebellion, the Guale coast was left without missionary influence for nearly twenty years. However, they were still subjected to the demands of the soldiers and citizens of Santa Elena and, to some extent, subjugated by the effects of disease. When Santa Catalina de Guale was reestablished in 1595, it was probably on St. Catherines Island (Hann 1990b:24; Jones 1978:183; Thomas 1993:32; cf. Geiger 1937). That "early" mission compound was destroyed in the Juanillo rebellion of 1597. When the church was again rebuilt (by 1604), it was described as being in the village of the chief of Guale.

Archaeological evidence indicates that the 1595 and 1604 Santa Catalina missions were constructed on the same site. A 20 percent transect survey of St. Catherines Island, conducted by David Hurst Thomas of the American Museum of Natural History (Thomas 1987, 1988a, 1988b), located only one possible mission site. At that site, there was good archaeological evidence for two Mission period occupational episodes. There was unequivocal evidence that the earlier of the two missions was burned, suggesting that it was the mission at the time of the 1597 rebellion. A second complex of buildings was erected over the first. These too were burned. This later burning correlates with the Spanish destruction of Santa Catalina prior to the abandonment of the mission after the Chichimeco attack of 1680 (see Bushnell 1994:146–147; Worth 1995:31).

Native Americans occupied St. Catherines Island again by 1743. At that time, Edward Kimber (1974) described eight or ten families with "several plantations of corn. It seems to be a most fruitful soil, and to have larger tracts of open land than any I have observed, and to abound in all kinds of game." It is unclear who these natives were or what part of St. Catherines Island they occupied. There is no evidence of an eighteenth-century Native American habitation site in the mission compound. In fact, the mission site is almost pristine; the most significant damage to structural features was done by large trees.

Evidence from the mission compound, the only area of the site reported to date, suggested that the location was not intensively occupied in the Irene phase. There were few, if any, subsurface features associated with the Irene phase and little or no Irene phase pottery. Broad-scale data generated by a power auger survey conducted at 10-meter intervals and extending more than 200 meters from the mission compound generated only 17 Irene sherds (but 251 "grit tempered stamped") as opposed to 882 Altamaha sherds (Thomas 1987:114, 149). This would seem to lend credence to the idea that the late-sixteenth-century mission was not founded in the chief's town. Of course, the compound could have been established in a plaza area, or the site may have been cleaned before the Spanish buildings were constructed. Research in the pueblo area will help to determine whether the mission was originally founded in an extant aboriginal town.

Descriptions of the site excavation methodology and the resulting definition of the buildings, including architectural characteristics, have been detailed elsewhere (Saunders 1990; Thomas 1987, 1988a, 1988b, 1993). Briefly then, the most visible set of structures were those from the seventeenth-century occupation (Figure 6.1). Burned wattle and daub rubble delineated the walls of a church, a convento, and a kitchen. All three structures were aligned in a quadrangle pattern on an orientation about 45 degrees west of north (Figure 6.1).

Low-level aerial photography initially suggested that two conventos were present. A visible drip line from the earlier structure ran about 10 degrees off the orientation of the burned daub rubble of the later structure. Excavation confirmed the presence of two structures. There were two sets of postholes, one with clean, mottled sand fill representing the early structural foundation and oriented with the drip line, and one set of rubble-filled postholes (the burned daub rubble derived from the remains of the earlier structure) oriented with the surface daub rubble of the later building (Figure 6.2).

Architectural information for the church and kitchen was not as clear. The presence of clean and rubble-filled postholes along the walls of the church indicated that the early and later structures were superimposed. However, the use of different building materials in different parts of

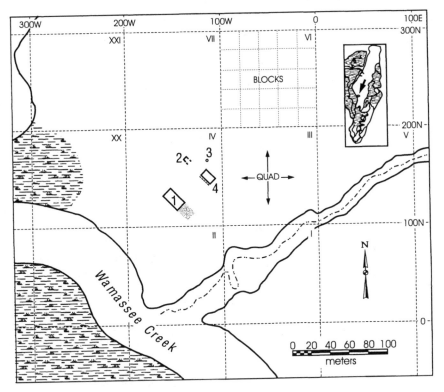

6.1. Santa Catalina de Guale Site Map. Key: 1 = Church; 2 = Kitchen; 3 = Well; 4 = Convento (from Thomas 1987; by permission).

the church, the addition of wall trenches, and burial activity within the church have obscured the relationship of many of the features. The kitchen was apparently a seventeenth-century addition to the mission compound (Thomas 1988a:103, 1988b:42); cooking may have taken place in the sixteenth-century convento.

During excavation, each structure was divided into a series of 2 × 2 meter units. These were originally aligned with a magnetic north grid (the A grid), though once the layout of the buildings was understood, the grid was shifted to align with the buildings (the B grid). The A zone corresponds to the soil above the daub rubble of the buildings; A zone materials were excavated on the A grid. Similarly, the B zone was defined as the soil associated with and beneath the building rubble to sterile tan sand. B zone materials were excavated on the B grid (see Thomas 1987:145, fn. 1). Because the area had been cleaned prior to erecting the second convento, artifacts from both these zones were considered to relate to the seventeenth-century

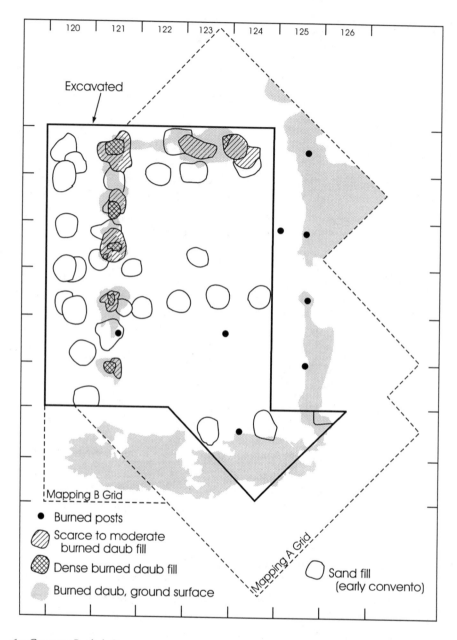

Excavated

120 121 122 123 124 125 126

Mapping B Grid

Mapping A Grid

● Burned posts

◨ Scarce to moderate
burned daub fill

◪ Dense burned daub fill

▨ Burned daub, ground surface

◯ Sand fill
(early convento)

6.2. Convento Posthole Patterns.

occupation. Pottery samples were taken from all structures and analyzed by the author. For the church, a set of sixteen systematically unaligned 2 × 2 meter units within the structure was chosen to be analyzed; A and B grid units were matched up as closely as possible. All pottery from those units was analyzed, though it was ultimately decided that only zone material (as opposed to features) would be used in the analysis.

Sampling strategy for the late convento assemblage was similar to that of the church—A zone materials from twenty-one units and B zone materials from another twelve units from the convento were analyzed. Fewer B zone proveniences were analyzed due to time constraints and the fact that there was little material in that zone away from daub debris. The few C zone (tan sand) proveniences that contained Altamaha phase materials in the selected units were included in this study. Those few artifacts were added to the B zone materials in the tables that follow. The pottery from forty-eight postholes was analyzed for early occupation materials.

The kitchen area was excavated differently from the two other structures. Initially, four test pits (TP) were placed in the area that would prove to be the southwest corner of the building. Materials from two of these, TP 1 and TP 2, were analyzed. These units revealed a 4 × 3 meter oval area filled with refuse (Feature 64). The floor of this feature appeared to have been covered several times with clay. Several olive jar vessels were embedded in the clay, and the clay surfaces were littered with food bone. The feature extended across four 2 × 2 meter units. Pottery was analyzed from one of those (W121) below TP 1 and TP 2.

The area of the kitchen occupied by Feature 64 may have had a special function over and above domestic food preparation for the friars. Donna Ruhl (Florida Museum of Natural History, personal communication, 1991), the ethnobotanist for the project, noted that almost no charred floral remains other than wood (which was abundant) were recovered from Feature 64. The absence of charred seed and vegetable foods, along with the preponderance of deer bone from the area, suggests that this portion of the kitchen may have been used to prepare meat for storage or perhaps even for export. The location of this hypothetical activity, close to the convento, suggests that it was tightly controlled by the friars. The pottery assemblage from the kitchen, then, may not have served a strictly domestic function, but was predominantly utilitarian.

Most of the proveniences from all structures were screened through 1/8-inch hardware cloth. Some A zone materials in the church were unscreened. Excavation procedures, however, ensured that sherds larger than 1 square centimeter were recovered. As in all other analyses, only sherds larger than 1 square centimeter were included in this study.

Stratigraphy, features, and structure function at Santa Catalina allowed for the analysis of pottery change along several lines. Prerebellion (1595–1597) pottery attributes were best studied from the least ambiguous contexts, that is, from the convento. Both early and late postholes provided closed contexts for the pottery of this earlier mission occupation. Initially the materials from the early occupation were compared with the results from the Meeting House Fields site. The data were then compared to the pottery recovered from the A and B zones. Because the site appeared to have been cleaned before the second convento was erected, pottery from both these strata was considered late. However, A zone and B zone materials were analyzed separately to determine whether there were any differences in pottery attributes. These were then compared to the feature materials.

The well-defined structure functions also provided the opportunity to determine variability in aboriginal ceramics within different contexts of use. Examining change within these functional contexts was considered imperative for understanding the role of, and, by extension, the possible reasons for, change in Guale Indian pottery in the overall mission context. For instance, given the fact that Santa Catalina appeared to have been a relatively well-supplied mission (Thomas 1988a), would there have been no necessity to use aboriginal wares in the church? If aboriginal wares were used, to what extent were their forms modified to conform to Spanish ideals, and how did this formal change affect both technological and stylistic attributes?

Similarly, were aboriginal wares incorporated into the domestic life of the friars in the convento? Data from St. Augustine indicated that in Spanish residences there, utilitarian ceramics were almost exclusively aboriginal and apparently unmodified, whereas serving dishes were European (Deagan 1983). Would the friars adopt this pattern, or would their commitment to poverty preclude the use of European ceramics? If serving wares were aboriginal, to what extent did the friars promote change (either formal or decorative) in the native pottery made for the their use? Finally, the kitchen area provided an assemblage of pottery with (presumably) only utilitarian functions. What forms were used there? Would they have been modified to prepare foods to Spanish tastes? How would they compare with contexts of use imbued with more ideotechnic or sociotechnic (*sensu* Binford 1962) functions?

It was expected that a different suite of vessel forms would appear in each structure. Because the Meeting House Fields material displayed some correlation of form and decoration, surface treatment and rim treatment were expected to be correlated with structure as well.

Results: The Prerebellion Component

Unfortunately, the sample size from the prerebellion component was small (n = 249). Nevertheless, there was enough information to observe that the change from Irene to Altamaha phase pottery was abrupt, at least at this mission site. There were no Irene wares. Even in this early component, curvilinear stamping was not present, and land and groove widths were well out of the range of Irene and comfortably within the range of the Altamaha in later contexts (see below). Because curvilinear stamping did appear in later contexts in very minor amounts, the absence of curvilinear stamping from the prerebellion context must be partially attributable to small sample size. Nevertheless, the assemblages from Meeting House Fields yielded between 30 percent (count) and 40 percent (weight) curvilinear stamping. The replacement of Irene filfot stamping with the rectilinear stamping of Altamaha phase pottery occurred either simultaneously (archaeologically speaking) with the beginning of the mission occupation or in the few years between the abandonment of Meeting House Fields and the mission occupation.

There were other surprising differences from the Irene phase. The incidence of stamping increased over that from Cluster 2 at the Meeting House Fields site (Table 6.1). In fact, the percentages were more like those from Cluster 1. This was true not only for the early context but also for the later mission contexts as well. Early context plain wares decreased in frequency as compared to both Clusters 1 and 2, though burnished plain wares reflected the values for Cluster 2. Incising also decreased in frequency. These results were contrary to those of Braley et al. (1986) at Harris Neck, where plain and incised wares increased in the Mission period (A.D. 1650) component. Check stamping, absent from Meeting House Fields Irene phase components, appeared on an Altamaha paste in very limited amounts in the early context. New "trade wares" appeared, the types St. Johns Check Stamped and St. Johns Plain. The former may have inspired the production of a local check stamp, but coeval interior Lamar assemblages also contain small amounts of check stamping.

The tempo of change reflected in the dramatic decrease in curvilinear stamping was also apparent in rim treatments. Although the difficulty of distinguishing some applique rim treatments from true folded rims at Meeting House Fields was noted (Chapter 4), there was no such ambiguity at Santa Catalina. There were no applique rims. Unfortunately, the rim sample (n = 18, Table 6.2) from the early context was too small to use for statistical comparisons. Some general observations can be made, however. Even in this early period, the most frequent rim treatment was the folded rim. These were most often cane punctated, but could also be fingernail punctated, stick punctated, or plain. Simple plain rims were the next most common rim treatment. There was only one decorated rim, and one ovoid pellet rim was recovered.

Vessel Form Analysis

The minimum number of vessels in the early context was just fourteen (Table 6.3). Simple bowls were the most prevalent identifiable form; one of the simple bowls had a scalloped lip. Including the two carinated bowls and the brimmed vessel, the seven serving vessels comprised half of the vessel assemblage in the early convento sample.

The brimmed vessel, a colono-ware form, was burnished and red filmed on the interior and exterior. In fact, three, or 21 percent, of these early vessels were red filmed, a seemingly high proportion probably related to sample size (see below). Filming occurred on the brimmed vessel noted above, one interior and exterior red filmed, straight-rimmed vessel (probably another brimmed vessel), and an interior-zoned red filmed and exterior-red filmed unidentified bowl.

The small sample size of the early context MNV may seriously affect the interpretation of the analysis of vessel form by other treatments. Again, some general observations can be made. Like Meeting House Fields, stamping was the most common surface decoration, and it was applied to all forms except the brimmed vessel (Table 6.3). The relatively high proportion of burnished plain vessels must be seen as the result of a small sample.

Other Attributes

All of the vessels defined were grit tempered save one, the brimmed vessel, which was sand tempered. Temper by sherd count (Table B.1) indicated that this attribute was not artificially depressed by the MNV approach; only 9 of 249 sherds were sand tempered. None of the sherds recovered from the early context were sooted.

The sherd count values for burnishing and red filming are given in Table B.2. Unburnished interiors were present on less than 20 percent of the sherds, a value more or less consistent with the Meeting House Fields total. Red filming and zoned red filming of interiors and exteriors were present at only 1 percent of the sample, indicating that the proportion of red filming in the vessel form analysis may be inflated.

Only four of the eight folded rims were measurable; mean rim depth was 17.7 millimeters. This was considerably deeper than the base of the Irene phase applique strips. Although it is probably unwise to make too much of this because of the small sample size, it is worth noting that the zone of rim decoration had moved down the vessel at this relatively early date.

Central dots (Table B.3) were visible in about the same percent of sherds as was found in the late Irene phase, or around 7 percent. This indicated that, as Brewer (1985) originally suggested, the central dot motif was the primary motif used at Santa Catalina.

Land and groove widths for the pottery from the early context were 2.0 and 2.4 millimeters, respectively. This represents a marked increase in the size of both attributes from the Cluster 2 Meeting House Fields values. Because pot lands were paddle grooves, the increase in land size might reflect the use of a different paddle carving tool.

Incising was characterized as bold (>1 millimeter), with designs comprised of few lands and grooves. Designs were more elaborate than those at Meeting House Fields, and they included the use of punctation with incising.

Summary and Implications of the Prerebellion Component

The analysis of the early context in the convento at Santa Catalina indicated that the transition from Irene phase to Altamaha phase wares must be seen as relatively abrupt, at least in archaeological time. In the proveniences examined, there were no Irene-like stamped wares. Before A.D. 1600, the brimmed plate and/or bowl was incorporated into the suite of traditional vessel forms; other colono-ware forms, such as foot rings and handles, were not found in the early component assemblage. The brimmed vessels, as well as more traditional forms, were red filmed. Red filming was not unknown in interior Georgia Lamar societies prior to the Mission period. It is reported as a minority treatment in Mississippian phase components in the Russell Reservoir, for instance (Anderson and Joseph 1988:250); rare instances of loop handles and red filming were recovered by Moore (1897) from coastal mounds containing no other evidence of contact. In general, though, red filming was not present in coastal Lamar sequences until the Mission period (contra Larson 1953:24). For this reason, red filming can be considered a development of the Mission period for Guale pottery. Why it should appear in the Mission period is something of a mystery. It might be worth noting that the Spanish had admired Taino Indian red filmed wares in the Caribbean: "Las Casas also noted and appreciated Taino pottery, writing that the Indians would offer the admiral [Columbus] 'water in earthenware jars, very well done and painted on the outside like red ochre' " (Las Casas 1965:273, quoted in Garcia-Arevalo 1990:276). Red slipped burnished wares also had a long history in Spain (Foster 1960:88–92). The evanescent presence of red filming in pre-Columbian times, and the above quotes, might indicate that red filming was encouraged by the Spanish.

Rim treatments also changed abruptly. Applique strips, which constituted around 30 percent of the rim treatments in the late Meeting House Fields component, were never used at the mission compound. Again, this is curious. Unless there were some compelling reasons to change, one would expect that a stylistic element would "drift" rather than be suddenly replaced. Perhaps the answer lies in a reconsideration of the rim strip and the folded rim. Rather than just decorative, both might very well have had a function, such as providing better purchase when moving a vessel. The rim fold, one piece with the vessel, would give the rim more strength and would be far less prone to break away than the applique strip. That said, and again considering the abrupt disappearance of the strip, one wonders whether the use of the folded rim could have been promoted by the Spanish.

This line of thought can be extended even further. Why should the design element change so abruptly? There are at least three possibilities, one functional, one social, and one ideological. First, paddles do have a function: to compress the coils of the pot and force air out of the vessel fabric. Paddles with deeper, wider lands would do this more effectively than the fine land and grooved Irene phase paddles. The friars might have asked that the lands and grooves be carved wider and deeper. If the paddle remained the same size and the proportions of the design were kept the same, the result would be that the terminal, curvilinear elements would drop out. Other "technological" explanations include changes in the woods used for paddles to a harder species, which would make curvilinear elements more difficult to carve; changes in the paddle carving tool that made curvilinear elements difficult to carve; or both.

The sociological reason is the more common explanation for the change in design content and execution. Perhaps by analogy to the design simplification that occurs in traditional pottery in market contexts (e.g., Lathrap 1976:203–207; Rice 1987:454), this line of reasoning suggests that Native American neophytes no longer had time to carve their intricate designs because of other labor demands, resulting in simplification with bolder elements. However, the cases are not truly analogous. Most studies on market effects have been done on painted pottery. The same time constraints do not apply to paddle stamped pottery because a single paddle can be used on a multitude of pots. In any case, because preexisting paddles could have been brought to the site, this explanation fails to explain the abrupt falloff in frequency of filfot cross motifs.

Finally, there is a possible ideological rationale for the change. If the Spanish understood that the Irene filfot cross was a cosmological symbol representing the sun and the cardinal directions, the friars could have discouraged the use of the motif. Also, if the Guale were truly converted, they might have ceased carving the design of their own volition. This explanation, like the first one, is not completely satisfactory either because the world symbol was still the principal motif throughout the mission occupation. It is possible that the Guale dropped the more noticeable curvilinear element and quietly went on producing the world symbol, confident that the friars (not unlike archaeologists of the distant future) would not recognize it. Wider and deeper lands and grooves would serve to obliterate the design all the better.

Although this kind of subterfuge is consistent with the sort of passive resistance described by Scott (1985), we lack independently derived data to choose between these (not necessarily mutually exclusive) alternatives. However, the absolute and abrupt replacement of Irene phase wares argues for some more direct intervention on the part of the Spanish than has usually been attributed to them. Keeping in mind that the Spanish quickly set up potting industries everywhere else they settled (Deagan 1983:234), it does not seem unwarranted to propose more directed change in some facets of Guale pottery production.

The Seventeenth-Century Ceramic Assemblage

Data from the early component confirmed that a fully new pottery complex, Altamaha, was in use at the mission compound before the seventeenth century. That complex changed little during the next eighty years at Santa Catalina.

Sample size for the late component was large (n = 2,476) and adequate for an analysis of pottery attributes by mission structure. The attribute with the largest sample size, surface decoration, was analyzed by structure and zone to determine whether there was any significant difference between the assemblage directly associated with the daub rubble of the church and convento (B zone) and that overlying them (A zone). Data for the kitchen could not be segregated in this manner, and the assemblage from that area was analyzed as a single provenience. These data are presented in Table 6.4.

A comparison of A and B zone surface decorations at the church indicated virtually no difference between the two. This may be due to mixing caused by the more than four hundred interments in the nave. More differences were observable at the convento, where plain wares increased through time and stamping and incising decreased. St. Johns wares, presumably imported from the St. Augustine area, are a relatively minor component of the assemblage, but appear to increase through time, as does a grit-tempered, presumably locally made, check stamped ware. However, some of these apparent changes, in particular the relative frequency of minority wares, may be due to sample size. There were more than four times as many sherds in the A zone sample as in the B zone sample.

Frequency distributions and a chi-square test (Tables 6.5 and 6.6) indicated that surface decorations were not distributed equally in space. Burnished plain wares were "over-represented" in the church; St. Johns pottery was absent (Table 6.4). This was an intuitively pleasing result, but it should be emphasized that no surface decoration was restricted to a single structure; stamping was overwhelmingly the most frequent surface decoration at the church, as it was elsewhere on the site. Plain wares were more prevalent at the convento than expected. In contrast to the church, St. Johns wares were present in relative abundance in the convento and in the kitchen, where percentage frequencies were about equal. In the kitchen area, plain wares were "under-represented"; the deviation from the expected frequency yielded the highest cell chi-square value in the test. This, too, conformed to the conventional wisdom, that is, that cooking wares were predominantly stamped vessels. However, note that decoration not commonly associated with cooking pots—incising and interior/exterior burnishing—were present at about the expected frequencies.

Vessel Form Analysis

One hundred and fifty-nine vessels were defined out of the sherd assemblage. Although the different sampling procedures used for the structures preclude a reliable comparison between structures on the basis of raw frequency, it is not surprising that the largest number of vessels came from the kitchen area.

Forms included all those from the late Irene phase as well as carinated bowls, brimmed vessels, and a restricted jar with a wide mouth (Table 6.7,

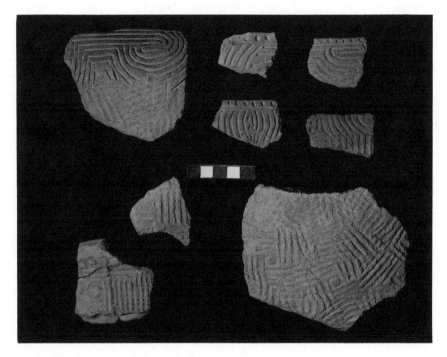

6.3. Representative Sherds from Santa Catalina de Guale. Scale in centimeters.

Figure 6.3). Vessel form was correlated with the same surface decorations as in the late Irene phase (Tables 6.8 and 6.9). Incising was correlated with bowls, both simple and carinated, and jars were most commonly stamped. As at Meeting House Fields and in the early Mission component, none of these associations were absolute. Still, carinated bowls were always either incised or stamped, never left plain. Brimmed vessels bore all categories of surface decoration except check stamping, though, like bowls and carinated bowls, they were most frequently incised. This indicates that brimmed vessels were assimilated into the design categories of more traditional bowls. One unusual brimmed vessel had a strongly notched rim (Figure 6.3). A single handle was found in the convento, another came from the kitchen, and four handles were recorded in the pottery sample from the church. No sherds in the sample selected had a foot ring, though one was recovered from the kitchen area in a provenience that was not included in this study.

Because surface decoration (by sherd) was associated with structures and because vessel forms were associated with surface decoration, it was surprising that a chi-square test indicated no association between vessel form and structure (Table 6.10). Whether figured by rim sherd total or by

MNV, chi-square test results indicated no difference in distribution (Table 6.11). However, the relative percentages of surface decorations changed quite a bit when analyzed by MNV. Incising rose from just 6 percent by sherd count (Table 6.5) to nearly 30 percent by MNV (Table 6.9). This is largely because incised vessels show a great deal more individual variation in execution than stamped vessels, and thus it is easier to tell them apart. Because the assemblage from the church was not a 100 percent sample and because the MNV method no doubt depressed the total number of stamped and plain vessels present, it seems best to take the sherd data at face value and conclude that there was a difference in the distribution of surface decoration at the site.

If a difference in the distribution of surface decoration is accepted, then the lack of correlation between vessel form and structure is curious. It may be that with the application of an appropriate design, different functions were assigned to a limited range of forms. Alternatively, structures may have had overlapping functions. For instance, all three structures might be expected to have numerous storage jars. These two hypotheses are not mutually exclusive. The former, that form was modified by decoration to serve a specific function, is given some weight by the association of rim treatment with structure (Tables 6.12 and 6.13). There were few folded rims in the church as compared with the convento or the kitchen.

Rim style showed the same association with vessels as was described for both Meeting House Fields and the early convento component (Table 6.14). There was an association between form and rim treatment (Tables 6.15 and 6.16). Bowl (including brimmed bowls and plates) rims were predominantly plain, whereas jar rims were folded. The incidence of decorated vessels was very low. This late pre-Columbian development, which is said to increase through time and reached 13.5 percent of the rim treatments in Cluster 2 at Meeting House Fields, was truncated in the Mission period. One rim treatment fell under the pellet/node category. However, the applique really fit no existing definition. It was a large circular addition, more in the size range of a lug, and was heavily punctated.

Rim elaborations associated with the various forms are given in Table 6.17. Cane punctation remained the dominant elaboration, followed by fingernail punctation. Note that if a bowl had a folded rim, it was never punctated, though a few brimmed vessel rims were, and one carinated bowl rim was pinched.

One new rim elaboration appeared in the late component. This was "triangle punctate" (one unidentified punctate sherd at the Meeting House

Fields site carried the comment "triangle?"). Six vessels bore this decoration. Unlike the other styluses used for punctation, the triangular stylus was used only on folded rims. Folded rims were also stamped with the same paddle as was used for the pot. There was a preponderance of cane punctation in the kitchen and stick impressions in the convento (Table 6.18).

Other Attributes

Although conspicuous, the amount of red and/or black filming was actually quite low (Table B.4). Just 2.3 percent of the sherds were interior filmed; twenty-five sherds, or 1.0 percent, had filming on the exterior. Only three vessels were identified as filmed: one bowl, one excurvate rim jar, and one brimmed vessel. Although the numbers were small, it appeared that both interior filming and exterior filming were more common in the convento than in the other structures. Contrary to expectations, filming was no more common at the church than in the kitchen.

Another surprising find was that virtually none of the sherds analyzed were sooted on the interior or exterior. Although this might have been expected in the church or even the convento, a high incidence of sooting was anticipated in the kitchen samples. As Table B.5 indicates, this was not the case.

Data from the late component indicated that the low incidence of sand tempering in the early convento component was not influenced by small sample size. Sand tempering was present in only 2 percent to 3 percent of the late Mission sample (Table B.6). These figures represented quite a drop from the values for the Meeting House Fields site, where 20 percent (sherd count/weight) to 36 percent (MNV count) of the assemblage was sand tempered. At the Mission site, plain sherds were most likely to be sand tempered, but sand tempering occurred in stamped and incised sherds as well. Sand tempering occurred in bowl, brimmed vessel, straight rim, and jar forms (Table B.7). Grog was added to the grit-tempered paste in a very few instances, including one brimmed vessel. The percentage of sherds with grit and grog tempering was identical to that at Meeting House Fields, so inspiration for grog temper cannot be said to have come from the Mocama area San Pedro wares (Ashley and Rolland 1997).

Land and groove widths averaged 1.8 millimeters for lands and 2.3 millimeters for grooves. These figures were virtually identical to those found for the early component (land 2.0, groove 2.4). There appeared to be no meaningful variation in land and groove width between structures; the average land and groove widths, respectively, were: church, 2.0 and

2.1 millimeters; convento, 1.8 and 2.8 millimeters; and kitchen, 1.7 and 1.9 millimeters. Land and groove widths were least proportional in the convento, but the significance of this, if any, is unknown.

Rim depth did vary between structures. The average depth for folded rims in the church was 13.2 millimeters; in the convento the average depth was 20.5 millimeters; and in the kitchen it was 18.3 millimeters. However, a difference of 0.5 centimeters in rim depth is unlikely to be culturally significant. Rim depth could vary to that degree on a single vessel. The overall average rim fold depth at the site was 17.3 millimeters.

Central elements were visible on between 5 percent (count) and a relatively large 14 percent (weight) of the stamped sherds (Table B.8). A comparison with the Meeting House Fields data on this attribute indicates that the world symbol remained the dominant motif. Curvilinear stamping, absent from the small early component sample, was present on only 0.5 percent of the sherds from the late component (Table B.9).

Motifs

As discussed, "San Marcos Complicated Stamped" was the primary motif used. Some sherds displayed a variation of the motif in which the central element was carved without a border (Figure 6.3). Single or double lines of checks were sometimes incorporated into the radiating lines. These unusual treatments may reflect the presence of another group of peoples with a slightly different traditional execution of the same design. As noted previously, the Satuache were incorporated into Santa Catalina by A.D. 1663. In addition, Yamassee from the interior Estatoe (Lamar) phase, where check stamping reaches 6 percent (Hally 1990:55), were arriving in Guale as refugees from Chichimeco attacks in A.D. 1661. There is no record that any lived at Santa Catalina, however. On the other hand, Santa Catalina natives might have begun carving innovative treatments under a variety of stimuli, resulting in a surge of creativity not unlike that noted by Charleton and Fournier (1993) in central Mexico.

Incising was almost all bold incising. Designs appeared to be principally scrolls, concentric semicircles, and filler. The most distinctive thing about the assemblage was the addition of punctation, which was not present in the Meeting House Fields assemblage or, indeed, in the interior Georgia Lamar incising tradition. Of the forty-nine different patterns of incising recorded (many of these were probably not discrete, but different portions of the same design), twenty-one, or 43 percent, had either rim punctation

immediately above the top of the incising or (rarely) punctation incorporated into the incised design.

Summary and Implications

It is now possible to answer some of the questions posed at the beginning of
this chapter. Clearly, even a well-supplied mission such as Santa Catalina
relied heavily on aboriginal wares. Colono-ware forms were made, but
remained a small part of the total assemblage. Colono-wares do not
appear significantly different in either paste or decorative qualities from
the aboriginal forms. Rather, it appears that colono-wares were assimilated
into the preexisting aboriginal formal categories and decorated accordingly.

With respect to contexts of use, data from the mission on St. Catherines
Island suggested that, contrary to expectations, there was little difference
in the frequencies of most pottery attributes between structures. Although
the relative frequency of different surface decorations did vary between
structures, this did not translate into differences in vessel form distribution.
Rather, it appeared that the same suite of forms was present in all structures
but that different decorations and rim treatments were applied to vessels
according to their context of use or function. It would be interesting to see
these results duplicated in other studies—the data presented here could
be anomalous. To anticipate a bit, however: the data from the Amelia
Island Santa Catalina mission at least partially substantiate these results
(see Chapter 7).

The use of surface treatment and rim styles to define vessel function
might represent the extension of an old strategy of the Guale. In comparing
Irene phase burial mound and midden contexts—the only contexts of
use compared thus far—researchers have concluded that there was no
difference in surface treatment or form between domestic and mortuary
wares with the exception of the small jars noted by Braley et al. (1986:88; also
see Cook 1980a; Pearson 1977b). In fact, domestic and mortuary wares may
have been one and the same. Many of the vessels accompanying burials at
the Kent Mound on St. Simons Island and Johns Mound on St. Catherines
Island were heavily sooted or showed other evidence of use before interment
(Cook 1980b:168; Larsen and Thomas 1982).[1] On the other hand, the most
elaborately incised vessels, often bearing Southeastern Ceremonial Cult
motifs, appear to occur predominantly in pottery caches in burial mounds
(e.g., Cook and Pearson 1989), and forms are not notably different from
utilitarian vessels. Instead, elaboration occurred solely in the incising. In
other words, form was modified by decoration to specify function.

Substantive data were available from the two occupations of the mission to indicate substantial breaks with the pre-Columbian past, changes that occurred simultaneously with or just prior to the initial mission occupation. Technological changes included the introduction of a new form, the brimmed vessel, made to copy the forms of majolica plates and bowls with which the Spanish were familiar. The form was assimilated into the "bowl" decorative category by the Guale.

Another technological change was the dramatic decrease in the use of sand as a tempering agent. At Meeting House Fields, as at Mission Santa Catalina, sand tempering was not restricted to one vessel form or one surface decoration. The reason why one vessel would be tempered with sand and another of the same form with grit is unknown. Both reasons discussed for the increase in sand tempering in the Meeting House Fields Cluster 2 assemblage might apply (in reverse) for the decrease at the mission. That is, grit deposits may have become more accessible, or vessels may have become larger. Most certainly, the selection of one temper over the other would alter functional attributes (firing characteristics as well as porosity, hardness, and strength) of the vessel (Rice 1987:347–369).

Although porosity, hardness, and strength were not recorded, as the study progressed it was decided to record fired color on a subsample of sherds. Fired color indicates the extent to which organic materials and iron compounds were oxidized during firing of the pot and, by extension, firing temperature (Rice 1987:343). Fired color is also influenced by particle size of the temper used, with coarser clays firing more thoroughly than fine clays (Rice 1987:89, Figure 4.3). Finally, firing affects hardness—high-fired vessels are harder than low-fired vessels. The subsamples consisted of a random selection of rims; rims were used so that location of the sherd on the vessel could be controlled.

Core color and interior and exterior color of a sample of rim sherds from Meeting House Fields and both Santa Catalina missions are shown in Tables 6.19, 6.20, and 6.21. Comparison of the samples indicated that the Georgia Santa Catalina sample had generally lighter (better oxidized) cores, lighter interiors, and, in particular, lighter exteriors than the Meeting House Fields sample. This might suggest that the Spanish influenced firing practices. Smith (1951:129) also observed that Mission period pottery was harder than pre-Columbian pottery and might indicate "improved techniques of firing learned from the Spanish." The Florida Santa María, in turn, had somewhat darker cores but much higher frequencies of light interiors and exteriors than the Georgia mission. This indicated that more pots were fired at high temperatures than at the earlier mission; firing duration, however, may have decreased. This may be some indirect evidence of wood shortages, which were reported to be severe around St. Augustine (Bushnell 1994:122) and on the barrier islands (Hann 1986b).

Again, this study was not designed to be a rigorous exploration into the technological changes of the two pottery types. The above data, however, suggest that such a study would be worthwhile. Taken together, the change in the ratios of temper types and the apparent change in firing practices may indicate another instance of Spanish influences in native pottery production.

Profound changes also occurred in decorative attributes (some of which may have had functional aspects). The use of applique rim strips was abandoned completely in favor of folded rims. The same elaborations that graced the strips were applied to folded rims. Both at Meeting House Fields and the mission, cane punctation was the dominant rim elaboration. Red and/or black filming was added as decoration, but would also decrease permeability of the vessel and perhaps inhibit loss of vessel strength due to cracks (Rice 1987:368). The stamped design changed abruptly, with no apparent intermediate steps. The design execution became much bolder, and, although the design continued to emphasize a central node with offset radiating lines, the curvilinear elements of the preceding phase almost completely disappeared. Incised designs also changed as they became uniformly bold and as punctation was incorporated into the motif.

Elsewhere in this chapter, the idea was advanced that many of the changes described above were stimulated by the Spanish. Although this hypothesis needs to be verified, it has been established that there were no significant changes in these attributes at Santa Catalina from 1595 to 1680. It is not surprising that these principally utilitarian wares did not change over the years. Utilitarian wares in general are quite resistant to change (Rice 1987:460, 465), and Spanish utilitarian wares in particular have been described as "monotonous" (Foster 1960:88). There may, in fact, have been little need for the introduction of new forms for cooking. Because both the Spanish peasant and the southeastern Indian relied principally on soups or stews for staple foods (though with different ingredients; see Hann 1996:97; Otto and Lewis 1974:106–110; Reitz 1990), independent but similar evolution of forms would not be unusual. The cooking pots depicted in a seventeenth-century Velasquez painting (Braudel 1981:231), though probably iron, were not that different in basic form from the Guale everted lip jar.

Table 6.1. Early Convento Surface Decoration.

Master Code	Stamp				Plain				Burnished Plain				Incised			
	Count		Weight		Count		Weight		Count		Weight		Count		Weight	
	Sum	Pct	Sum	Pct	Sum	Pct	Sum	Pct	Sum	Pct	Sum	Pct	Sum	Pct	Sum	Pct
	201	80.7	2389.1	85.5	22	8.84	207.3	7.42	14	5.62	90.8	3.25	7	2.81	53.6	1.92

Master Code	Check				St. Johns				All			
	Count		Weight		Count		Weight		Count		Weight	
	Sum	Pct	Sum	Pct	Sum	Pct	Sum	Pct	Sum	Pct	Sum	Pct
	2	0.80	40.5	1.45	3	1.20	13.4	0.48	249	100	2794.7	100

Table 6.2. Early Convento Rim Style.

Rim Treatment									
Plain				Decorated				Folded	
Style									
Plain		Incised		Decorated		Pellet/Node		Folded Plain	
Count	Weight	Count	Weight	Count	Weight	Count	Weight	Count	Weight
N	Pct	N	Pct	N	Pct	N	Pct	N	Pct	N	Pct	N	Pct	N	Pct	N	Pct	N	Pct

Count		Weight		Count		Weight		Count		Weight		Count		Weight		Count		Weight	
N	Pct	N	Pct	N	Pct	N	Pct	N	Pct	N	Pct	N	Pct	N	Pct	N	Pct	N	Pct
6	100	79.4	100	2	100	19.3	100	1	100	3.6	100	1	100	17.9	100	1	100	4.4	100

Rim Treatment							All		
Folded									
Style									
Folded Cane		Folded Stamp		Folded Stick					
Count		Weight		Count		Weight		Count		Weight		Count		Weight	
N	Pct	N	Pct	N	Pct	N	Pct	N	Pct	N	Pct	N	Pct	N	Pct
3	100	32.7	100	2	100	11.2	100	1	100	4.2	100	18	100	184.2	100

Table 6.3. Early Convento Vessel Forms by Surface Decoration.

Vessel Form	Master Code											
	Uid		Stamp		Plain		B Plain		Incised		All	
	Count		Count		Count		Count		Count		Count	
	Sum	Pct	Sum	Pct	Sum	Pct	Sum	Pct	Sum	Pct	Sum	Pct
Bowl	1	25.0	2	50.0	.	.	1	25.0	.	.	4	100
Straight (UID)	1	20.0	2	40.0	1	20.0	1	20.0	.	.	5	100
Jar	1	50.0	1	50.0	.	.	.	.	.	.	2	100
Carinated Bowl	.	.	1	50.0	.	.	.	.	1	50.0	2	100
Brimmed Vessel	.	.	.	.	.	.	1	100	.	.	1	100
All	3	21.4	6	42.9	1	7.1	3	21.4	1	7.1	14	100

Table 6.4. Surface Decoration by Structure/Zone.

Church

	Master Code											
	Stamp				Plain				Burnished Plain			
	Count		Weight		Count		Weight		Count		Weight	
Zone	N	Pct	N	Pct	N	Pct	N	Pct	N	Pct	N	Pct
A	208	69.1	2666.7	71.6	40	13.3	431.7	11.6	25	8.31	311.1	8.35
B	244	68.9	3157.8	73.8	55	15.5	491.2	11.5	19	5.37	146.9	3.44
All	452	69.0	5824.5	72.8	95	14.5	922.9	11.5	44	6.72	458.0	5.72

	Master Code											
	Incised				Check				All			
	Count		Weight		Count		Weight		Count		Weight	
Zone	N	Pct	N	Pct	N	Pct	N	Pct	N	Pct	N	Pct
A	18	5.98	212.0	5.69	10	3.32	103.5	2.78	301	100	3725	100
B	21	5.93	296.8	6.94	15	4.24	183.3	4.29	354	100	4276.0	100
All	39	5.95	508.8	6.36	25	3.82	286.8	3.58	655	100	8001.0	100

Table 6.4 (cont).

Convento

	Master Code												
	Stamp				Plain				Burnished Plain				Incised
	Count		Weight		Count		Weight		Count		Weight		Count
Zone	N	Pct	N	Pct	N	Pct	N	Pct	N	Pct	N	Pct	N	Pct
A	486	67.5	3881.0	70.8	133	18.5	968.2	17.7	24	3.33	142.6	2.60	44	6.11
B	124	72.5	1387.1	81.8	21	12.3	137.2	8.09	7	4.09	33.6	1.98	16	9.36
All	610	68.5	5268.1	73.4	154	17.3	1105.4	15.4	31	3.48	176.2	2.45	60	6.73

	Master Code												
	Incised		Check				St. Johns				All			
	Weight		Count		Weight		Count		Weight		Count		Weight	
Zone	N	Pct	N	Pct	N	Pct	N	Pct	N	Pct	N	Pct	N	Pct
A	316.7	5.78	15	2.08	153.8	2.80	18	2.50	21.2	0.39	720	100	5483.5	100
B	121.7	7.18	1	0.58	11.6	0.68	2	1.17	3.8	0.22	171	100	1695.0	100
All	438.4	6.11	16	1.80	165.4	2.30	20	2.24	25.0	0.35	891	100	7178.5	100

Table 6.4 (cont).

Kitchen

	Master Code													
	Stamp				Plain				Burnished Plain				Incised	
	Count		Weight		Count		Weight		Count		Weight		Count	
Zone	N	Pct	N	Pct	N	Pct	N	Pct	N	Pct	N	Pct	N	Pct
All	604	77.8	9007.7	81.6	45	5.80	347.0	3.14	26	3.35	260.8	2.36	42	5.41

	Master Code															
	Incised				Check				St. Johns				All			
	Count		Weight		Count		Weight		Count		Weight		Count		Weight	
Zone	N	Pct	N	Pct	N	Pct	N	Pct	N	Pct	N	Pct	N	Pct	N	Pct
All	31	3.99	599.8	5.43	28	3.61	695.7	6.30			126.6	1.15	776	100	11038	100

Table 6.5. Surface Decoration by Structure.

Frequency Percent Row Pct Col Pct	Master Code				
	Stamp	Plain	Burnished Plain	Incised	Total
Church	477 20.98 72.82 27.45	95 4.18 14.50 32.31	44 1.93 6.72 43.56	39 1.72 5.95 27.66	655 28.80
Kitchen	635 27.92 84.89 36.54	45 1.98 6.02 15.31	26 1.14 3.48 25.74	42 1.85 5.61 29.79	748 32.89
Convento	626 27.53 71.87 36.02	154 6.77 17.68 52.38	31 1.36 3.56 30.69	60 2.64 6.89 42.55	871 38.30
Total	1738 76.43	294 12.93	101 4.44	141 6.20	2274 100.00

Table 6.6. Chi-Square Test, Surface Decoration by Structure.

Frequency Expected Deviation Cell Chi-Square	Master Code				
	Stamp	Plain	Burnished Plain	Incised	Total
Church	477	95	44	39	655
	500.61	84.683	29.092	40.613	
	-23.61	10.317	14.908	-1.613	
	1.1136	1.2568	7.6396	0.0641	
Kitchen	635	45	26	42	748
	571.69	96.707	33.223	46.38	
	63.31	-51.71	-7.223	-4.38	
	7.011	27.647	1.5702	0.4136	
Convento	626	154	31	60	871
	665.7	112.61	38.686	54.007	
	-39.7	41.391	-7.686	5.9934	
	2.3674	15.213	1.5269	0.6651	
Total	1738	294	101	141	2274

Statistics for Table of Structure by Surface Decoration

Statistic	DF	Value	Prob
Chi-Square	6	66.488	<0.001

Table 6.7. Vessel Form by Structure.

Frequency Percent Row Pct Col Pct	Vessel Form								
	Bowl	Straight	X Unrest	X Rest	X Uid	Rsmjar	Car bowl	Brim	Total
Church	16 10.06 34.78 41.03	7 4.40 15.22 20.00	2 1.26 4.35 40.00	1 0.63 2.17 33.33	6 3.77 13.04 19.35	2 1.26 4.35 40.00	6 3.77 13.04 42.86	6 3.77 13.04 22.22	46 28.93
Kitchen	14 8.81 21.21 35.90	17 10.69 25.76 48.57	2 1.26 3.03 40.00	1 0.63 1.52 33.33	15 9.43 22.73 48.39	2 1.26 3.03 40.00	6 3.77 9.09 42.86	9 5.66 13.64 33.33	66 41.51
Convento	9 5.66 19.15 23.08	11 6.92 23.40 31.43	1 0.63 2.13 20.00	1 0.63 2.13 33.33	10 6.29 21.28 32.26	1 0.63 2.13 20.00	2 1.26 4.26 14.29	12 7.55 25.53 44.44	47 29.56
Total	39 24.53	35 22.01	5 3.14	3 1.89	31 19.50	5 3.14	14 8.81	27 16.89	159 100.0

X Unrest = excurvate unrestricted
X Rest = excurvate restricted
X Uid = excurvate unidentified

Rsmjar = restricted mouth jar
Carbowl = carinated bowl
Brim = brimmed vessel

Table 6.8. Chi-Square Test, Vessel Form by Structure.

Frequency Expected Deviation Cell Chi-Square	Vessel Form					
	Bowl	Straight	Jar	Carbowl	Brim	Total
Church	16	7	11	6	6	46
	11.283	10.126	12.73	4.0503	7.8113	
	4.717	-3.126	-1.73	1.9497	-1.811	
	1.972	0.9649	0.235	0.9385	0.42	
Kitchen	14	17	20	6	9	66
	16.189	14.528	18.264	5.8113	11.208	
	-2.189	2.4717	1.7358	0.1887	-2.208	
	0.2959	0.4205	0.165	0.0061	0.4348	
Convento	9	11	13	2	12	47
	11.528	10.346	13.006	4.1384	7.8911	
	-2.528	0.6541	-0.006	-2.138	4.0189	
	0.5545	0.0414	0.000	1.1049	2.0237	
Total	39	35	44	14	27	159

Statistics for Table of Structure by Vessel Form

Statistic	DF	Value	Prob
Chi-Square	8	9.577	0.296

Table 6.9. Surface Decoration by Vessel Form.

Frequency Percent Row Pct Col Pct	Surface Decoration						
	Uid	Stamp	Plain	Burnished Plain	Incised	Check	Total
Bowl	1 0.63 2.56 5.26	11 6.92 28.21 16.92	4 2.52 10.26 25.00	3 1.89 7.69 30.00	20 12.58 51.28 43.48	0 0.00 0.00 0.00	39 24.53
Straight (UID)	11 6.92 31.43 57.89	16 10.06 45.71 24.62	2 1.26 5.71 12.50	3 1.89 8.57 30.00	3 1.89 8.57 6.52	0 0.00 0.00 0.00	35 22.01
Jar	6 3.77 13.64 31.58	22 13.84 50.00 33.85	6 3.77 13.64 37.50	3 1.89 6.82 30.00	4 2.52 9.09 8.70	3 1.89 6.82 100.00	44 27.67
Carinated Bowl	0 0.00 0.00 0.00	6 3.77 42.86 9.23	0 0.00 0.00 0.00	0 0.00 0.00 0.00	8 5.03 57.14 17.39	0 0.00 0.00 0.00	14 8.81
Brimmed Vessel	1 0.63 3.70 5.26	10 6.29 37.04 15.38	4 2.52 14.81 25.00	1 0.63 3.70 10.00	11 6.92 40.74 23.91	0 0.00 0.00 0.00	27 16.98
Total	19 11.95	65 40.88	16 10.06	10 6.29	46 28.93	3 1.89	159 100.00

Table 6.10. Chi-Square Test, Surface Decoration by Vessel Form.

Frequency Expected Deviation Cell Chi-Square	Master Code			
	Stamp	Plain	Incised	Total
Bowl	25	12	39	76
	36.348	14.319	25.333	
	-11.35	-2.319	13.667	
	3.5428	0.3755	7.3728	
Straight	16	5	3	24
	11.478	4.5217	8	
	4.5217	0.4783	-5	
	1.7813	0.0506	3.125	
Jar	25	9	4	38
	18.174	7.1594	12.667	
	6.8261	1.8406	-8.667	
	2.5639	0.4732	5.9298	
Total	66	26	46	138

Note: Unidentified deleted; Burnished Plain combined with Plain.

Statistics for Table of Vessel Form by Surface Decoration

Statistic	DF	Value	Prob
Chi-Square	4	25.215	<0.001

Table 6.11. Chi-Square Test, Surface Decoration by Structure (MNV).

Frequency Expected Deviation Cell Chi-Square	Master Code			
	Stamp	Plain	Incised	Total
Church	23 22 1 0.0455	9 8.6667 0.3333 0.0128	14 15.333 -1.333 0.1159	46
Kitchen	28 24.87 3.1304 0.394	7 9.7971 -2.797 0.7986	17 17.333 -0.333 0.0064	52
Convento	15 19.13 -4.13 0.8918	10 7.5362 2.4638 0.8055	15 13.333 1.6667 0.2083	40
Total	66	26	46	138

Note: Unidentified deleted; Burnished Plain combined with Plain.

Statistics for Table of Structure by Surface Decoration

Statistic	DF	Value	Prob
Chi-Square	4	3.279	0.512

Table 6.12. Rim Treatment by Structure.

Structure	Rim Treatment				
Frequency Percent Row Pct Col Pct	Plain	Decorated	Pel/Node	Folded	Total
Church	33 22.00 73.33 39.76	3 2.00 6.67 50.00	0 0.00 0.00 0.00	9 6.00 20.00 15.00	45 30.00
Kitchen	29 19.33 46.77 34.94	2 1.33 3.23 33.33	1 0.67 1.61 100.00	30 20.00 48.39 50.00	62 41.33
Convento	21 14.00 48.84 25.30	1 0.67 2.33 16.67	0 0.00 0.00 0.00	21 14.00 48.84 35.00	43 28.67
Total	83 55.33	6 4.00	1 0.67	60 40.00	150 100.0

Frequency Missing = 9

Table 6.13. Chi-Square Test, Rim Treatment by Structure.

Frequency Expected Deviation Cell Chi-Square	Rim Treatment		
	Plain	Folded	Total
Church	34 24.958 9.042 3.2758	9 18.042 -9.042 4.5315	43
Kitchen	28 33.664 -5.664 0.9531	30 24.336 5.6643 1.3184	58
Convento	21 24.378 -3.378 0.468	21 17.622 3.3776 0.6474	42
Total	83	60	143

Statistics for Table of Structure by Rim Treatment

Statistic	DF	Value	Prob
Chi-Square	2	11.194	0.004

Table 6.14. Late Rim Styles (see key below for abbreviations).

		Rim Treatment														
		Plain						Decorated						Pel/Node	
	UID/Other	Elaboration				Pinch		Elaboration						Elab	
		Plain		Incised				Dec Cane		Dec Finger		Dec Stick		Incised	
Vessel Form	N	Pct	N	Pct	N	Pct	N	Pct	N	Pct	N	Pct	N	Pct	N	Pct
Bowl	1	2.9	16	47.1	17	50.0	.	.	.	.	.	.	.	.	1	100.
Straight	.	.	9	75.0	3	25.0	.	.	1	100.	.	.	.	.	.	.
Excurve Unrestr	.	.	.	.	.	.	.	.	.	.	.	.	.	.	.	.
Excurve Restr	.	.	2	100.	.	.	.	.	.	.	.	.	.	.	.	.
Excurve UID	.	.	2	66.7	1	33.3	.	.	1	50.0	1	50.0	.	.	.	.
Restr Neck Jar	.	.	1	50.0	1	50.0	.	.	.	.	.	.	.	.	.	.
Carinated Bowl	1	10.0	2	20.0	6	60.0	1	10.0	.	.	1	100	.	.	.	.
Brimmed Vessel	1	5.0	13	65.0	6	30.0	.	.	.	.	.	.	2	100	.	.
All	3	3.6	45	54.2	34	41.0	1	1.2	2	33.3	2	33.3	2	33.3	1	100

Pel/node = Pellet or Node
Dec = Decorated
Excurve Unrestr = Excurvate, Unrestricted Vessel (probable jar)

Excurve Restr = Excurvate, Restricted Vessel (probable jar)
Excurve UID = Excurvate Vessel (probable jar)
Restr Neck Jar = Restricted Neck Vessel

Table 6.14 (cont).

Vessel Form	Folded — Elaboration						Folded — Elaboration				Folded — Elab.				ALL	
	Fld Plain		Fld Cane		Fld Finger		Fld Triangle		Fld Stamp		Fld Stick		Fld Incised			
	N	Pct	N	Pct	N	Pct	N	Pct	N	Pct	N	Pct	N	Pct	N	Pct
Bowl	1	33.3	.	.	.	.	.	.	1	4.5	.	.	2	66.7	38	100
Straight	3	13.6	8	36.4	4	18.2	2	9.1	1	4.5	3	13.6	1	4.5	35	100
Excurve Unrestr	.	.	1	25.0	1	25.0	1	25.0	.	.	.	.	.	.	4	100
Excurve Restr	.	.	.	.	.	.	.	.	.	.	.	.	1	100	3	100
Excurve UID	.	.	9	37.5	7	29.2	3	12.5	2	8.3	3	12.5	.	.	29	100
Restr Neck Jar	1	33.3	.	.	1	33.3	.	.	.	.	1	33.3	.	.	5	100
Carinated Bowl	.	.	.	.	.	.	.	.	.	.	.	.	.	.	12	100
Brimmed Vessel	.	.	1	100	.	.	.	.	.	.	.	.	.	.	23	100
All	5	8.5	19	32.2	13	22.0	6	10.2	4	6.8	7	11.9	5	8.5	149	100

Fld = Folded rim
Excurve Unrestr = Excurvate, Unrestricted Vessel (probable jar)
Excurve Restr = Excurvate, Restricted Vessel (probable jar)
Excurve UID = Excurvate Vessel (probable jar)
Restr Neck Jar = Restricted Neck Vessel

Table 6.15. Rim Treatment by Vessel Form.

Frequency Percent Row Pct Col Pct	Rim Treatment				
	Plain	Decorated	Pel/Node	Folded	Total
Bowl	34	0	1	3	38
	22.82	0.00	0.67	2.01	25.50
	89.47	0.00	2.63	7.89	
	40.96	0.00	100.00	5.08	
Straight	12	1	0	22	35
	8.05	0.67	0.00	14.77	23.49
	34.29	2.86	0.00	62.86	
	14.46	16.67	0.00	37.29	
Jar	7	2	0	32	41
	4.70	1.34	0.00	21.48	27.52
	17.07	4.88	0.00	78.05	
	8.43	33.33	0.00	54.24	
Carinated Bowl	10	1	0	1	12
	6.71	0.67	0.00	0.67	8.05
	83.33	8.33	0.00	8.33	
	12.05	16.67	0.00	1.69	
Brimmed Vessel	20	2	0	1	23
	13.42	1.34	0.00	0.67	15.44
	86.96	8.70	0.00	4.35	
	24.10	33.33	0.00	1.69	
Total	83	6	1	59	149
	55.70	4.03	0.67	39.60	100.0

Frequency Missing = 10

Table 6.16. Chi-Square Test, Rim Treatment by Vessel Form.

Frequency Expected Deviation Cell Chi-Square	Vessel Form					Total
	Bowl	Straight	Jar	Carinated Bowl	Brimmed Vessel	
Plain	34	12	7	10	20	83
	21.627	19.873	22.796	6.429	12.275	
	12.373	-7.873	-15.8	3.5704	7.7254	
	7.0791	3.1192	10.945	1.9827	4.8621	
Folded	3	22	32	1	1	59
	15.373	14.127	16.204	4.5704	8.7254	
	-12.37	7.8732	15.796	-3.57	-7.725	
	9.9587	4.388	15.398	2.7892	6.84	
Total	37	34	39	11	21	142

Statistics for Table of Rim Treatment by Vessel Form

Statistic	DF	Value	Prob
Chi-Square	4	67.362	<0.001

Table 6.17. Rim Elaboration by Vessel Form.

Frequency / Percent / Row Pct / Col Pct	Rim Elaboration								Total
	Plain	Incised	Finger	Cane	Stick	Triangle	Fld/St	Pinch	
Bowl	17 / 10.97 / 44.74 / 33.33	21 / 13.55 / 55.26 / 43.75	0 / 0.00 / 0.00 / 0.00	0 / 0.00 / 0.00 / 0.000	0 / 0.00 / 0.00 / 0.00	0 / 0.00 / 0.00 / 0.00	0 / 0.00 / 0.00 / 0.00	0 / 0.00 / 0.00 / 0.00	38 / 24.52
Straight	12 / 7.74 / 34.29 / 23.53	4 / 2.58 / 11.43 / 8.33	4 / 2.58 / 11.43 / 26.67	9 / 5.81 / 25.71 / 42.86	3 / 1.94 / 8.57 / 33.33	2 / 1.29 / 5.71 / 33.33	1 / 0.65 / 2.86 / 25.00	0 / 0.00 / 0.00 / 0.00	35 / 22.58
All Jar	7 / 4.5 / 16.28 / 13.73	4 / 2.58 / 9.30 / 8.33	10 / 6.45 / 23.26 / 66.67	11 / 7.10 / 25.58 / 52.38	4 / 2.58 / 9.30 / 44.44	4 / 2.58 / 9.30 / 66.67	3 / 1.94 / 6.98 / 75.00	0 / 0.00 / 0.00 / 0.00	43 / 27.74
Carinated Bowl	2 / 1.29 / 14.29 / 3.92	10 / 6.45 / 71.43 / 20.83	1 / 0.65 / 7.14 / 6.67	0 / 0.00 / 0.00 / 0.00	0 / 0.00 / 0.00 / 0.00	0 / 0.00 / 0.00 / 0.00	0 / 0.00 / 0.00 / 0.00	1 / 0.65 / 7.14 / 100.00	14 / 9.03
Brimmed Vessel	13 / 8.39 / 52.00 / 25.49	9 / 5.81 / 36.00 / 18.75	0 / 0.00 / 0.00 / 0.00	1 / 0.65 / 4.00 / 4.76	2 / 1.29 / 8.00 / 22.22	0 / 0.00 / 0.00 / 0.00	0 / 0.00 / 0.00 / 0.00	0 / 0.00 / 0.00 / 0.00	25 / 16.13
Total	51 / 32.90	48 / 30.97	15 / 9.68	21 / 13.55	9 / 5.81	6 / 3.87	4 / 2.58	1 / 0.65	155 / 100.00

Frequency Missing = 4

Table 6.18. Rim Elaboration by Structure.

Frequency Percent Row Pct Col Pct	Rim Elaboration								
	Plain	Incised	Finger	Cane	Stick	Triangle	Fld/St	Pinch	Total
Church	22 14.19 47.83 43.14	14 9.03 30.43 29.17	2 1.29 4.35 13.33	3 1.94 6.52 14.29	1 0.65 2.17 11.11	1 0.65 2.17 16.67	3 1.94 6.52 75.00	0 0.00 0.00 0.00	46 29.68
Kitchen	15 9.68 23.81 29.41	21 13.55 33.33 43.75	9 5.81 14.29 60.00	14 9.03 22.22 66.67	0 0.00 0.00 0.00	3 1.94 4.76 50.00	0 0.00 0.00 0.00	1 0.65 1.59 100.00	63 40.65
Convento	14 9.03 30.43 27.45	13 8.39 28.26 27.08	4 2.58 8.70 26.67	4 2.58 8.70 19.05	8 5.16 17.39 88.89	2 1.29 4.35 33.33	1 0.65 2.17 25.00	0 0.00 0.00 0.00	46 29.68
Total	51 32.90	48 30.97	15 9.68	21 13.55	9 5.81	6 3.87	4 2.58	1 0.65	155 100.00

Frequency Missing = 4

Table 6.19. Firing Characteristics,
Meeting House Fields (see key for Table 6.21).

Core	Count	Pct
Hd	11	12.5
Hm	52	59.1
Lc	6	6.8
Mc	9	10.2
Nc	10	11.4
TOTAL	88	100.0

Interior	Frequency	Percent
1	40	45.5
2	12	13.6
3	30	34.1
4	6	6.8
TOTAL	88	100.0

Ext	Frequency	Percent
1	27	30.7
2	11	12.5
3	42	47.7
4	8	9.1
TOTAL	88	100.0

Table 6.20. Firing Characteristics,
Santa Catalina de Guale, Georgia (see key, Table 6.21).

Core	Frequency	Percent
Hd	55	34.4
Hm	47	29.4
Lc	21	13.1
Mc	18	11.3
Nc	19	11.9
TOTAL	160	100.0

Frequency Missing = 2

Interior	Frequency	Percent
.	4	2.5
1	57	36.3
2	44	28.0
3	44	28.0
4	8	5.1
TOTAL	157	100.0

Frequency Missing = 5

Exterior	Frequency	Percent
1	54	34.0
2	50	31.4
3	47	29.6
4	8	5.0
TOTAL	159	100.0

Frequency Missing = 3

Table 6.21. Firing Characteristics,
Santa Catalina de Santa Maria, Florida.

Core	Frequency	Percent
Hd	29	22.3
Hm	73	56.2
Lc	5	3.8
Mc	20	15.4
Nc	3	2.3
TOTAL	130	100.0

Interior	Frequency	Percent
1	81	62.3
2	15	11.5
3	33	25.4
4	1	0.8
130	100.0	

Exterior	Frequency	Percent
1	65	50.0
2	21	16.2
3	42	32.3
4	2	1.5
TOTAL	130	100.0

Table 6.21 Key:

Nc: no coring, well oxidized throughout

Lc: light coring, up to 30% of cross section is dark and core color is same as either Hm or Hd.

Mc: moderate coring, 30-60% of cross section is dark and core color same as either Hm or Hd.

Hm: heavy medium coring, at least 60% of cross section is dark and core is 10yr to 5y values >=3 and <=5.

Hd: heavy dark coring, at least 60% of cross section is dark and core is 2.5y or 5y with values <3 and chromas <2.

1: hues 5yr to 10yr, values >4, chromas 3-6. Well oxidized.

2: hues 10yr to 5y, values 4-6, chromas 1-2. Moderately oxidized.

3: hues 10yr to 5y, values 3-4, chromas 1-2. Poorly oxidized.

4: hues 10yr to 5y, values <3, chromas <2. Extremely poor oxidation.

7

Mission Santa Catalina de Santa María, Amelia Island, Florida

After the Chichimeco attack of 1680, Santa Catalina de Guale on St. Catherines Island was burned by its own inhabitants and abandoned.[1] The population, previously amalgamated with Satuache, relocated to the Guale mission of San José de Sápala on Sapelo Island. Also on Sapelo at this time were immigrants from Santa Clara de Tupiqui, a mainland mission that was relocated in 1674. At least for the former inhabitants of Santa Catalina, the stay was projected to be temporary. The Spanish, recognizing the importance of St. Catherines Island as a breadbasket for St. Augustine, intended to resettle the mission with a stronger garrison. These plans never materialized, however. An attack on Fort Matanzas and raids on the Cumberland Island missions perpetrated by the French pirate Grammont in 1683 persuaded the Spanish to cut their loses on the Georgia coast—to favor the core over the periphery (Bushnell 1994).

Grammont's activities also disturbed the Yamassee in Guale and Mocama. According to Worth (1995:37; Bushnell 1994:165), the Grammont raid was all the evidence the Yamassee needed to conclude that life under Spanish protection was too dangerous, and they shifted allegiance, en masse, to the British. The emigration, involving some three hundred people, effectively halved the number of Native Americans under Spanish control in Guale and Mocama (Worth 1995:37–38).

Until this defection, one enclave of Yamassee was established at the mission of Santa María de los Yamases, on Isla Santa María, or what has become known as Amelia Island, Florida (Bushnell 1986). There was a church at this mission (Saunders 1993), but rarely a priest, and visitation records refer to the inhabitants as *infieles* (infidels). With the area abandoned in 1683, the caciques of "the four places" on Sapelo Island requested to move to Santa María, where there was a "good landing place, plenty of fish, shellfish, and cassina, and enough tillable land to feed 80 families" (Bushnell 1994:165).[2] The Santa Catalina, Satuache, and Sápala Guale had moved to the new mission by August 22, 1684 (Worth 1995:39, 45).[3] That mission site, dubbed Santa Catalina de Santa María,[4] has been positively identified by the recovery of the seal of Santa Catalina from the floor of the structure identified as the convento (Hardin 1986). Santa María is located on the marsh side of Amelia Island, adjacent to Harrison Creek, a tidal creek leading to the South Amelia River (Figure 7.1). The Guale church is just 50 meters from what is presumed to be the church of Santa María de los Yamases.

Pottery from several different contexts of use at Santa Catalina de Santa María provides the final data for this study. The most serendipitous aspect of comparing the two Santa Catalinas is that the primary population of the Amelia Island mission consisted of the same families, perhaps even some of the same individuals, responsible for the ceramic assemblage from St. Catherines Island. Indeed, other things being equal, the continuity of family groups between sites, and therefore the continuity of pottery production units and "style pools," would be expected to produce an assemblage of pottery attributes very similar to that on St. Catherines Island. However, the aggregation on Sapelo Island, and the amalgamation of at least some of the Sápala into Santa María, might have produced some changes in pottery.[5] In addition, while Guale men probably interacted to some extent with different tribes before relocating, Guale women may have been brought into more direct contact with the Timucua and other groups than they had experienced on St. Catherines or Sapelo Island. This population amalgamation might produce a more heterogenous stylistic assemblage than that of Saint Catherines Island, unless environmental or social factors (e.g., the use of pottery decoration to signal social affiliation) were operating to decrease the number of stylistic elements used. Santa María, then, offered a unique opportunity for the study of change in Guale pottery. Although containing a strong element of continuity with the Georgia tradition, the site was a good laboratory to study the effects of an increasingly heterogenous population on traditional pottery of the late Mission period.

Besides the relatively high degree of continuity, the site had other advantages. It was absolutely distinct, both spatially and temporally, from the earlier sites associated with Irene and Altamaha phase pottery. In addition, the site was occupied for a very short time. The period of the

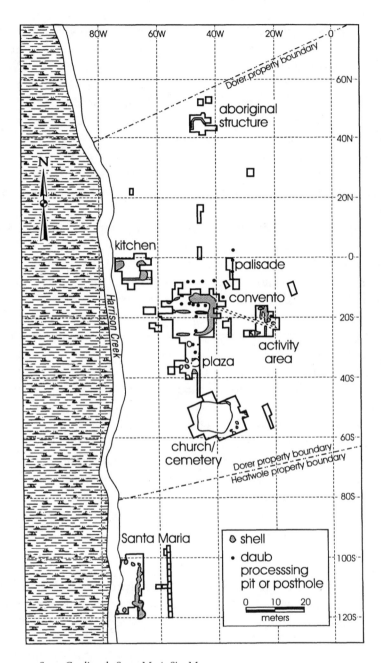

80W 60W 40W 20W 0

Dorer property boundary

60N

aboriginal
structure

40N

N

20N

kitchen

0

palisade

convento

20S

activity
area

plaza

40S

church/
cemetery

Dorer property boundary
Heatwole property boundary

60S

80S

Santa Maria

shell

daub
processsing
pit or posthole

0   10   20
meters

100S

120S

Harrison Creek

7.1. Santa Catalina de Santa María Site Map.

eighteen years it existed (1684–1702) is shorter than the life span of a single generation. A brief occupation was ideal for descriptive and comparative purposes. Comparison of the Amelia Island pottery assemblage to the pottery assemblage from the mission on St. Catherines Island also furnished an opportunity to compare San Marcos and Altamaha pottery directly and to determine the discreteness of the two types.

The site structure and mission architecture have been described in detail elsewhere (Saunders 1990, 1991, 1993). Only a brief discussion of the contexts used for this report and how they compare with those from the mission on St. Catherines Island is presented here. At the outset it should be noted that the two mission sites differed in archaeological integrity. Whereas the site on St. Catherines Island was relatively undisturbed (Thomas 1987:142), the Amelia Island site was reoccupied around 1790 by a British planter and more or less continuously occupied until the present. All Mission period proveniences examined from Amelia Island were impacted to some degree by Plantation period and more modern activities. However, because the short time of Mission period occupation precluded questions of temporal change in the Mission period materials, the mixing of artifacts resulting from these multiple occupations was not perceived as a problem. The site also contained a significant Savannah phase component radiocarbon dated to between A.D. 1300–1550. In general, however, it was not difficult to segregate the Savannah phase wares from the Mission period wares on the basis of surface treatment, fired color, and sherd thickness. Some sand-tempered plain wares were more difficult to distinguish. The treatment of those sherds is discussed in the temper section.

Seven different Mission period "contexts of use" were intensively excavated (Figure 7.1), and four were selected for intrasite and/or intersite comparisons. These included the convento; the church[6]; a possible kitchen area; and an aboriginal structure probably located outside the mission compound proper. Thus, in addition to the site-specific questions enumerated above, the same questions outlined for the St. Catherines Island mission can be addressed at the Amelia Island site.

The Santa María convento was quite different architecturally from the one on St. Catherines Island. Most distinctive were the shell "sleepers" or surface foundations. The convento shares this attribute with only one other known mission structure, that of the church of Santa María de los Yamases 80 meters south of the convento (see Saunders 1993). The later convento, however, was clearly aligned with a different church some 20 meters south of its southern shell sleeper. Squared post construction and the use of wrought iron nails and spikes confirmed that the convento had been constructed under Spanish supervision. The recovery of the seal of Santa Catalina (Figure 7.2; see Hardin 1986), used to impress the wax closure in official correspondences from the friar, clinched the functional as well as the ecclesiastical identification.

The Santa María church was constructed differently from both the St. Catherines Island church and that of the Yamassee to the south. The area was disturbed by Plantation period and modern activities, but as best as could be determined, it was a far less substantial structure than either one of those earlier constructions. This was true despite the fact that Santa María, like its predecessor Santa Catalina, was the administrative center of the Province of Guale in the late Mission period. Nevertheless, the presence of burials, a disturbed clay floor, and large postholes indicated that a church had been present.

No area excavated at the Amelia Island site contained features similar to the complex of features identified as the kitchen on St. Catherines Island. The possible kitchen area on Amelia Island had a thick Mission period shell midden and midden-filled posthole pattern that was extrapolated to represent a *ramada,* or shedlike structure. If this was the kitchen, the pottery from it might not be directly comparable with the pottery from the portion of the kitchen on St. Catherines Island, which, as noted previously, might have been used to prepare comestibles for export. Thus, the two structures were compared as utilitarian food processing areas rather than as kitchens per se.

The pueblo to the northwest of the St. Catherines Island mission has not been excavated, and no native house sites were excavated at Wamassee Head. Consequently, materials comparable to those recovered from the aboriginal structure on Amelia were not available. The pottery from the Amelia Island aboriginal structure was analyzed for comparison with the more "Spanish" contexts within the site. Strictly speaking, however, this aboriginal structure was not a village habitation site. The pueblo associated with Santa María (probably both the Yamassee and Guale incarnations) was to the south of the mission, where Hemmings and Deagan (1973) conducted tests in 1971. The aboriginal structure uncovered during this project was located a little more than 50 meters north of the convento, between the mission compound and another Spanish structure and box well excavated by Robert Johnson (personal communication, 1989). These structures, including the aboriginal structure, might have been associated with the Spanish garrison attached to the mission. Nevertheless,

7.2. The Seal of Santa Catalina of Alexandria Found at Santa María; top = face of seal; bottom = seal in profile.

the construction techniques used were clearly aboriginal. Despite the presence of a good deal of Savannah phase, Plantation period, and modern activity, the presence of San Marcos pottery as the most recent artifacts in the wall trench describing the building indicated that it most likely dated to the Mission period. Although not from the village proper, the pottery assemblage associated with the structure probably represented that used by Guale.

All San Marcos pottery from the block excavations in the four mission contexts was used in this analysis. Other contemporaneous Mission period wares, San Pedro[7] for example, were excluded because it is likely that they were made by the Mocama, and their inclusion would confuse the issue of change in Guale pottery (see discussion under Other Attributes). Most of the collections were analyzed by the author. However, some proveniences from the church and the convento that were excavated early in the project were analyzed by others under the supervision of the author. Zone A (modern humus and overlying Plantation period materials mixed with Mission period materials in gray fine sand) was either ½-inch or ¼-inch screened. Zone B (slightly humic brown fine sand with predominantly Mission period materials) was ¼-inch screened. As for the Georgia sites reported in Chapters 5 and 6, only pottery larger than 1 square centimeter was studied.

Comparisons

A total of 16,232 San Marcos sherds were recovered from the four contexts of use examined for this study. The distribution of surface decoration by structure for Santa María is displayed in Table 7.1, and a chi-square test for the significance of the distribution is presented in Table 7.2. Significant deviations from expectations in the chi-square test were the relatively high incidence of incising at the aboriginal structure and the lack of plain wares in the area hypothesized to have been the kitchen. Stamped wares were "over-represented" in the kitchen. The reverse was true for the convento, where the bulk of the incised sherds occurred. In the church, burnished plain wares were more frequent than expected. These distributions were remarkably similar to those found at the mission site on St. Catherines Island.

Not only were the distributions similar, but percentage totals for the different surface decorations at each site were almost identical as well. The major difference was the decrease in incised wares as a whole, from around 6 percent on St. Catherines Island (at both Meeting House Fields and Mission Santa Catalina) to just 1.4 percent on Amelia. This decrease was not unexpected. Although Smith (1948) reported incised wares as a minority occurrence in post-1686 proveniences in St. Augustine, incising was apparently absent from all First Spanish period contexts at 8SA16–23 (Otto and Lewis 1974; they may not have considered incised wares to be locally produced; see Piatek 1985). The decrease in incising may well be related to the kind of time constraints cited in Chapter 6 as an explanation for the simplification of designs. Incised pots must be paddled and then smoothed and incised, and they were often heavily burnished—all of which require more time and skill than stamping. On the other hand, if incised designs were "permeated" with religious significance, as Speck (1909:54) noted for the Catawba, the decrease in incising may reflect either the loss of religious beliefs or a shift in the Guale conception of what is appropriate decoration for pottery. They may no longer have felt the need to display cosmological concepts on vessels or may have come to believe that such a display was inappropriate.

Vessel Form Analysis

Four hundred and seventy-seven vessels were defined from the assemblage of 16,232 San Marcos sherds (Table 7.3). Unidentified straight rims (probably of jars, though some bowl and brimmed vessel sherds might also be included) constituted the most frequent vessel form, followed by excurvate rim jars. Brimmed plates or bowls were the next most frequent form, followed by simple bowls. These four forms were far and away the most common vessels. Other jar forms, carinated bowls, and unidentified forms that were nevertheless recognized as nontraditional (colono-ware) forms completed the list of vessels present.

A comparison of the relative frequencies of forms at the Georgia and Florida missions indicates that there was a slight decrease in the percentage of bowls (carinated and simple) and an increase in the number of jars at the Florida site. Brimmed vessels were slightly more common at the Amelia Island site.

A chi-square test for the significance of the distribution of forms was conducted with all jars collapsed into a single category. The result of that test is displayed in Table 7.4. The structure with the most diversity in forms was the convento. Nevertheless, just as at the St. Catherines Island mission, the dominant forms were more or less evenly distributed between structures. This included the aboriginal structure, which had as many brimmed vessels as it had simple bowls. In fact, there was a striking correspondence between the number of bowls and the number of brimmed vessels in each context at Santa María.

Vessels showed the same correlation with surface decoration as was exhibited at the Santa Catalina mission in Georgia and at Meeting House Fields: simple bowls were most commonly incised, and jars were more likely to be stamped (Tables 7.5 and 7.6). Simple bowls were also more frequently burnished than other forms. This could not be tested against the other site assemblages because there were too few burnished plain vessels in those samples. Other forms displayed all surface decorations in more or less equal proportions. Note that in the vessel form analysis, the percentage of incising increased compared to the values for sherds. This was also observed for the St. Catherines Island vessel form analysis. Again, this was due to ease of recognition of individual variation in incising, and the total of 9 percent is considered inflated (or rather, the other values considered depressed) relative to the other totals. If the percentages of incised vessels at each site are taken at face value, however, the drop in incising in the Santa María is even more dramatic: from nearly 30 percent of the vessels on St. Catherines Island to only 9.0 percent on Amelia Island.

When surface decoration was reanalyzed using only the MNV, and with related surface decorations collapsed (Table 7.7), there was still a correlation between structure and surface decoration. It may be recalled that a correlation between MNV and surface decoration was present but not statistically significant at Santa Catalina (Table 6.11). As in the sherd analysis, this derived from the high frequency of stamped vessels and the lack of plain vessels in the possible kitchen, along with the relatively high incidence of burnished plain wares in the church.

A complete listing of all rim styles by vessel form is given in Table 7.8. Rim styles are broken down into rim treatments and rim elaborations in Tables 7.9, 7.10, 7.11, and 7.12. When compared with the assemblage from the mission on St. Catherines Island, differences between the two assemblages appeared negligible. Folded rims were present on 46 percent of the vessels from Amelia and 40 percent of the vessels on St. Catherines; there was a consequent 7 percent decrease in the percentage of plain rims at Santa María. If applique rims are regarded as the stylistic equivalent of the folded rim, in the long run there was a trend toward the use of more folded rims: from 34.2 percent applique rims at Meeting House Fields (29.5 percent for Cluster 2 only), to 39.6 percent folded rims at Mission Santa Catalina in Georgia, to 46.5 percent folded rims at Santa María. The frequencies of decorated and noded rims remained about the same.

The association of specific rim treatments with certain vessel forms was similar to the St. Catherines Island mission and represents a continuum from the pre-Columbian period Meeting House Fields site. Bowls were much more likely to have plain than folded or decorated rims; the reverse was true for jars. This was a statistically significant association (Table 7.10). Carinated bowls generally had plain rims. Although the number of brimmed vessels with folded rims increased, the percentage of brimmed vessels with folded rims remained about the same.

Although the association was not statistically significant, frequencies of rim treatments were different between structures. As at the St. Catherines Island mission, there were fewer folded and more plain rims in the church than expected (Table 7.11). On the other hand, there were more folded and fewer plain rims at the proposed kitchen.

The overall increase in folded rims was accompanied by a diversification in the implements used to punctate those rims. In addition to the common cane and fingernail punctation and the less common triangular punctation and stamped folds found on St. Catherines Island, there were a variety of new styluses, including sharks' teeth, shells, thumbs, an unidentified square tool, an oval implement, and something that looked like an animal tooth impression (Table 7.8). A few folded rims were incised. Nevertheless, despite the increase in the diversity of rim elaborations, there was a net increase in the use of cane punctation (Table 7.12). The incidence of the other, more common elaborations (except incising) remained surprisingly stable. A hypothesis that the more unusual rim styles were not locally made received some support from the paucity of such rims in the aboriginal structure. However, their absence could be due to the small size of the sample from that context.

Perhaps the most interesting treatments were the rarest ones. One straight rim had an applique rim strip, another vessel had applique nodes (Figure 7.3), and one other had a lug (Table 7.8). The strip and lug were found at the convento, and the noded vessel was from the church. As noted in Chapter 6, there were no rim strips and only one noded vessel at the mission on St. Catherines Island. Because neither of these treatments existed in Florida in pre-Columbian times, their appearance in the Amelia Island assemblage indicates that these traditional styles remained part of the "style pool" and, furthermore, that the cultural continuum responsible for the transmission of those style concepts had not broken down. The lug treatment, on the other hand, though in the Lamar tradition, is not

7.3. Representative Sherds from Santa Catalina de Santa María. Scale in centimeters.

described for Irene sites. It may suggest inspiration from the Leon-Jefferson phase to the west.

It is tempting to see in the reappearance of the applique rim and the node some nativistic overtones. Certainly the conditions in the late seventeenth-century coastal missions were deplorable (e.g., Hann 1987:22–23, 1990a; Larsen 1994; Saunders 1998). Spanish labor demands were seen by the natives as excessive, as was the physical abuse meted out both by friars and by soldiers. Those communities with attached garrisons were doubly encumbered. They were expected to provision friars and soldiers[8]; soldiers apparently had no compunction against stealing what was not given freely (e.g., Bushnell 1994:175). Official correspondences alluded to widespread defections of the mission Indians, who fled from Spanish control to the sanctuary of the woods (e.g., Bushnell 1990; Hann 1990a, 1991:80; Saunders 2000b). Indians who remained in Spanish territory were aware that they were in constant danger of attack by pirates or natives loyal to the British. The Spanish friars and their religion could not succor the neophytes as promised.

Other Attributes

Other pottery attributes that might be used to substantiate a renewed emphasis on pre-Columbian religious principles did not support this premise, however. Curvilinear stamped sherds were only slightly more common at the mission on Amelia than on St. Catherines Island (1.1 percent versus .45 percent, Table C.1). More important, central elements (Table C.2) were visible in only 2.3 percent (count) and 4.4 percent (weight) of the sherd assemblage, amounts that did appear to be a significant decrease from the St. Catherines Island totals. Taken together, stylistic attributes do not suggest a revitalization movement among the Indians who chose to stay at the mission. Although the size of the collection was relatively small and the significance unknown, it is interesting that no sherds with central elements were recovered from the aboriginal structure.

Although the overwhelming majority of San Marcos sherds were grit tempered (Tables C.3 and C.4), there was a higher incidence of sand tempering at the Amelia Island site than was recorded for the St. Catherines Island mission (2.3 percent versus 4.8 percent by count, for St. Catherines and Amelia, respectively). This apparent increase in sand tempering at the later mission might suggest that some pre-Columbian sand-tempered plain sherds were included in this total. However, in this analysis, sand-tempered sherds were considered San Marcos only if they had the characteristic stamping, were filmed, or displayed a form not characteristic of the Savannah phase pottery found on Amelia Island. Thus, if anything, the number of San Marcos sand-tempered sherds, and particularly plain sherds, was more likely to be depressed than inflated.

Grog-tempered sherds were handled similarly. Grog tempering was used in minor amounts in the Wilmington/Savannah phase in coastal southern Georgia and northeast Florida. Grog tempering increased in the Contact period (Borremans 1985:210, 286; DesJean 1985:149) with the appearance of San Pedro wares. San Pedro pottery was present at both Santa Catalina de Santa María and Santa María de los Yamases on Amelia Island. Sherds identified as San Pedro by surface treatment, distinctive paste, and/or surface color were removed from the sample. The grog tempering in Tables C.3 and C.4 is believed to be in San Marcos wares on the basis of surface decoration. As such, less than 1 percent of the San Marcos assemblage was determined to have been tempered with grog or grog and grit.

Another group of peoples represented in both the pre-Columbian and Mission period components at the site were Timucuans, who made their distinctively chalky St. Johns pastes for nearly two millennia. Some of this surely arrived on site during the Mission period. No colono-wares were found with St. Johns pastes, however, and because of the inability to segregate the St. Johns pottery associated with the late pre-Columbian component on the site from that associated with the mission, St. Johns phase materials were not included in this study.

Limestone tempering, absent from the St. Catherines Island assemblage, appeared in minute amounts, as did shell tempering. Otto and Lewis (1974:101) remarked that shell and limestone were present in San Marcos wares only as incidental inclusions in the sand used for tempering or in the clay sources. Indeed, a few of the sherds coded as containing shell on Amelia carried the note "incidental?" though other sherds had larger quantities of shell and/or limestone. Apparently, true shell tempering did appear on pastes with San Marcos–like surface decorations in St. Augustine (Jim Cusick, personal communication, 1991). However, at the present time little is known about either the temporal or ethnic associations of that ware. Because limestone outcrops are not found on Amelia Island (Hemmings and Deagan 1973:16), and no limestone or shell-tempered wares were found in the village area excavated by Hemmings and Deagan, the limestone-tempered vessels in the mission compound probably were brought from St. Augustine.

Sand and shell tempering occurred in one bowl and in two straight rim forms. Shell-, grit-, and limestone-tempered pastes occurred only in brimmed vessels (Table C.4). One of the latter was stamped, one burnished plain, and the remainder were plain. All shell- or limestone-tempered wares came from either the church or the convento. None were recovered from the kitchen or the aboriginal structure; nor, for that matter, were any recovered from the village area (Hemmings and Deagan 1973:16). This may be more evidence for importation of vessels from St. Augustine by the friars.

A chi-square test of the association of temper with vessel form was conducted for the sand-tempered and grit-tempered vessels and with jar forms collapsed (Table C.5). As at the earlier sites, there was no 100 percent association of temper and form, but the test indicated significance at a probability greater than .005. This resulted from the high percentage of simple bowls that were sand tempered. The low percentage of sand-tempered jars and high number of sand-tempered carinated bowls and colono-ware vessels also contributed.

The complete inventory of interior and exterior surface treatments (excluding burnished plain) is shown in Table C.6. On a sherd basis, around

20 percent of the total assemblage had unburnished interiors. Again, this figure was quite similar to the totals from the Meeting House Fields site and the mission on St. Catherines Island. Unlike the earlier mission, where the lowest frequency of interior burnishing was at the kitchen, at Santa María the kitchen area had the highest proportion of interior burnishing. This may reflect the different hypothetical functions of the two kitchens.

Because red-filmed sherds were so visible, it was again surprising to find that their frequency was quite low. Less than 5 percent (count) of the assemblage had red filming, zoned red filming, and, very rarely, red and black filming on vessel interiors. Less than 2 percent of the sample had these treatments on vessel exteriors, either alone or in combination with filmed interiors. These figures were higher, however, than the number of filmed sherds from the Georgia mission.

Similar to those at the Georgia mission, filmed sherds were slightly more likely to be found in the convento than elsewhere. Red filming was present at the aboriginal structure. A little more than 2 percent of the sherds from that area were filmed, a lower total than from the church or convento, but higher than the kitchen area. Red filming was also present in the pueblo portion of the mission to the south (Hemmings and Deagan 1973:16).

There was so little filming in the St. Catherines Island sample that an association between form and filming could not be tested. However, the test for the Santa María assemblage (Table C.7) indicated a strong association between filming and brimmed vessels. Few jars were filmed, and no carinated bowls were filmed.

Another similarity with the northern Georgia mission was the extremely low incidence of sooting—less than 1 percent (Table C.8). A comparison of counts and weights for the incidence of sooting indicated that there was no significant difference in the distribution of sooted sherds except, perhaps, for the absence of sooting at the aboriginal structure.

The final attributes measured on sherds were folded rim width and land and groove measurements. The average folded rim width for the site as a whole was 18.8 millimeters, only 1.5 millimeters deeper than the St. Catherines Island mission average of 17.3 millimeters. Averages were 18.9, 20.1, and 17.8 millimeters at the convento, church, and kitchen, respectively. Because the standard deviation was larger than the difference between these averages, they were considered insignificant. Land and groove widths were also similar to those from St. Catherines; they were 2.0 and 2.1 millimeters, respectively, compared with 2.0 and 2.4 millimeters from the earlier mission.

Motifs

As might be expected, there was a wider variety of motifs at Santa María than at Santa Catalina. Most appeared to be a reinterpretation of the world symbol. Even the few curvilinear complicated stamped elements (Figure 7.3) were probably central to a four-field background similar to that depicted by Smith (1948, see Figure 4.3). One sherd may have a cross-in-circle motif (too poorly defined to be photographed). The world symbol was as implicit in this design as it was in the filfot cross. The frequency of sherds with unusual designs, however, was quite low, around .1 percent (a count of twenty sherds) of the total number of sherds.

Despite the decrease in incising, there did not appear to be much difference in the designs incised by the Guale at Santa Catalina and those incised at Santa María. Some fine-line incising was present (Figure 7.3), but the bulk of the incising was bold. Punctation continued to be used frequently with incising.

Implications

Beyond the goal of the presentation of the descriptive characteristics of the assemblage at Santa Catalina de Santa María on Amelia Island and a comparison with its predecessors, two questions were proposed: (1) what would be the effect on the pottery assemblage of the increasingly heterogeneous populations of the late Mission period, and (2) is there enough variation between the St. Catherines Island mission assemblage and the Amelia Island assemblage to justify the use of two separate types?

Heterogeneity

As expected, the assemblage on Amelia Island did become more diverse as compared with the St. Catherines Island assemblage. There was an increase in temper types, and new or reworked designs appeared, as did a wide variety of new rim elaborations. Nevertheless, these experiments remained infrequent in the overall assemblage. Shell or limestone inclusions, for instance, were found in only 1.2 percent of the sherds. The amount of shell or limestone tempering at the mission is much lower than what is found in St. Augustine, where San Marcos sherds with these tempers constitute between 7.5 percent and 65.7 percent of assemblages (Jim Cusick, personal communication, 1991). Vessels with these temper types were probably brought to Amelia Island from St. Augustine.

New rim elaborations constituted a larger percentage of the assemblage than new tempers; about 5 percent of the rim elaborations were not found on St. Catherines Island. These rim elaborations were not copied from other styles, but represented new creations. One would not expect a great deal of creativity on utilitarian pottery if it was produced under constraints. In addition, there were a number of colono-ware forms not found at the earlier site.[9] Two colono-ware olive jar–like rims were found, both from the church; there were another sixteen unidentified colono-ware vessels. In addition, nine handles and eight footed or ringed bases were recovered from the convento, another four handles and two footed or ringed bases came from the church, one ringed base was found in the kitchen area, and the aboriginal structure excavation block yielded one ringed base and one handle. Although there are no comparable analyses from St. Augustine reporting the proportion of colono-wares (either sherd data or MNV) compared to traditional forms, it would appear that Deagan (1990b) was correct in positing greater formal diversity in the colono-wares at mission sites than in urban St. Augustine.

Although the San Marcos assemblage did become more heterogenous, the diversity was not accompanied by any loss of creativity or technical excellence. New motifs were generated, but constituted a very small part of the assemblage. As far as technical excellence is concerned, no loss is reflected in the remarkable stability in the proportion of interior burnished sherds from the late Irene phase through the Mission period.

It is possible that many or all of the unusual designs, rim elaborations, and forms, along with the unusual tempers, were produced off site, perhaps at a workshop. For that matter, all of the pottery produced for Spanish use on the site could have been produced elsewhere or by a single individual at the site. With the use of one datum measuring individual variation (Hill and Gunn 1977; Saunders 1985, 1986a)—rim fold depth—it appears that more than one individual produced the folded rim pots. Standard deviation around the mean was higher on Amelia Island (4.6 millimeters) than at the Meeting House Fields site (2.0 millimeters for Cluster 1 and 3.5 millimeters for Cluster 2), where production for use was expected. This is but one small bit of evidence that the pottery was made by a number of different individuals, probably on site. This question needs to be pursued further, however.

Other data indicate increasing standardization. The tendency for bowls to be sand tempered was present in the late Irene phase. At Meeting House Fields, between 30 percent and 38 percent of the vessels of other forms were sand tempered, and 44 percent of the bowl forms were sand tempered. Sand tempering declined dramatically in the succeeding Mission period; only

5 percent of the simple bowls at the St. Catherines Island mission were sand tempered. By the late Mission period on Amelia Island, though the incidence of sand tempering by sherd was about the same (3.1 percent on St. Catherines Island, 4.8 percent of Amelia Island), 30 percent of bowls were sand tempered. Red filming, slightly more prevalent at the later mission than the earlier one, became associated with brimmed vessels.

Although it is tempting to see the red-filmed brimmed vessels as elite (Spanish) wares, possibly produced for market, it is important to remember that approximately the same proportion of red-filmed wares was present in the village area (about 4.7 percent) as within the mission compound. Brimmed vessels were also present in the village. These data may argue against workshop production for red-filmed wares and brimmed vessels.

Types

Braley (1990:100) drew a distinction between the Altamaha phase wares recovered at the Harris Neck Wildlife Refuge and San Marcos pottery: "By the seventeenth century, complicated stamped designs became more sloppily applied, and the curvilinear filfot cross was abandoned in favor of rectilinear designs. However, the complicated stamped wares resemble their prehistoric counterparts more than they do the San Marcos wares found in St. Augustine. The San Marcos cross-simple stamped motif, so common in post-1660 contexts in St. Augustine, . . . is rarely represented at site 9MC41." It was possible to test Braley's assertion that there was more over-stamping in the later wares. The five principal stamped codes—accounting for 80.6 percent of all stamped sherds (excluding obliterated stamped) on St. Catherines Island and 80.9 percent on Amelia Island—were simple stamped, simple stamped paddle zoned (commonly called line blocked—perpendicular lines are present on the paddle), simple stamped and cross-simple stamped, cross-simple stamped, and simple stamped paddle zoned with cross-simple stamping. The first two codes were not overstamped, and the latter three were. In fact, there was more overstamping on St. Catherines Island (79 percent of the sherds were overstamped) than Amelia Island (70 percent overstamped).

Indeed, the comparison of most pottery attributes on the Altamaha wares from the St. Catherines Island mission and the San Marcos wares from Amelia Island suggests that the two should not be separate types. As the above analysis has demonstrated, there was little difference between the two in either stylistic or formal attributes, at least in mission contexts. The most these designations accomplish is the recognition of the geographical location of the site (northern Georgia versus southern Georgia and northeast Florida). Such "extrinsic" data (Rice 1987:276) is not necessarily improper in typologies. However, as the sole basis for the typological distinction, it begs more questions than it answers.

Clearly the criteria used to distinguish Altamaha from San Marcos (Chapter 3) need revision. Punctation directly on the vessel body was not confined to the north Georgia wares, and the incidence of this attribute remained stable throughout the Mission period. Other attributes cited to distinguish Altamaha, stamping and incising on the same vessel and whole-rather than half-cane punctate, also occur on San Marcos vessels. Whole-cane punctation occurred on 50 of 123 (40.6 percent) cane-punctated sherds on Amelia Island and 23 of 67 (34.3 percent) cane-punctated sherds on St. Catherines Island. Whole-cane punctation was significantly more frequent at the Meeting House Fields site, where 75 percent of cane punctations were whole cane. As with the other stylistic attributes, significant change occurred at the juncture of the Irene and Altamaha phases, not between the Altamaha and the San Marcos types. Stamping on vessels with incised rims was less frequent on Amelia Island (nine sherds versus sixteen sherds on St. Catherines), but this is probably related to the overall decrease in incised wares at the later site. This last attribute, the decrease in incising, is a significant difference between the two phases. However, it could not be used to distinguish individual sherds of one "type" from the other. Although the assemblages from the two Santa Catalinas might be expected to be more similar than assemblages from less-related sites, the data compiled here argue against a typological distinction between Guale pottery produced in north Georgia and that produced in Florida.

Unfortunately, these terms are embedded in the literature, and it will be difficult to correct the phraseology without creating confusion. Frankly, I prefer the term *Altamaha* because it more accurately reflects the origin of the type, but *San Marcos* has precedence in the literature. However, as mentioned earlier, that type definition is too broad and encompasses motifs that have not been demonstrated to be associated with the Guale. Then there is Brewer's San Marcos Complicated Stamped, the concept of which, if not the term, should be incorporated into the list of varieties for Guale pottery. Before a complete reworking is attempted, however, more comparisons should be done between mission, urban, rural, and other contexts to define more precisely the nature of temporal and spatial variation in Guale pottery.

Table 7.1. Surface Decoration by Structure.

	Master Code											
	Stamp				Plain				Burnished Plain			
	Count		Weight		Count		Weight		Count		Weight	
Structure	Sum	Pct	Sum	Pct	Sum	Pct	Sum	Pct	Sum	Pct	Sum	Pct
Convento	8038	74.4	50325.0	76.2	1866	17.3	9978.3	15.1	426	3.9	2486.6	3.8
Kitchen	2549	82.6	16728.0	81.8	306	9.9	1947.6	9.5	100	3.2	757.6	3.7
Church	1468	74.5	10263.0	75.9	317	16.1	2037.3	15.1	95	4.8	620.0	4.6
Abo Str	293	77.5	1642.1	78.6	60	15.9	276.8	13.2	9	2.4	89.3	4.3
All	12348	76.1	78958.1	77.3	2549	15.7	14240.0	13.9	630	3.9	3953.5	3.9

Table 7.1 (cont).

Structure	Master Code								All			
	Incised				Check							
	Count		Weight		Count		Weight		Count		Weight	
	Sum	Pct	Sum	Pct	Sum	Pct	Sum	Pct	Sum	Pct	Sum	Pct
Convento	135	1.3	770.5	1.2	333	3.1	2472.8	3.7	10798	100	66033.2	100
Kitchen	50	1.6	312.1	1.5	80	2.6	713.0	3.5	3085	100	20459.3	100
Church	36	1.8	228.9	1.7	55	2.8	371.9	2.8	1971	100	13521.1	100
Abo Str	13	3.4	73.6	3.5	3	0.8	7..3	0.3	378	100	2089.1	100
All	234	1.4	1385.1	1.4	471	2.9	3565.0	3.5	16232	100	102102.7	100

Table 7.2. Chi-Square Test, Surface Decoration by Structure.

Frequency Expected Deviation Cell Chi-Square	Master Code				
	Stamp	Plain	Burnished Plain	Incised	Total
Convento	8371	1866	426	135	10798
	8527.6	1695.7	419.09	155.66	
	-156.6	170.33	6.9056	-20.66	
	2.8748	17.11	0.1138	2.743	
Kitchen	2629	306	100	50	3085
	2436.3	484.45	119.74	44.473	
	192.66	-178.5	-19.74	5.5267	
	15.2360	65.736	3.253	0.6868	
Church	1523	371	95	36	1971
	1556.6	309.52	76.499	28.414	
	-33.57	7.4831	18.501	7.5861	
	0.724	0.1809	4.4745	2.0254	
Aboriginal Structure	296	60	9	13	378
	298.52	59.359	14.671	5.4492	
	-2.52	0.6406	-5.671	7.5508	
	0.0213	0.0069	2.1921	10.463	
Total	12819	2549	630	234	16232

Statistics for Table of Structure by Surface Decoration

Statistic	DF	Value	Prob
Chi-Square	9	127.840	<0.001

Table 7.3. Vessel Form by Structure.

Frequency Percent Row Pct Col Pct	Vessel Form										
	Bowl	Straight	X Unr	X Res	XUid	Lnj	Rsmjar	Car Bowl	Uclno	Brim	Total
Convento	45 9.43 15.05 55.56	62 13.00 20.74 56.88	25 5.24 8.36 96.15	11 2.31 3.68 64.71	67 14.05 22.41 65.05	1 0.21 0.33 100.00	6 1.26 2.01 54.55	14 2.94 4.68 70.00	13 2.73 4.35 76.47	55 11.53 18.39 59.78	299 62.68
Kitchen	14 2.94 17.95 17.28	24 5.03 30.77 22.02	0 0.00 0.00 0.00	2 0.42 2.56 11.76	16 3.35 20.51 15.53	0 0.00 0.00 0.00	2 0.42 2.56 18.18	4 0.84 5.13 20.00	1 0.21 1.28 5.88	15 3.14 19.23 16.30	78 16.35
Church	18 3.77 21.95 22.22	18 3.77 21.95 16.51	1 0.21 1.22 3.85	4 0.84 4.88 23.53	16 3.35 19.51 15.53	0 0.00 0.00 0.00	3 0.63 3.66 27.27	2 0.42 2.44 10.00	2 0.42 2.44 11.76	18 3.77 21.95 19.57	82 17.19
Native Structure	4 0.84 22.22 4.94	5 1.05 27.78 4.59	0 0.00 0.00 0.00	0 0.00 0.00 0.00	4 0.84 22.22 3.88	0 0.00 0.00 0.00	0 0.00 0.00 0.00	0 0.00 0.00 0.00	1 0.21 5.56 5.88	4 0.84 22.22 4.35	18 3.77
Total	81 16.98	109 22.85	26 5.45	17 3.56	103 21.59	1 0.21	11 2.31	20 4.19	17 3.56	92 19.29	477 100.00

XUnr = excurvate unrestricted
XRes = excurvate restricted
XUid = excurvate unidentified
Lnj = long necked jar

Rsmjar = restricted mouthed jar
Car bowl = carinated bowl
Brim = brimmed vessel
Uclno = unidentified colono ware

Table 7.4. Chi-Square Test, Vessel Form by Structure.

Frequency Expected Deviation Cell Chi-Square	Vessel Form					
	Bowl	Straight	Jar	Carinated Bowl	Brimmed	Total
Convento	45	62	110	14	55	286
	49.711	67.142	99.422	12.912	56.813	
	-4.711	-5.142	10.578	1.088	-1.813	
	0.4465	0.3938	1.1252	0.0917	0.0578	
Kitchen	14	24	20	4	15	77
	13.384	18.077	26.767	3.4763	15.296	
	0.6163	5.9233	-6.767	0.5237	-0.296	
	0.284	1.9409	1.711	0.0789	0.0057	
Church	18	18	24	2	18	80
	13.905	18.781	27.81	3.6117	15.892	
	4.0948	-0.781	-3.81	-1.612	2.1084	
	1.2058	0.0325	0.5221	0.7192	0.2797	
Total	77	104	154	20	88	443

Statistics for Table of Structure by Vessel Form

Statistic	DF	Value	Prob
Chi-Square	8	8.639	0.374

Table 7.5. Surface Decoration by Vessel Form.

Frequency Percent Row Pct Col Pct	Master Code					
	UID	Stamp	Plain	B Plain	Incised	Total
Bowl	4	34	13	10	20	81
	0.84	7.13	2.73	2.10	4.19	16.98
	4.94	41.98	16.05	12.35	24.69	
	4.60	13.99	17.57	33.33	46.51	
Straight	28	53	18	5	5	109
	5.87	11.11	3.77	1.005	1.05	22.85
	25.69	48.62	16.51	4.59	4.59	
	32.18	21.81	24.32	16.67	11.63	
Jar	45	86	14	7	6	158
	9.43	18.03	2.94	1.47	1.26	33.12
	28.48	54.43	8.86	4.43	3.80	
	51.72	35.39	18.92	23.33	13.95	
Carinated Bowl	0	16	1	1	2	20
	0.00	3.35	0.21	0.21	0.42	4.19
	0.00	80.00	5.00	5.00	10.00	
	0.00	6.58	1.35	3.33	4.65	
UID Colono	2	0	12	2	1	17
	0.42	0.00	2.52	0.42	0.21	3.56
	11.76	0.00	70.59	11.76	5.88	
	2.30	0.00	16.22	6.67	2.33	
Brimmed Bowl/Plate	8	54	16	5	9	92
	1.68	11.32	3.35	1.05	1.89	19.29
	8.70	58.70	17.39	5.43	9.78	
	9.20	22.22	21.62	16.67	20.93	
Total	87	243	74	30	43	477
	18.24	50.94	15.51	6.29	9.01	100.00

Table 7.6. Chi-Square Test, Surface Decoration by Vessel Form.

Frequency Expected Deviation Cell Chi-Square	Master Code				
	Stamp	Plain	B Plain	Incised	Total
Bowl	34	13	10	20	77
	49.896	12.731	5.7493	8.624	
	-15.9	0.2693	4.2507	11.376	
	5.0642	0.0057	3.1427	15.006	
Straight	53	18	5	5	81
	52.488	13.392	6.048	9.072	
	0.512	4.608	-1.048	-4.072	
	0.005	1.5855	0.1816	1.8277	
Jar	86	14	7	6	113
	73.224	18.683	8.4373	12.656	
	12.776	-4.683	-1.437	-6.656	
	2.2291	1.1737	0.2449	3.5005	
Carinated Bowl	16	1	1	2	20
	12.96	3.3067	1.4933	2.24	
	3.04	-2.307	-0.493	-0.24	
	0.7131	1.6091	0.163	0.0257	
Brimmed Vessel	54	16	5	9	84
	54.432	13.888	6.272	9.408	
	-0.432	2.112	-1.272	-0.408	
	0.0034	0.3212	0.258	0.0177	
Total	243	62	28	42	375

Statistics for Table of Vessel Form by Surface Decoration

Statistic	DF	Value	Prob
Chi-Square	12	13.078	<0.001

Table 7.7. Chi-Square Test, Surface Decoration by Structure (MNV).

Frequency Expected Deviation Cell Chi-Square	Master Code				
	Stamp	Plain	B Plain	Incised	Total
Convento	151	52	12	29	244
	152.91	45.547	18.869	26.677	
	-1.907	6.4533	-6.869	2.3227	
	0.0238	0.9143	2.5008	0.2022	
Kitchen	45	4	5	4	58
	36.347	10.827	1.1853	6.3413	
	8.6533	-6.827	0.5147	-2.341	
	2.0602	4.3045	0.0591	0.8645	
Church	39	14	12	8	73
	45.747	13.627	5.6453	7.9813	
	-6.747	0.3733	6.3547	0.0187	
	0.995	0.0102	7.1531	0.0000	
Total	235	70	29	41	375

Note: aboriginal structure deleted for adequate cell size.

Statistics for Table of Structure by Surface Decoration

Statistic	DF	Value	Prob
Chi-Square	6	19.088	0.004

Table 7.8. Rim Style by Vessel Form.

	Rim Treatment																					
	UID		Plain						Decorated										Folded			
	Elab		Elaboration						Elaboration							Pelnode Elab		Applique Elab		Elaboration			
	UID		Plain		Incised		Shark		Cane		Finger		Stick		Pelnode		Cane		Plain		Cane	
	Count		Count		Count		Count		Count		Count		Count		Count		Count		Count		Count	
Vessel	N	Pct	N	Pct	N	Pct	N	Pct	N	Pct	N	Pct	N	Pct	N	Pct	N	Pct	N	Pct	N	Pct
Bowl	2	2.5	44	55.7	15	19.0	1	1.3	2	2.5	1	1.3	·	·	1	1.3	·	·	5	6.3	2	2.5
Straight	·	·	37	34.6	4	3.7	·	·	4	3.7	1	0.9	·	·	·	·	1	0.9	8	7.5	25	23.4
X Unrest	·	·	5	20.8	1	4.2	·	·	1	4.2	·	·	·	·	1	4.2	·	·	3	12.5	6	25.0
X Rest	·	·	4	25.0	2	12.5	·	·	1	6.2	1	6.2	·	·	·	·	·	·	3	18.8	3	18.8
X Uid	1	1.0	9	8.8	2	2.0	·	·	7	6.9	1	1.0	1	1.0	·	·	·	·	5	4.9	28	27.5
Lnj	·	·	1	100	·	·	·	·	·	·	·	·	·	·	·	·	·	·	·	·	·	·
Rsmjar	·	·	1	9.1	·	·	·	·	·	·	·	·	·	·	·	·	·	·	1	9.1	4	36.4
CarBowl	2	10.0	14	70.0	1	5.0	·	·	·	·	·	·	·	·	·	·	·	·	1	5.0	·	·
Uchno	13	81.2	2	12.5	1	6.2	·	·	·	·	·	·	·	·	·	·	·	·	·	·	·	·
Brim	6	6.5	61	66.3	9	9.8	·	·	1	1.1	·	·	·	·	·	·	·	·	1	1.1	8	8.7
All	24	5.1	178	38.0	35	7.5	1	0.2	16	3.4	4	0.9	1	0.2	2	0.4	1	0.2	27	5.8	76	16.2

Lnj = long necked jar
Uchno = UID colono-ware form
All other vessel forms, see key, Table 6.7

Table 7.8. (cont).

Rim Treatment — Folded — Elaboration

Vessel	Finger		Triangle		Stamp		Stick		Incised		UID		Shark		Oval		Molar		Squares		Pinch	
	Count		Count		Count		Count		Count		Count		Count		Count		Count		Count		Count	
	N	Pct	N	Pct	N	Pct	N	Pct	N	Pct	N	Pct	N	Pct	N	Pct	N	Pct	N	Pct	N	Pct
Bowl	1	1.3	.	.	.	.	1	1.3	3	3.8	.	.	.	.	.	.	.	.	.	.	.	.
Straight	8	7.5	5	4.7	2	1.9	7	6.5	.	.	1	0.9	1	0.9	2	1.9	1	0.9	.	.	.	.
X Unrest	5	20.8	.	.	.	.	1	4.2	.	.	.	.	1	4.2	.	.	.	.	.	.	.	.
X Rest	1	6.2	1	6.2	.	.	.	.	.	.	.	.	.	.	.	.	.	.	.	.	.	.
X Uid	20	19.6	9	8.8	5	4.9	6	5.9	.	.	1	1.0	2	2.0	1	1.0	1	1.0	1	1.0	1	1.0
Lnj	.	.	.	.	.	.	.	.	.	.	.	.	.	.	.	.	.	.	.	.	.	.
Rsmjar	2	18.2	.	.	.	.	.	.	.	.	.	.	1	9.1	.	.	.	.	2	18.2	.	.
CarBowl	.	.	.	.	.	.	.	.	1	5.0	.	.	.	.	.	.	.	.	.	.	.	.
Uclno	.	.	.	.	.	.	.	.	.	.	.	.	.	.	.	.	.	.	.	.	.	.
Brim	2	2.2	.	.	.	.	3	3.3	.	.	.	.	.	.	.	.	1	1.1	.	.	.	.
All	39	8.32	15	3.2	7	1.5	18	3.8	4	0.9	2	0.4	5	1.1	3	0.6	3	0.6	3	0.6	1	0.2

Table 7.8. (cont).

Vessel	Rim Treatment				All	
	Folded					
	Elaboration					
	Pushed		Thumb			
	Count		Count		Count	
	N	Pct	N	Pct	N	Pct
Bowl	.	.	1	1.3	79	100
Straight	.	.	.	.	107	100
X Unrest	.	.	.	.	24	100
X Rest	.	.	.	.	16	100
Uid	1	1.0	.	.	102	100
Lnj	.	.	.	.	1	100
Rsmjar	.	.	.	.	11	100
CarBowl	.	.	1	5.0	20	100
Uclno	.	.	.	.	16	100
Brim	.	.	.	.	92	100
All	1	0.2	2	0.4	468	100

Note: For abbreviations, see Table 6.7

Table 7.9. Rim Treatment by Vessel Form.

Frequency Percent Row Pct Col Pct	Rim Treatment						
	UID	Plain	Decorate	Pel/Node	Applique	Folded	Total
Bowl	3 . . .	60 13.48 76.92 28.04	3 0.67 3.85 14.29	1 0.22 1.28 50.00	0 0.00 0.00 0.00	14 3.15 17.95 6.76	78 17.53
Straight	2 . . .	41 9.21 38.32 19.16	5 1.12 4.67 23.81	0 0.00 0.00 0.00	1 0.22 0.93 100.00	60 13.48 56.07 28.99	107 24.04
Jar	5 . . .	25 5.62 16.34 11.68	12 2.70 7.84 57.14	1 0.22 0.65 50.00	0 0.00 0.00 0.00	115 25.84 75.16 55.56	153 34.38
Carinated Bowl	2 . . .	15 3.37 83.33 7.01	0 0.00 0.00 0.00	0 0.00 0.00 0.00	0 0.00 0.00 0.00	3 0.37 16.67 1.45	18 4.04
UID Colono	14 . . .	3 0.67 100.00 1.40	0 0.00 0.00 0.00	0 0.00 0.00 0.00	0 0.00 0.00 0.00	0 0.00 0.00 0.00	3 0.67
Brimmed Vessel	6 . . .	70 15.73 81.40 32.71	1 0.22 1.16 4.76	0 0.00 0.00 0.00	0 0.00 0.00 0.00	15 3.37 17.44 7.25	86 19.33
Total	. .	214 48.09	21 4.72	2 0.45	1 0.22	207 46.52	445 100.00

Table 7.10. Chi-Square Test, Rim Treatment by Vessel Form.

Frequency Expected Deviation Cell Chi-Square	Rim Treatment		Total
	Plain	Folded	
Bowl	60	14	74
	37.354	36.646	
	22.646	-22.65	
	13.729	13.994	
Straight	41	60	101
	50.983	50.017	
	-9.983	9.9833	
	1.9549	1.9926	
Jar	25	115	140
	70.67	69.33	
	-45.67	45.67	
	29.514	30.084	
Carinated Bowl	15	3	18
	9.0861	8.9139	
	5.9139	-5.914	
	3.8492	3.9235	
Brimmed Vessel	70	15	85
	42.907	42.093	
	27.093	-27.09	
	17.108	17.439	
Total	211	207	418

Statistics for Table of Vessel Form by Rim Treatment

Statistic	DF	Value	Prob
Chi-Square	4	133.588	<0.001

Table 7.11 Chi-Square Test, Rim Treatment by Structure.

Structure	Rim Treatment		Total
Frequency Expected Deviation Cell Chi-Square	Plain	Folded	
Convento	132 131.61 0.3871 0.0011	128 128.39 -0.387 0.0012	260
Kitchen	29 35.434 -6.434 1.1683	41 34.566 6.4342 1.1977	70
Church	43 36.953 6.0471 0.9896	30 36.047 -6.047 1.0144	73
Total	204	199	403

Statistics for Table of VF by Rim Treatment

Statistic	DF	Value	Prob
Chi-Square	2	4.372	0.112

Table 7.12. Rim Elaboration by Structure.

Frequency Percent Row Pct Col Pct	UID	Plain	Incised	Finger	Cane	Stick	Triangle	Stamp	Total
Convento	26	128	28	28	54	13	9	6	292
	5.59	27.53	6.02	6.02	11.61	2.80	1.94	1.29	62.80
	8.90	43.84	9.59	9.59	18.49	4.45	3.08	2.05	
	70.27	61.84	71.79	65.12	57.45	56.52	60.00	85.71	
Kitchen	6	29	2	7	20	5	4	1	74
	1.29	6.24	0.43	1.51	4.30	1.08	0.86	0.22	15.91
	8.11	39.19	2.70	9.46	27.03	6.76	5.41	1.35	
	16.22	14.01	5.13	16.28	21.28	21.74	26.67	14.29	
Church	4	41	7	5	17	5	2	0	81
	0.86	8.82	1.51	1.08	3.66	1.08	0.43	0.00	17.42
	4.94	50.62	8.64	6.17	20.99	6.17	2.47	0.00	
	10.81	19.81	17.95	11.63	18.09	21.74	13.33	0.00	
ABO Structure	1	9	2	3	3	0	0	0	18
	0.22	1.94	0.43	0.65	0.65	0.00	0.00	0.00	3.87
	5.56	50.00	11.11	16.67	16.67	0.00	0.00	0.00	
	2.70	4.35	5.13	6.98	3.19	0.00	0.00	0.00	
Total	37	207	39	43	94	23	15	7	465
	7.96	44.52	8.39	9.25	20.22	4.95	3.23	1.51	100.00

8

Continuity and Change

As discussed in Chapter 1, the object of this study was to determine the nature and timing of change in Guale pottery from the late pre-Columbian Irene phase through the Mission period of Spanish colonial Florida (A.D. 1300–1702). The database consisted of pottery assemblages from five temporally sequential contexts—two Irene phase components from the Meeting House Fields site on St. Catherines Island; early and late proveniences from the Santa Catalina mission compound, also on St. Catherines Island, Georgia; and selected proveniences from the late Mission period site Santa Catalina de Santa María on Amelia Island, Florida. In addition to temporal changes, different "contexts of use," defined as the different structures in the Spanish missions, were studied to determine whether pottery assemblages would vary according to structure function. Once the descriptive characteristics of the respective assemblages were defined, it was thought it would be possible to correlate differences between the assemblages with changes in demography, subsistence patterns, residence rules, or the organization of labor brought about by Spanish colonization.

Guale pottery was contrasted with that of some other peoples in colonial environments. Several influential studies indicated that change attributable to the effects of colonization were subtle or were limited to simplification or assimilation. However, change in Guale pottery after contact has been obvious to archaeologists for some time, at least as regards design motif. The only motif on paddle stamped pottery prior to contact appears to have been the filfot cross, a representation of the world symbol reflecting the cosmology of Southeastern peoples. Sometime during the early Mission period, the curvilinear elements of the cross disappeared, and the design became bolder and, it was thought, devolved into a series of perpendicular lines. Previous work indicated that through time there would also be a change in rim treatment, from applique strips to folded rims and that some changes would occur in the relative frequencies of surface decorations.

The comparison of the pottery from the late Irene (Pine Harbor) phase Meeting House Fields site (Cluster 2, circa A.D. 1550) and the early component of the St. Catherines Island mission (A.D. 1595–1597) indicated that the transition from the Irene phase to the Mission period Altamaha phase was abrupt, at least in archaeological terms. No curvilinear elements were present in the designs on the sherds from the early mission context, designs were bolder, and there were no applique strips in that context or in later ones from the site (Table 8.1). However, the motif on the pottery continued to emphasize a central element (the sun) surrounded by four sets of lines radiating in the four cardinal directions.

A number of possible explanations—functional, social, and ideological—were forwarded to explain the change in the execution of the world symbol (Chapter 6). Although none of the possibilities could be eliminated with the available data, the ostensibly abrupt change in this trait on St. Catherines Island, along with the simultaneous adoption of the folded, punctated rim and better firing techniques, implicated the Spanish in these changes to a larger degree than had been anticipated.

This conclusion was surprising. It was expected that changes in Irene pottery would begin before effective missionization (i.e. before A.D. 1600). Certainly there must have been profound changes in Guale society before the establishment of the Santa Catalina mission in 1595. The French had lived among the Guale in the 1560s, perhaps in the same village (Hann 1990b:13), and Menéndez placed a garrison and blockhouse in the principal Guale town. The Guale provided food for the Spanish colony at Santa Elena, sometimes under duress, from its inception in 1566 until its abandonment in 1587. And prior to the early Franciscan mission, at least four epidemics struck the Guale coast. The first epidemic emanated from the Ayllón colony of 1526 (*contra* DePratter 1994), the second was reported by Father Sedeño in 1570, the third appeared after the Spanish reprisals for the 1576 Guale rebellion, and a fourth occurred in 1582. As noted in Chapter 2, by the time the first Franciscan mission was established (1595), the mortality rate among the Guale could have been approaching 90 percent.

Despite these turbulent conditions, the pottery from the later contexts at the Meeting House Fields site, which *could have been* occupied during early Spanish forays on St. Catherines Island, showed no characteristics that could be considered transitional to Altamaha pottery. The changes that did occur appeared to represent a continuation of the changes in the Lamar tradition in general and to be a result of drift. For instance, Cluster 2 at Meeting House Fields differed from the slightly earlier Cluster 1 in having more plain and incised wares, more decorated vessels, and fewer applique strips. The attribute most connected with the change from Irene to Altamaha phase pottery, curvilinear versus rectilinear stamping, showed no change over time at Meeting House Fields.

There was, however, significantly more sand tempering in Cluster 2. This may be a factor of vessel size—smaller vessels tended to be sand tempered at Harris Neck—and might be some indirect evidence of population loss, but the data are not adequate for a strong argument for this at present. The incidence of sand tempering returned to the same low frequency as was found in Cluster 1 in the early (and late) mission components. There was also a slight decrease in the number of burnished sherds in Cluster 2, but the percentage of burnished plain vessels in Clusters 1 and 2 was virtually the same.

The trend toward more plain and incised wares over time in the late Irene phase was not continued into the Mission period. Instead, the percentages of stamped and plain wares from both St. Catherines Island Mission period assemblages resembled the Cluster 1 totals more than those from Cluster 2. In addition, the incidence of sand tempering declined, burnishing remained about the same, and decorated vessels declined. Attributes that might have been expected to decline gradually, for instance, curvilinear designs with the eventual loss or breakage of all paddles with the filfot cross, were absent from the 1595–1597 context at mission Santa Catalina. The applique strip was also absent from early (and later) mission contexts.

It is difficult to associate any of the changes between Irene and Altamaha pottery with the further disruption of Guale lifeways once missions were established. Population loss was probably severe before A.D. 1595. If population loss, in the form of the disruption of traditional teaching and pottery production groups, was a primary cause of pottery change, some of its effects should have appeared in the late contexts at Meeting House Fields.

The results from studies of pottery changes in other areas of the Spanish colonial empire that suffered severe population losses would seem to indicate that craft traditions were extremely tenacious despite high morbidity and mortality rates. This may be precisely because pottery production was not specialized in most of the areas studied. In the case of the Guale, the repertoire of designs was quite small, and, as a comparison of rim elaborations between middens at Meeting House Fields indicates, rim styles did not correspond to household units. Both technique and style could be passed down by any female member of the group. Thus, there were no major differences in the frequency of different rim elaborations between the Irene and the Altamaha phases, and it would appear that these attributes were not sensitive to changes in residence patterns.

Although a redirection of traditional labor patterns is well chronicled, the idea that the execution of the world symbol with larger lands and grooves changed because of time constraints did not explain the sheer drop-off of this attribute (see Chapter 6). Also, changes in labor patterns would not explain the complete rejection of the applique strip in favor of the folded rim. Functional reasons were proposed to explain the evolution of both of these attributes; it was suggested that the Spanish may have been instrumental in these changes. Of course, more data are needed from other sites before the hypothesis presented here, that the Spanish directed change in Guale more than is commonly acknowledged, can be accepted. In fact, data from several previously excavated sites seem to indicate that, at least in some areas, the transition to Altamaha wares was much more gradual than it appeared in the St. Catherines Island data.

The first data set is from Sapelo Island. Sapelo Island was the location of the mission of San José de Sápala and later Tupiqui; the Santa Catalina Guale and Satuache fled to Sapelo after Santa Catalina was abandoned. There is some indication that the Bourbon Field site was the location of an aspect of one or the other of these mission incarnations, though the data are unclear (see Worth 1995:194). Some level of interaction with the Spanish is indicated at the site by the presence of olive jar sherds at the site.

At Bourbon Fields (see Figure 5.1), Crook (1981:18; see also Crook 1980) defined an "Irene-San Marcos pottery nexus." Crook (1981:18) thought that Irene pottery and San Marcos pottery were both produced at the same time by the same peoples: "Significant correlations among members of the nexus provide an excellent indication that all are components of a single pottery complex." In other words, the horizontal distribution of frequencies of Irene and San Marcos wares were correlated across the site. The problem with this interpretation is that, as the name implies, the site had been heavily plowed. Postdepositional factors, for instance erosion, might account for some of this correlation. It is also possible that during the occupation of the site from a hypothetical late Irene to Mission period, activity areas remained the same. Without better site integrity, it is impossible to determine whether these two pottery types were related in time.

Other data come from St. Simons Island, which is nominally south of the area of Irene phase occupation. The sites discussed below illustrate the problems of determining chronologies based on ceramics at the spatial and temporal boundaries of culture areas. Late prehistoric and contact period sites should contain Savannah phase cordmarked wares unless the southern boundaries of the Irene phase need to be redrawn. By 1661, the Guale had moved in to the area. The northern end of the island was the location of Santo Domingo de Asao at that time (Worth 1995:195). There was a refugee population of pagan Colones two leagues south of Asao and another community of Yamassee one league south of the Colones.[1] The location of Asao has not been positively identified; Worth (1995:195), following Larson (1980b), thought the site might be at Cannon's Point.

Wallace (1975) excavated three sites at the northern end of the island: Couper Field, Indian Field, and the Taylor Mound. Couper Field was identified as a Savannah phase charnel house; Indian Field was the associated village. In addition to using Couper Field material to demonstrate that Savannah phase peoples were present in the area during the contact period, Wallace did an attribute analysis of the pottery at Couper Field and at Indian Field. His results indicated that San Marcos and "Pine Harbor" (Irene) Complicated Stamped were used contemporaneously at those sites.[2] In the case of Couper and Indian Fields, however, once again the sites had been plowed. In addition, pottery was assigned to type on the basis of rectilinear versus curvilinear stamping. As the analysis of Meeting House Fields has shown, rectilinear stamping is the most frequent design recovered on sherds even in Irene phase pottery assemblages. The essential attributes needed to discriminate the two types on a sherd-by-sherd basis are land and groove width and depth. Irene and San Marcos are hopelessly conflated in this analysis.

A quick review of these assemblages at the Florida Museum of Natural History indicated that both types were present, but co-occurred predominantly in zone, presumably plowed, material. I examined eight closed context features at Couper Field that were indicated to have both San Marcos and Irene sherds. Six of these had no San Marcos wares, only Irene, and greater or lesser amounts of Savannah, St. Johns, and San Pedro wares. One of the two exceptions, Pit F (FS 118), had a single sherd identified as San Marcos; it was obliterated stamped and could not be confidently typed to one ware or the other. Area I (FS 32), identified as a sherd concentration, had San Marcos and a bold incised sherd that was identified as Irene but that could easily be Altamaha Incised. All other features at Couper Field were Savannah phase. Indian Field had very few closed contexts, but no clear association of Irene and San Marcos emerged from reviewing those features either. Area II, also referred to as "Surface," did have what I would consider San Marcos (Altamaha), Irene, and Savannah wares, but the significance of this association is unclear. In sum, the data from these two components were not useful in discussion of the transition from Irene to Altamaha. However, a complete reanalysis of these assemblages would be most interesting in terms of interaction between contemporaneous Savannah and Irene peoples.

More compelling evidence for the contemporaneity of Irene and San Marcos wares came from Taylor Mound. The Taylor Mound was a low (45 to 85 centimeters high) sand mound built over a prepared shell core. A portion of the mound was first excavated by Pearson (1977a) in 1971. He proposed a three-stage construction sequence of a central shell core, overlying sand fill, and a later sand "apron" on the eastern side of the mound. The shell core is typical of both Savannah and Irene phase burial mounds. Pearson's excavations extended west from the apron, through the center of the mound and several meters to the west. In all excavations, Pearson (1977a:76) recovered only Savannah ceramics.

Thirteen burials were uncovered, all either intrusive into the shell core or into the flanking sand apron. Two burials, one of which contained two individuals, were associated with Contact period materials, the most diagnostic of which were Nueva Cadiz beads. Nine *maravedis* (copper coins) were also recovered, but the mint date for these is controversial (Pearson 1977a; Saunders 2001); Pearson thought 1540–1560 was a reasonable date for these two burials. Pearson considered the other burials to date to the pre-contact Savannah phase. Wallace (1975) revisited the site and expanded on Pearson's previous excavations. He interpreted both the topography and construction sequence differently from Pearson, mapping a more symmetrical shape and four construction stages (Wallace 1975:55, Figure 6). He found no other burials associated with European artifacts, though several nails and spikes were recovered near the top of the mound fill. Wallace did find an east side pottery cache containing at least five vessels and several wrought iron spikes. According to Wallace (1975:52, 57–58), the cache originated at the level of old humus and was covered with mound fill. He interpreted his data to indicate that all mound construction occurred after contact.

Pottery types within the cache were described as "San Marcos (rectilinear complicated stamped), Irene Incised, Irene Filfot, and Irene Plain" (Wallace 1975:58). Four of these vessels are reconstructed at the Florida Museum of Natural History; two vessels are depicted in Figure 8.1. Two are incised and obliterated stamped, and the others are stamped. Both stamped vessels are jars with slightly excurvate lips. They have plain rims decorated with whole-cane punctation. One of these has San Marcos–like stamping (broad, deep lands and grooves) and a high-fired exterior. The other jar is obliterated stamped, probably San Marcos, and is also relatively highly fired (Figure 8.1a). Both incised vessels have more complex forms. One is a small (diameter = 14 centimeters) collared jar with an excurvate rim. This shape may be associated with the carinated jar that Braley et al. (1986) identified as a mortuary ware. The collar is plain and the rim stick punctated (Figure 8.1b). Elaborately incised scrolls (seven lands per scroll) decorate the vessel shoulder. The dark body of the vessel is stamped with obliterated Irene filfot crosses. The other incised vessel is a long-necked jar. The neck is plain, and the simple rim is cane punctated. The vessel shoulder is incised with pendant semi-ovals and filler. Incising on this vessel is not as well executed as that on the collared jar. The vessel body is obliterated stamped and could not be typed. None of the vessels examined were sooted.

Both Irene and San Marcos wares, then, were manifestly present in the Taylor Mound. The problem thus becomes how to determine when the cache was deposited. It is doubtful that the age of the cache can be derived from the terminus post quem of the Contact period burials excavated by Pearson.[3] The absence of San Marcos in Pearson's excavation area, and the presence of San Marcos throughout the mound fill in Wallace's,[4] leads me

8.1. Two of the Vessels in the Cache at Taylor Mound; a = 16 centimeters in diameter, b = 14 centimeters in diameter.

to suspect that Pearson's stratigraphic interpretation was more accurate—there were both prehistoric and historic construction episodes. However, on the basis of the artifacts, I might suggest two different postcontact activities at the mound. The first would consist of the Contact period burials—no San Marcos sherds were found in this excavation area—and the second would entail the final construction episode that included a sand mound fill with quite a bit of San Marcos and the vessel cache.[5] Unfortunately, no diagnostic materials were recovered, and this construction episode cannot be dated. Nevertheless, and in contrast to the St. Catherines Island data, information from Taylor Mound suggests that San Marcos–like stamping may have been used contemporaneously with Irene, at least in ceremonial contexts away from centers of Spanish settlement.[6]

Larson (1980b) and Cook (1980a) excavated a mound and village site along the Guale coast proper, the Pine Harbor site. Larson (1980b:40) described the site as "a site that I presently feel was occupied at the beginning of the Spanish mission activity on the Georgia coast." The site extends for more than a mile along high ground abutting the marsh between the Sapelo and White Chimney Rivers (Larson 1984:67). The village area contained more than two hundred middens; Larson recovered charred maize cobs and kernels along with native plant remains in the middens. Cook (1980a) recovered good evidence indicating that the mound was in continuous use from the early through the late Irene and up to the late sixteenth or early seventeenth century. Log tomb, mass burials were present in the latest inhumations. Pine Harbor, which was located in a pivotal area—the population center for Guale and hence near the Ayllón colony—could be key to understanding pottery change among the Guale.

No Altamaha traits were present in fifteen mortuary vessels associated with the latest burials in the Pine Harbor mound, though they did display elaborate Southeastern Ceremonial Complex incising (Cook 1980a; Cook and Pearson 1989; Cook and Snow 1983). After reviewing a portion of the ceramic assemblage from Larson's 1953 excavations in the village area, I thought the site contained at least two components. An early component was represented by numerous incurved, burnished plain bowls with applique pellets and by stamped sherds with rosettes and possibly some crude incising. As did Larson, I noted Savannah sherds in the early collection. The later occupation contained *a few* filfot stamped vessels with deeply folded cane punctate rims and two colono-ware forms—shallow saucers and brimmed bowls—along with more typical late Irene Pine Harbor phase forms and treatments. I did see some stamped sherds with motifs that appeared to consist of concentric circles only, but I observed nothing else that could not be construed as a portion of a filfot cross.

This component should be contemporaneous with Midden M and possibly some other Cluster 2 proveniences at Meeting House Fields. It may also have been contemporaneous with the 1595–1597 Santa Catalina mission and perhaps with the early occupation of the later Santa Catalina—the terminus post quem on the European artifacts in the mound was circa 1600. No European materials were present in the village materials I examined.

Thus, the Pine Harbor site might manifest a more gradual transition from Irene to Altamaha than is evident in the contexts studied on St. Catherines Island. In retrospect, this might be expected. St. Catherines Island populations may have been rapidly co-opted into the mission environment and, in this context, may have begun producing a fairly homogeneous ware for Spanish consumption. Pine Harbor inhabitants had the "luxury" of picking and choosing what interested them. Although I would never advocate using the frequency of nonnative attributes as a one-to-one measure of *acculturation* (e.g., Quimby and Spoehr 1951; Quimby 1966), in this case there may be some correspondence between native and nonnative (folded rims, modified filfot cross, colono-wares) attributes and level of *interaction*.

Pine Harbor site pottery may also display attributes indicative of population loss prior to effective Spanish colonization, changes that were absent at Meeting House Fields. DePratter (1991:190) noted an increase in motifs at this and other late sites. At least some of this increase in motifs, particularly the production of crosses (Figure 8.2), might be attributable to the same behavioral response that produced the elaborate Southeastern Ceremonial Complex vessels in the mound—a marked increase in ceremonial behavior in the face of drastic changes in the physical (in terms of disease) and sociopolitical realms (see Cook 1980a). That some of this ceremonial response was transferred to village pottery should be expected in terms of the cosmological content of the previously ubiquitous filfot cross. DePratter also noted an increase in land and groove widths, "sloppier" stamping, and more overstamping in later Pine Harbor phase materials. I do not have data on these attributes for the Pine Harbor site; no such differences were recorded in the Meeting House Fields results. However, an increase in land and groove width and sloppier stamping in combination with new, simplified motifs such as concentric circles (which I did observe) suggests some inexperienced paddle carvers—just what one would suspect in areas of high mortality rates.

8.2. Cross Motif from the Pine Harbor Site (from South and
DePratter 1996; by permission).

An answer to the question of when Irene phase pottery became Altamaha
phase pottery remains elusive. As noted in Chapter 3, pottery change along
the Guale coast probably kept pace with local events. Different sites with
different local histories (especially as regards mortality and the amount
of direct and indirect European contact) will yield different answers.
Indeed, the interpretations of the data used in this study depend on the
acceptance of the dating of the proveniences examined. In particular, the
Meeting House Fields Cluster 2 material could be earlier than suggested. As
discussed for another context below, both the absolute and relative dating
methods available are at present too imprecise to yield unequivocal answers
to the complex question of the timing of culture change.

Not only are our dating methods imprecise but the database at hand
offers too few sites that are too widely scattered over the coast to construct
a reliable chronology. Many previously identified sites are known only
through surface survey (e.g., Larson 1953) or have been impacted by
agriculture or other modern developments. The Pine Harbor site has been
completely destroyed. The last decade has seen a resurgence of interest in

Contact period sites. Nevertheless, the rate of site destruction along the coast will render it impossible to understand the process of culture change unless we intensify our efforts.

In order to fully understand the transition between the phases, we need to study (in addition to more sites with characteristics similar to those under discussion here) two other contexts. The first, obviously, is the mission pueblo, particularly the pueblos of early missions. Initially, the Spanish may have been more concerned with directing change in pottery produced for their own use. Associated village pottery may have retained some pre-Columbian attributes longer. Pottery produced by Guale living in villages not directly associated with missions might also have changed less dramatically.

Second, we need to know more about the pottery of the Guale who eschewed Spanish domination, those who "put a piece of forest between themselves and the long arm of the invaders" (Axtell 1988a:54; Chapter 1). One might predict that the pottery of those peoples would remain Irene, and therein lies a problem. Possibly many previously identified sites with Irene pottery have been considered pre-Columbian but actually represent the occupations of those refugees. Those hypothetical sites will be almost impossible to date. Radiocarbon dating is not accurate enough, and it is likely that in evading the Spanish, those Guale also either shunned European material culture or had little access to it prior to the arrival of English traders after 1670. Unless some diagnostic European artifacts are present, site locations away from the centers of Spanish occupation and in environs not typically occupied by the pre-Columbian Guale may be the only criteria for identifying such occupations. Snow (1990) may have located such sites in the Pine Barrens of south-central Georgia. Some of the sites discovered by Larson (1953) in McIntosh and Liberty Counties might also qualify.

The problem of the identification of those sites aside, if refugee sites have "Altamaha" pottery, a (somewhat arbitrary) date of A.D. 1600 was a true watershed, a time when a number of complex and interrelated variables culminated in the replacement of Irene phase pottery with a different type. As demonstrated in Chapters 6 and 7, the changes wrought in the Guale pottery of the early seventeenth century quickly stabilized. Except for a large decrease in the frequency of incising, values for relative frequencies of surface decoration, rim treatments and elaborations, and even the distributional patterns of surface decorations and vessel forms were quite similar between the St. Catherines Island and Amelia Island missions (Table 8.1). These data suggested that Altamaha and San Marcos should not be separate types.

In the two mission sites, contexts of use proved to have subtle but intriguing effects on assemblages. Contrary to expectations, vessel forms showed little correlation with structure. Instead, pottery assemblages from the structures varied along "stylistic" as opposed to "functional" attributes. Assemblages from utilitarian contexts had higher percentages of stamped wares, and churches had more plain and burnished plain pottery. Although in most cases these differences were statistically significant, they were not absolute. However, these data did suggest that certain "stylistic" properties were desirable for vessels used in each structure. Other differences between structures included a slightly higher percentage of red-filmed wares in the convento and relatively low percentages of folded rims in the churches.

Two not necessarily mutually exclusive hypotheses were offered for the similarity between pottery assemblages from the different structures. First, structures probably did have overlapping functions; for instance, kitchens, conventos, and church sacristies could all be used for storage. However, the overall lack of difference between structures probably emerged from the relatively undifferentiated set of forms in both the pre-Columbian Guale and Spanish potting traditions. One attribute not measured in this study, vessel diameter, might have evoked stronger differences in contexts of use. Folk taxonomies of pottery in Spain and Mexico use vessel size, measured in *cuartillos,* as a major distinguishing criterion (Foster 1960:90–91; the referent, however, is not capacity but the number of pots that could be purchased for a fourth of a real). Vessel size also appeared related to context in the comparison of Guale pottery from mounds and middens (Braley et al. 1986:90), though only for certain forms.

The world symbol continued to be used on pottery after the Guale were removed from the Georgia coast to Amelia Island. However, the frequency of the design did appear to decrease. Although paddles continued to exhibit the four sets of radiating lines, many motifs no longer had central "suns." The result is the Line Block motif noted by many researchers. At the same time, a few long-disused attributes, such as the rim strip and the applique node, reappeared (though in minute quantities), so it was unlikely that the loss of the central dot was due to a breakdown in the transmission of design concepts from one generation to another.

Was the decline in the use of the world symbol evidence of the adoption of a different worldview by some of the Guale at the mission on Amelia Island? Very likely. Fray Pareja noted as early as 1616 that (as in most cultures undergoing rapid change) "the younger generation makes fun of and laughs at some old men and women who carelessly have recourse to these abuses (the aboriginal customs)" (Milanich and Sturtevant 1972:4; Oré 1936:106). However, unless one is willing to believe that many carvers continued to produce paddles with customary designs then bereft of meaning, some Guale Indian women continued to believe in pre-Columbian cosmological concepts. Documentary evidence (see especially Milanich and Sturtevant 1972 and Hann 1991) does not indicate that friars put less emphasis on indoctrinating women into the Christian fold than men. The continued use of the world symbol should not be construed as a difference in acculturation between men and women in mission contexts (an idea for which there is very little evidence; see Saunders 1986b). In any event, when one reflects on the continuity between Irene and San Marcos pottery, the overall impression is that the Guale retained their formal and decorative categories for pottery throughout a period of rapid demographic and cultural change. Because these categories often signal group affiliation (see the discussion in Saunders 1986a, 1986c), the results of this study suggest that the Guale may have maintained a strong sense of their social identity as well.

Table 8.1. Summary of Proveniences and Selected Attributes.

Provenience	Date	Surface Decoration (%)				Rim Treatment (%)				
		Stamp	Plain	B Plain	Incise	Plain	Dec	Pel/Node	Appl	Fold
MHF Cluster 1	ca. A.D. 1420	71.7	19.2	8.9	0.1	25.0	10.7	14.3	50.0	0.0
MHF Cluster 2	ca. A.D. 1550	52.4	35.4	5.5	6.6	53.7	14.7	0.0	29.5	2.1
Sta. Catalina, GA Early	A.D. 1594-1597	80.7	8.8	5.6	2.8	44.4	5.6	5.6	0.0	44.4
Sta. Catalina, GA Late	A.D. 1604-1680	76.4	12.9	4.4	6.2	55.3	4.0	0.7	0.0	40.0
Sta. Maria	A.D. 1684-1702	79.1	15.7	3.9	1.4	48.1	4.7	0.5	0.2	46.5

Note: Radiocarbon dates based on uncorrected/uncalibrated radiocarbon year for comparative purposes. Date presented was selected as most appropriate on the basis of stylistic attributes.

Appendix A
Meeting House Fields: Tables

Table A.1. Meeting House Fields Surface Decoration by Midden/Level.

Midden 12

LEVEL	Master Code												All			
	Stamped				Plain				Burnished Plain							
	Count		Weight		Count		Weight		Count		Weight		Count		Weight	
	N	Pct	N	Pct	N	Pct	N	Pct	N	Pct	N	Pct	N	Pct	N	Pct
1	47	58.0	291.4	64.9	27	33.3	139.8	31.2	7	8.6	17.5	3.9	81	100	448.7	100
2	47	65.3	408.5	71.8	15	20.8	89.0	15.6	10	13.9	71.2	12.5	72	100	568.7	100
3	57	90.5	651.4	94.1	4	6.3	64.0	4.9	2	3.2	6.7	1.0	63	100	692.1	100
4	11	78.6	121.1	77.5	3	21.4	35.1	22.5	.	.	.	.	14	100	156.2	100
All	162	70.4	1472.4	78.9	49	21.3	297.9	16.0	19	8.3	95.4	5.1	230	100	1865.7	10

Table A.1. (cont.).

Midden 21

LEVEL	Master Code												All			
	Stamp				Plain				Burnished Plain							
	Count		Weight		Count		Weight		Count		Weight		Count		Weight	
	N	Pct	N	Pct	N	Pct	N	Pct	N	Pct	N	Pct	N	Pct	N	Pct
1	9	56.2	42.7	55.7	6	37.5	30.5	39.8	1	6.2	3.5	4.6	16	100	76.7	100
2	109	68.1	509.6	67.2	32	20.0	169.4	22.3	19	11.9	79.7	10.5	160	100	758.7	100
3	89	93.7	808.4	95.6	6	6.3	36.8	4.4	.	.	.	.	95	100	845.2	100
4	29	82.9	320.5	79.4	4	11.4	66.3	16.4	2	5.7	17.0	4.2	35	100	403.8	100
5	2	100	23.1	100	.	.	.	.	.	.	.	.	2	100	23.1	100
6	.	.	.	.	1	100	0.4	100	.	.	.	.	1	100	0.4	100
All	238	77.0	1704.3	80.9	49	15.9	303.4	14.4	22	7.1	100.2	4.8	309	100	2107.9	100

Table A.1 (cont.).

Midden B

LEVEL	Master Code												All			
	Stamp				Plain				Burnished Plain							
	Count		Weight		Count		Weight		Count		Weight		Count		Weight	
	N	Pct	N	Pct	N	Pct	N	Pct	N	Pct	N	Pct	N	Pct	N	Pct
3	2	66.7	18.2	87.9	1	33.3	2.5	12.1	.	.	.	.	3	100	20.7	100
4	7	46.7	71.2	63.5	7	46.7	37.9	33.8	1	6.7	3.0	2.7	15	100	112.1	100
5	4	66.7	29.3	80.1	1	16.7	3.7	10.1	1	16.7	3.6	9.8	6	100	36.6	100
6	7	58.3	101.1	67.0	5	41.7	45.4	31.0	.	.	.	.	12	100	146.5	100
7	4	44.4	93.6	61.9	4	44.4	48.8	32.3	1	11.1	8.7	5.8	9	100	151.1	100
9	4	80.0	35.6	69.9	1	20.0	15.3	30.1	.	.	.	.	5	100	50.9	100
10	2	100	48.5	100	.	.	.	.	.	.	.	.	2	100	48.5	100
All	30	57.7	397.5	70.2	19	36.5	153.6	27.1	3	5.8	15.3	2.7	52	100	566.4	100

Table A-1 (cont.).

Midden D

	Master Code																			
	Stamped				Plain				Burnished Plain				Incised				All			
	Count		Weight		Count		Weight		Count		Weight		Count		Weight		Count		Weight	
LEVEL	N	Pct	N	Pct	N	Pct	N	Pct	N	Pct	N	Pct	N	Pct	N	Pct	N	Pct	N	Pct
1					5	100	28	100									5	100	27.8	100
2	.	.	.	.	1	100	37	00				.	.	.	.	.	1	100	3.7	100
4	4	50.0	38.5	67.1	3	37.5	13.8	24.0	1	2.5	5.1	8.9	.	.	.	.	8	100	57.4	100
5	5	35.7	103.1	56.6	8	57.1	74.0	40.7	1	7.1	4.9	2.7	.	.	.	.	14	100	182.0	100
6	8	57.1	105.5	66.9	3	21.4	26.7	16.9	2	14.3	19.0	12.0	1	7.1	6.6	4.2	14	100	157.8	100
7	10	55.6	89.7	65.7	7	38.9	40.2	29.5	1	5.6	6.6	4.8	.	.	.	.	18	100	136.5	100
8	1	100	6.8	100	.	.	.	.	.	.	.	.	.	.	.	.	1	100	6.8	100
All	28	45.9	343.6	60.1	27	44.3	186.2	32.6	5	8.2	35.6	6.2	1	1.6	6.6	1.2	61	100	572.0	100

Table A-1 (cont.).

Midden E

LEVEL	Stamped				Plain				Burnished Plain				Incised				All			
	Count		Weight		Count		Weight		Count		Weight		Count		Weight		Count		Weight	
	N	Pct	N	Pct	N	Pct	N	Pct	N	Pct	N	Pct	N	Pct	N	Pct	N	Pct	N	Pct
1	46	55.4	430.7	70.1	26	31.3	141.4	23.0	·	·		·	11	13.3	42.6	6.9	83	100	614.7	100
2	34	33.0	468.8	45.1	49	47.6	430.1	41.4	3	2.9	28.4	2.7	17	16.5	112.0	10.8	103	100	1039.3	100
3	46	73.0	577.1	71.6	10	15.9	85.4	10.6	3	4.8	76.2	9.5	4	6.3	67.0	8.3	63	100	805.7	100
4	50	72.5	678.0	85.1	17	24.6	108.8	13.7	1	1.4	6.2	0.8	1	1.4	3.9	0.5	69	100	796.9	100
5	38	58.5	468.0	64.5	23	35.4	242.1	33.4	2.	3.1	11.7	1.6	2	3.1	3.6	0.5	65	100	725.4	100
6	71	64.5	893.8	73.4	28	25.5	240.0	19.7	1	0.9	4.2	0.3	10	9.1	78.9	6.5	110	100	1216.9	100
7	66	49.3	944.2	61.5	58	43.3	508.0	33.1	2	1.5	19.2	1.3	8	6.0	64.4	4.2	134	100	1535.8	100
8	115	61.2	1237.9	67.8	66	35.1	528.1	28.9	1	0.5	12.7	0.7	6	3.2	47.9	2.6	188	100	1826.6	100
9	31	66.0	266.1	74.8	14	29.8	79.6	22.4	·	·		·	2	4.3	10.0	2.8	47	100	355.7	100
10	3	60.0	17.2	61.0	1	20.0	7.5	26.6	·	·		·	1	20.0	3.5	12.4	5	100	28.2	100
All	500	57.7	5981.8	66.9	292	33.7	2371.0	26.5	13	1.5	158.6	1.8	62	7.2	433.8	4.8	867	100	8945.2	100

Table A-1 (cont.).

Midden H

LEVEL	Master Code																			
	Stamped				Plain				Burnished Plain				Incised				All			
	Count		Weight		Count		Weight		Count		Weight		Count		Weight		Count		Weight	
	N	Pct	N	Pct	N	Pct	N	Pct	N	Pct	N	Pct	N	Pct	N	Pct	N	Pct	N	Pct
1	69	51.5	694.8	64.7	51	38.1	276.4	25.7	8	6.0	39.30	3.6	6	4.5	63.3	5.9	134	100	1073.5	100
2	22	22.2	260.7	32.5	35	35.4	237.9	29.7	24	24.2	154.6	19.3	18	18.2	148.5	18.5	99	100	801.7	100
3	12	38.7	205.8	41.7	19	61.3	287.3	58.3	.	.	.	.	.	.	.	.	31	100	493.1	100
4	4	40.0	72.0	41.5	5	50.0	84.0	48.5	1	5.0	4.8	1.3	1	10.0	17.3	10.0	10	100	173.3	100
5	14	70.0	310.9	83.8	5	25.0	55.3	14.9	.	.	.	.	.	.	.	.	20	100	357.0	100
6	10	62.5	261.8	73.3	6	37.5	95.2	26.7	.	.	.	.	.	.	.	.	16	100	357.0	100
7	24	58.5	350.8	69.1	17	41.5	156.7	30.9	.	.	.	.	.	.	.	.	41	100	507.5	100
8	8	66.7	129.2	85.2	3	25.0	17.7	11.7	1	8.3	4.8	3.2	.	.	.	.	12	100	151.7	100
9	1	100	3.9	100	.	.	.	.	.	.	.	.	.	.	.	.	1	100	3.9	100
All	164	45.1	2289.9	58.2	141	38.7	1210.5	30.8	34	9.3	203.2	5.2	25	6.9	229.1	5.8	364	100	3932.7	100

Table A-1 (cont.).

Midden J

	Master Code															
	Stamped				Plain				Burnished Plain				Incised			
	Count		Weight		Count		Weight		Count		Weight		Count		Weight	
LEVEL	N	Pct	N	Pct	N	Pct	N	Pct	N	Pct	N	Pct	N	Pct	N	Pct
1	46	60.5	567.4	64.5	21	27.6	172.2	19.6	9	11.8	139.9	15.9	.	.	.	.
2	.	.	.	.	14	100	197.7	100	.	.	.	.	.	.	.	.
3	1	16.7	7.0	7.0	.	.	.	.	5	83.3	93.2	93.0	.	.	.	.
4	1	10.0	14.2	15.1	.	.	.	.	9	90.0	79.6	84.9	.	.	.	.
5	13	86.7	270.5	89.9	2	13.3	30.4	10.1	.	.	.	.	.	.	.	.
6	15	100	344.1	100	.	.	.	.	.	.	.	.	.	.	.	.
7	22	91.7	427.6	93.0	1	4.2	26.8	5.8	.	.	.	.	1	4.2	5.3	1.2
8	16	88.9	288.9	95.6	2	11.1	13.2	4.4	.	.	.	.	.	.	.	.
All	114	64.0	1919.7	71.7	40	22.5	440.3	16.4	23	12.9	312.7	11.7	1	0.6	5.3	0.2

Table A-1 (cont).

Midden J (cont).

LEVEL	All					
	Count			Weight		
	N	Pct		N	Pct	
1	76	100		879.5	100	
2	14	100		197.7	100	
3	6	100		100.2	100	
4	10	100		93.8	100	
5	15	100		300.9	100	
6	15	100		344.1	100	
7	24	100		459.7	100	
8	18	100		302.1	100	
All	178	100		1678.0	100	

Table A-1 (cont.).

Midden M

	Master Code															
	Stamped				Plain				Burnished Plain				Incised			
	Count		Weight		Count		Weight		Count		Weight		Count		Weight	
LEVEL	N	Pct	N	Pct	N	Pct	N	Pct	N	Pct	N	Pct	N	Pct	N	Pct
1	3	16.7	32.6	22.3	6	33.3	48.0	32.9	8	44.4	62.1	42.5	1	5.6	3.4	2.3
2	23	33.3	278.8	35.2	26	37.7	228.2	28.8	14	20.3	237.6	30.0	6	8.7	46.9	5.9
3	70	60.9	824.1	65.4	35	30.4	308.8	24.5	5	4.3	102.5	8.1	5	4.3	24.3	1.9
4	20	40.8	302.2	49.2	22	44.9	199.4	32.4	4	8.2	85.8	14.0	3	6.1	27.3	4.4
5	19	61.3	241.0	49.8	6	19.4	48.5	10.0	6	19.4	194.7	40.2	.	.	.	.
6	12	37.5	142.1	46.7	13	40.6	132.6	43.6	.	.	.	.	7	21.9	29.4	9.7
7	1	50.0	7.7	26.6	1	50.0	21.3	73.4	.	.	.	.	.	.	.	.
All	148	46.8	1828.5	50.4	109	34.5	986.8	27.2	37	11.7	682.7	18.8	22	7.0	131.3	3.6

Table A-1 (cont).

Midden M (cont).

LEVEL	All Count N	All Count Pct	All Weight N	All Weight Pct
1	18	100	146.1	100
2	69	100	791.5	100
3	115	100	1259.7	100
4	49	100	614.7	100
5	31	100	484.2	100
6	32	100	304.1	100
7	2	100	29.0	100
All	316	100	3629.3	100

Table A-1 (cont.).

All

LEVEL	Stamped				Plain				Burnished Plain				Incised				All			
	Count		Weight		Count		Weight		Count		Weight		Count		Weight		Count		Weight	
	N	Pct	N	Pct	N	Pct	N	Pct	N	Pct	N	Pct	N	Pct	N	Pct	N	Pct	N	Pct
1	220	53.3	2059.6	63.0	142	34.4	836.1	25.6	33	8.0	262.0	8.0	18	4.4	109.3	3.3	413	100	3267.0	100
2	235	45.4	1926.4	46.3	172	33.2	1356.0	32.6	70	13.5	571.5	13.7	41	7.9	307.4	7.4	518	100	4161.3	100
3	277	73.7	3092.0	73.3	75	19.9	754.8	17.9	15	4.0	278.6	6.6	9	2.4	91.3	2.2	376	100	4216.7	100
4	126	60.0	1617.7	67.2	61	29.0	545.3	22.6	18	8.6	196.7	8.2	5	2.4	48.5	2.0	210	100	2408.2	100
5	95	62.1	1445.9	68.1	45	29.4	454.0	21.4	11	7.2	219.7	10.3	2	1.3	3.6	0.2	153	100	2123.2	100
6	123	61.5	1848.4	73.2	56	28.0	540.3	21.4	3	1.5	23.2	0.9	18	9.0	114.9	4.5	200	100	2526.8	100
7	127	55.7	1913.6	67.9	88	38.6	801.8	28.4	4	1.8	34.5	1.2	9	3.9	69.7	2.5	228	100	2819.6	100
8	140	63.9	1662.8	72.7	71	32.4	559.0	24.4	2	0.9	17.5	0.8	6	2.7	47.9	2.1	219	100	2287.2	100
9	36	67.9	305.6	74.4	15	28.3	94.9	23.1	·	·	·	·	2	3.8	10.0	2.4	53	100	410.5	100
10	5	71.4	65.7	85.7	1	14.3	7.5	9.8	·	·	·	·	1	14.3	3.5	4.6	7	100	76.7	100
All	1384	58.2	15938	65.6	726	30.5	5949.7	24.5	156	6.6	1603.7	6.6	111	4.7	806.1	3.3	2377	100	24297	100

Master Code

Table A-2. Meeting House Fields Rim Style by Midden/Level.

Midden 12

	Style															
	Plain				Pellet/Node				Decorated Cane				Strip Segmented			
	Count		Weight		Count		Weight		Count		Weight		Count		Weight	
LEVEL	Sum	Pct	Sum	Pct	Sum	Pct	Sum	Pct	Sum	Pct	Sum	Pct	Sum	Pct	Sum	Pct
1	.	.	.	.	.	.	.	.	.	.	.	.	.	.	.	.
2	1	25.0	4.2	9.2	.	.	.	.	1	25.0	6.1	13.3	1	25.0	7.3	15.9
3	.	.	.	.	1	33.3	9.6	24.4	.	.	.	.	.	.	.	.
4	1	33.3	2.5	4.8	1	33.3	25.2	48.4	.	.	.	.	1	33.3	24.4	46.8
All	2	13.3	6.7	4.2	2	13.3	34.8	21.6	1	6.7	6.1	3.8	2	13.3	31.7	19.7

Table A.2 (cont).

Midden 12 (cont).

LEVEL	Style – Strip Cane				Style – Strip Cane/Segmented				All			
	Count		Weight		Count		Weight		Count		Weight	
	Sum	Pct	Sum	Pct	Sum	Pct	Sum	Pct	Sum	Pct	Sum	Pct
1	1	20.0	3.4	14.4	4	80.0	20.2	856	5	100	23.6	100
2	1	25.0	28.3	61.7	.	.	.	.	4	100	45.9	100
3	2	66.7	29.7	75.6	.	.	.	.	3	100	39.3	100
4	.	.	.	.	.	.	.	.	3	100	52.1	100
All	4	26.7	51.4	38.2	4	26.7	20.2	12.6	15	100	160.9	100

Table A-2 (cont.).

Midden 21

		Strip														
	Plain				Pellet/Node				Decorated Cane				Strip Segmented			
	Count		Weight		Count		Weight		Count		Weight		Count		Weight	
Level	Sum	Pct	Sum	Pct	Sum	Pct	Sum	Pct	Sum	Pct	Sum	Pct	Sum	Pct	Sum	Pct
2	3	21.4	7.3	15.8	3	21.4	12.8	27.7	1	7.1	2.0	4.3	3	21.4	8.9	19.3
3	2	50.0	6.5	36.9	·	·	·	·	·	·	·	·	1	25.0	4.1	23.3
4	1	25.0	3.1	2.7	1	25.0	38.2	33.2	·	·	·	·	·	·	·	·
All	6	27.3	16.9	9.5	4	18.2	51.0	28.5	1	4.5	2.0	1.1	4	18.2	13.0	7.3

Table A.2 (cont).

Midden 21 (cont).

Level	Style												All			
	Strip Cane				Strip Cane/Segmented				Strip Pinch				Count		Weight	
	Count		Weight		Count		Weight		Count		Weight					
	Sum	Pct	Sum	Pct	Sum	Pct	Sum	Pct	Sum	Pct	Sum	Pct	Sum	Pct	Sum	Pct
2	4	28.6	15.2	32.9	.	.	.	.	.	.	.	.	14	100	46.2	100
3	.	.	.	.	1	25.0	7.0	39.8	.	.	.	.	4	100	17.6	100
4	1	25.0	18.6	16.2	.	.	.	.	1	25.0	55.0	47.9	4	100	114.9	100
All	5	22.7	33.8	18.9	1	4.5	7.0	3.9	1	4.5	55.0	30.8	22	100	178.7	100

Table A-2 (cont.).

Midden B

	Style							All			
	Decorated Cane				Strip Cane						
	Count		Weight		Count		Weight		Count		Weight	
Level	Sum	Pct	Sum	Pct	Sum	Pct	Sum	Pct	Sum	Pct	Sum	Pct
4	.	.	.	.	1	100	3.8	100	1	100	3.8	100
6	1	50.0	8.1	61.4	1	50.0	5.1	38.6	2	100	13.2	100
All	1	33.3	8.1	47.6	2	66.7	8.9	52.4	3	100	17.0	100

Table A.2 (cont).

Midden D

	Style												All			
	Plain				Decorated Cane				Strip Cane							
	Count		Weight		Count		Weight		Count		Weight		Count		Weight	
Level	Sum	Pct	Sum	Pct	Sum	Pct	Sum	Pct	Sum	Pct	Sum	Pct	Sum	Pct	Sum	Pct
2	1	100	3.7	100	.	.	.	.	.	.	.	.	1	100	3.7	100
5	1	100	5.7	100	.	.	.	.	.	.	.	.	1	100	5.8	100
7	1	50.0	3.1	40.3	.	.	.	.	1	50.0	4.6	59.7	2	100	7.7	100
8	.	.	.	.	1	100	6.8	100	.	.	.	.	1	100	6.8	100
All	3	60.0	12.6	52.5	1	20.0	6.8	28.3	1	20.0	4.6	19.2	5	100	24.0	100

Table A.2 (cont).

Midden E

	Style															
	Plain				Decorated Cane				Decorated Fingernail				Decorated Stamped			
	Count		Weight		Count		Weight		Count		Weight		Count		Weight	
Level	Sum	Pct	Sum	Pct	Sum	Pct	Sum	Pct	Sum	Pct	Sum	Pct	Sum	Pct	Sum	Pct
1	2	22.2	8.4	24.3	1	11.1	3.1	9.0	.	.	.	.	.	.	.	.
2	5	38.5	84.4	48.7	2	15.4	34.5	19.9	.	.	.	.	.	.	.	.
3	.	.	.	.	.	.	.	.	1	20.0	18.1	29.6	.	.	.	.
4	2	28.6	6.8	13.5	.	.	.	.	.	.	.	.	.	14.3	3.0	6.0
5	3	50.0	45.1	55.6	.	.	.	.	1	16.7	10.2	12.6	.	.	.	.
6	5	41.7	86.8	52.5	3	25.0	34.5	20.9	.	.	.	.	1	8.3	3.0	1.8
7	9	52.9	61.2	44.3	3	17.6	12.2	8.8	.	.	.	.	.	.	.	.
8	6	33.3	25.0	9.2	2	11.1	65.3	24.1	.	.	.	.	.	.	.	.
9	2	66.7	23.5	83.3	.	.	.	.	.	.	.	.	.	.	.	.
All	34	37.8	341.2	34.0	11	12.2	149.6	14.9	2	2.2	28.3	2.8	2	2.2	6.0	0.6

Table A.2 (cont).

Midden E (cont).

	Style															
	Strip Segmented				Strip Cane				Strip Pinch				Incised			
	Count		Weight		Count		Weight		Count		Weight		Count		Weight	
Level	Sum	Pct	Sum	Pct	Sum	Pct	Sum	Pct	Sum	Pct	Sum	Pct	Sum	Pct	Sum	Pct
1									2	22.2	12.9	37.4	4	44.4	10.1	29.3
2	1	7.7	12.9	7.4	.	.	.	.					5	38.5	41.4	23.9
3	.	.	.	.	1	20.0	20.0	32.7					3	60.0	23.1	37.7
4	3	42.9	29.2	58.2	1	14.3	11.2	22.3					.	.	.	.
5	.	.	.	.	.	.	.	.	1	16.7	24.5	30.2	1	16.7	1.3	1.6
6	.	.	.	.	.	.	.	.					3	25.0	40.9	24.8
7	1	5.9	18.1	13.1	3	17.6	44.6	32.2					1	5.9	2.2	1.6
8	5	27.8	117.8	43.4	3	16.7	52.2	19.2					2	11.1	11.0	4.1
9	.	.	.	.	1	33.3	4.7	16.7					.	.	.	.
All	10	11.1	178.0	17.7	9	10.0	132.7	13.2	3	3.3	37.4	3.7	19	21.1	130.0	13.0

Table A.2 (cont).

Midden E (cont).

| Level | All | | | |
| | Count | | Weight | |
	Sum	Pct	Sum	Pct
1	9	100	34.5	100
2	13	100	173.2	100
3	5	100	61.2	100
4	7	100	50.2	100
5	6	100	81.1	100
6	12	100	165.2	100
7	17	100	138.3	100
8	18	100	271.3	100
9	3	100	28.2	100
All	90	100	1003.2	100

Table A.2 (cont).

Midden H

LEVEL	Plain				Decorated Cane				Strip Segmented				Strip Cane			
	Count		Weight		Count		Weight		Count		Weight		Count		Weight	
	Sum	Pct	Sum	Pct	Sum	Pct	Sum	Pct	Sum	Pct	Sum	Pct	Sum	Pct	Sum	Pct
1	4	28.6	76.4	39.6	.	.	.	.	9	64.3	113.6	58.9	1	7.1	2.8	1.5
2	3	60.0	21.1	69.4	1	20.0	3.6	11.8	.	.	.	.	1	20.0	5.7	18.8
3	5	100	48.1	100	.	.	.	.	.	.	.	.	.	.	.	.
4	2	66.7	35.6	67.3	.	.	.	.	.	.	.	.	.	.	.	.
5	2	50.0	40.8	40.6	.	.	.	.	2	50.0	59.6	59.4	.	.	.	.
6	3	75.0	172.2	80.9	.	.	.	.	1	25.0	40.6	19.1	.	.	.	.
7	2	28.6	8.2	7.8	4	57.1	83.6	79.4	.	.	.	.	.	.	.	.
8	.	.	.	.	.	.	.	.	.	.	.	.	.	.	.	.
All	21	48.8	402.4	53.8	5	11.6	87.2	11.7	12	27.9	213.8	28.6	2	4.7	8.5	1.1

Table A.2 (cont).

Midden H (cont).

	Style								All			
	Food Plain				Incised							
	Count		Weight		Count		Weight		Count		Weight	
Level	Sum	Pct	Sum	Pct	Sum	Pct	Sum	Pct	Sum	Pct	Sum	Pct
1	.	.	.	.	.	.	.	.	14	100	192.8	100
2	.	.	.	.	.	.	.	.	5	100	30.4	100
3	.	.	.	.	.	.	.	.	5	100	48.1	100
4	.	.	.	.	1	33.3	17.3	32.7	3	100	52.9	100
5	.	.	.	.	.	.	.	.	4	100	100.4	100
6	.	.	.	.	.	.	.	.	4	100	212.8	100
7	1	14.3	13.5	12.8	.	.	.	.	7	100	105.3	100
8	1	100	5.4	100	.	.	.	.	1	100	5.4	100
All	2	4.7	18.9	2.5	1	2.3	17.3	2.3	43	100	748.1	100

Table A.2 (cont).

Midden J

	Style															
	Plain				Decorated Cane				Strip Segmented				Strip Cane			
	Count		Weight		Count		Weight		Count		Weight		Count		Weight	
Level	Sum	Pct	Sum	Pct	Sum	Pct	Sum	Pct	Sum	Pct	Sum	Pct	Sum	Pct	Sum	Pct
0	.	.	.	.	.	.	.	.	2	66.7	14.0	48.6	1	33.3	14.8	51.4
5	.	.	.	.	1	100	16.7	100	.	.	.	.	.	.	.	.
7	1	100	26.8	100	.	.	.	.	.	.	.	.	.	.	.	.
8	.	.	.	.	.	.	.	.	.	.	.	.	.	.	.	.
All	1	16.7	26.8	34.5	1	16.7	16.7	21.5	2	33.3	14.0	18.0	1	16.7	14.8	19.0

Table A.2 (cont).

Midden J (cont).

	Style				All			
	Strip Pinch							
	Count		Weight		Count		Weight	
Level	Sum	Pct	Sum	Pct	Sum	Pct	Sum	Pct
0	.	.	.	.	3	100	28.8	100
5	.	.	.	.	1	100	16.7	100
7	.	.	.	.	.1	100	26.8	100
8	1	100	5.4	100	1	100	5.4	100
All	1	16.7	5.4	6.9	6	100	77.7	100

Table A.2 (cont).

Midden M

		Style														
	Plain				Decorated Cane				Strip Segmented				Strip Cane			
	Count		Weight		Count		Weight		Count		Weight		Count		Weight	
Level	Sum	Pct	Sum	Pct	Sum	Pct	Sum	Pct	Sum	Pct	Sum	Pct	Sum	Pct	Sum	Pct
1	.	.	.	.	.	.	.	.	.	.	.	.	1	100	7.7	100
2	4	66.7	157.6	93.9	.	.	.	.	1	16.7	3.3	2.0	.	.	.	.
3	8	66.7	143.3	76.5	.	.	.	.	2	16.7	25.2	13.4	2	16.7	18.9	10.1
4	1	25.0	4.5	10.3	.	.	.	.	.	.	.	.	2	50.0	24.1	54.9
5	1	50.0	6.3	50.4	1	50.0	6.2	49.6	.	.	.	.	.	.	.	.
6	.	.	.	.	.	.	.	.	.	.	.	.	.	.	.	.
7	.	.	.	.	.	.	.	.	.	.	.	.	1	100	7.7	100
All	14	51.9	311.7	72.6	1	3.7	6.2	1.4	3	11.1	28.5	6.6	6	22.2	58.4	13.6

Table A.2 (cont).

Midden M (cont).

	Style				All			
	Incised							
	Count		Weight		Count		Weight	
Level	Sum	Pct	Sum	Pct	Sum	Pct	Sum	Pct
1	.	.	.	.	1	100	7.7	100
2	1	16.7	6.9	4.1	6	100	167.8	100
3	.	.	.	.	12	100	187.4	100
4	1	25.0	15.3	34.9	4	100	43.9	100
5	.	.	.	.	2	100	12.5	100
6	1	100	2.5	100	1	100	2.5	100
7	.	.	.	.	1	100	7.7	100
All	3	11.1	24.7	5.8	27	100	429.5	100

Table A.2 (cont).

All

	Style															
	Plain				Pellet/Node				Decorated Cane				Decorated Fingernail			
	Count		Weight		Count		Weight		Count		Weight		Count		Weight	
Level	Sum	Pct	Sum	Pct	Sum	Pct	Sum	Pct	Sum	Pct	Sum	Pct	Sum	Pct	Sum	Pct
0	.	.	.	.	.	.	.	.	.	.	.	.	.	.	.	.
1	6	20.7	84.8	32.8	.	.	.	.	1	3.4	3.1	1.2	.	.	.	.
2	17	39.5	278.3	59.6	.	7.0	12.8	2.7	5	11.6	46.2	9.9	.	.	.	.
3	15	51.7	197.9	56.0	1	3.4	9.6	2.7	.	.	.	.	1	3.4	18.1	5.1
4	7	31.8	52.5	16.5	2	9.1	63.4	19.9	.	.	.	.	.	.	.	.
5	7	50.0	98.0	45.3	.	.	.	.	2	14.3	22.9	10.6	1	7.1	10.2	4.7
6	8	42.1	259.0	65.8	.	.	.	.	4	21.1	42.6	10.8	.	.	.	.
7	13	46.4	99.3	34.7	.	.	.	.	7	25.0	95.8	33.5	.	.	.	.
8	6	28.6	25.0	8.7	.	.	.	.	3	14.3	72.1	25.0	.	.	.	.
9	2	66.7	23.5	83.3	.	.	.	.	.	.	.	.	.	.	.	.
All	81	38.4	1118.3	42.4	6	2.8	85.8	3.3	22	10.4	282.7	10.7	2	0.9	28.3	1.1

Table A.2 (cont).

All

Level	Decorated Stamped				Strip Segmented				Strip Cane				Strip Cane/ Segmented			
	Count		Weight		Count		Weight		Count		Weight		Count		Weight	
	Sum	Pct	Sum	Pct	Sum	Pct	Sum	Pct	Sum	Pct	Sum	Pct	Sum	Pct	Sum	Pct
0	.	.	.	.	2	66.7	14.0	48.6	1	33.3	14.8	51.4	.	.	.	.
1	.	.	.	.	9	31.0	113.6	43.9	3	10.3	13.9	5.4	4	13.8	20.2	7.8
2	.	.	.	.	6	14.0	32.4	6.9	6	14.0	49.2	10.5	.	.	.	.
3	.	.	.	.	3	10.3	29.3	8.3	5	17.2	68.6	19.4	1	3.4	7.0	2.0
4	1	4.5	3.0	0.9	4	18.2	53.6	16.9	5	22.7	57.7	18.2	.	.	.	.
5	.	.	.	.	2	14.3	59.6	27.5	.	.	.	.	.	.	.	.
6	1	5.3	3.0	0.8	1	5.3	40.6	10.3	1	5.3	5.1	1.3	.	.	.	.
7	.	.	.	.	1	3.6	18.1	6.3	5	17.9	56.9	19.9	.	.	.	.
8	.	.	.	.	5	23.8	117.8	40.8	3	14.3	52.2	18.1	.	.	.	.
9	.	.	.	.	.	.	.	.	1	33.3	4.7	16.7	.	.	.	.
All	2	0.9	6.0	0.2	33	15.6	479.0	18.2	30	14.2	323.1	12.2	5	2.4	27.2	1.0

Table A.2 (cont).

All (cont.).

	Style															
	Strip Pinch				Folded Plain				Incised				All			
	Count		Weight		Count		Weight		Count		Weight		Count		Weight	
Level	Sum	Pct	Sum	Pct	Sum	Pct	Sum	Pct	Sum	Pct	Sum	Pct	Sum	Pct	Sum	Pct
0	.	.	.	.	.	.	.	.	.	.	.	.	3	100	28.8	100
1	2	6.9	12.9	5.0	.	.	.	.	4	13.8	10.1	3.9	29	100	258.6	100
2	.	.	.	.	.	.	.	.	6	14.0	48.3	10.3	43	100	467.2	100
3	.	.	.	.	.	.	.	.	3	10.3	23.1	6.5	29	100	353.6	100
4	1	4.5	55.0	17.3	.	.	.	.	2	9.1	32.6	10.3	22	100	317.8	100
5	1	7.1	24.5	11.3	.	.	.	.	1	7.1	1.3	0.6	14	100	216.5	100
6	.	.	.	.	.	.	.	.	4	21.1	43.4	11.0	19	100	393.7	100
7	.	.	.	.	1	3.6	13.5	4.7	1	3.6	2.2	0.8	28	100	285.8	100
8	1	4.8	5.4	1.9	1	4.8	5.4	1.9	2	9.5	11.0	3.8	21	100	288.9	100
9	.	.	.	.	.	.	.	.	.	.	.	.	3	100	28.2	100
All	5	2.4	97.8	3.7	2	0.9	18.9	0.7	23	10.9	172.0	6.5	211	100	2639.1	100

Table A.3. Meeting House Fields Vessel Form by Midden.

Midden	Bowl Count		Straight Count		Jar Count		Bottle Count		All	
	Sum	Pct	Sum	Pct	Sum	Pct	Sum	Pct	Sum	Pct
12	2	16.7	4	33.3	6	50.0	.	.	12	100
21	2	15.4	4	30.8	7	53.8	.	.	13	100
B	.	.	1	33.3	2	66.7	.	.	3	100
D	1	25.0	1	25.0	2	50.0	.	.	4	100
E	8	16.0	14	28.0	26	52.0	2	4.0	50	100
H	6	27.3	8	36.4	6	27.3	2	9.1	22	100
J	.	.	4	80.0	1	20.0	.	.	5	100
M	4	22.2	4	22.2	8	44.4	2	11.1	18	100
All	23	18.1	40	31.5	58	45.7	6	4.7	127	100

Table A.4. Temper by Cluster.

CLUSTER	Temper												All			
	Grit				Sand				Grit & Grog							
	Count		Weight		Count		Weight		Count		Weight		Count		Weight	
	N	Pct	N	Pct	N	Pct	N	Pct	N	Pct	N	Pct	N	Pct	N	Pct
1	694	92.0	6270.5	92.9	60	8.0	477.6	7.1	.	.	.	.	754	100	6748.1	100
2	1225	72.1	13935.5	77.8	467	27.5	3925.6	21.9	7	0.4	47.5	0.3	1699	100	17908	100
All	1919	78.2	20206.0	81.9	527	21.5	4403.2	17.9	7	0.3	47.5	0.2	2453	100	24656	100

Table A.5. Temper By Vessel Form.

Vessel	Temper				All	
	Grit		Sand			
	Count		Count		Count	
	Sum	Pct	Sum	Pct	Sum	Pct
Bowl	13	56.5	10	43.5	23	100
Straight	24	61.5	15	38.5	39	100
Jar	39	67.2	19	32.8	58	100
Bottle	4	66.7	2	33.3	6	100
All	80	63.5	46	36.5	126	100

Chi-Square value (bottles deleted) = 0.895
Prob = 0.64

Table A.6. Burnishing by Cluster.

Cluster	Interior Surface								All			
	Unburnished				Burnished							
	Count		Weight		Count		Weight		Count		Weight	
	Sum	Pct	Sum	Pct	Sum	Pct	Sum	Pct	Sum	Pct	Sum	Pct
1	114	15.0	897.6	13.1	646	85.0	5943	86.9	760	100	6841	100
2	368	21.6	3396	18.9	1339	78.4	14542	81.1	1707	100	17937	100
All	482	19.5	4293	17.3	1985	80.5	20485	82.7	2467	100	24778	100

Table A.7. Frequency of Rectilinear vs. Curvilinear Stamping.

Cluster	Master Code									All						
	Rectilinear				Curvilinear											
	Count		Weight		Count		Weight			Count		Weight				
	Sum	Pct	Sum	Pct	Sum	Pct	Sum	Pct		Sum	Pct	Sum	Pct			
1	319	70.9	2657	59.1	131	29.1	1835.6	40.9		450	100	4492.6	100			
2	487	71.1	5498.5	63.1	198	28.9	3216.0	36.9		685	100	8714.5	100			
All	806	71.0	8155.5	61.8	329	29.0	5051.6	38.2		1135	100	13207	100			

Table A.8. Frequency of Dots on Stamped Sherds.[1]

	Master Code												
	Stamped				Dot				All				
	Count		Weight		Count		Weight		Count		Weight		
Cluster	Sum	Pct	Sum	Pct	Sum	Pct	Sum	Pct	Sum	Pct	Sum	Pct	
1	414	92.0	4045.1	90.0	36	8.0	447.5	10.0	450	100	4492.6	100	
2	644	94.0	7997.2	91.8	41	6.0	717.3	8.2	685	100	8714.5	100	
All	1058	93.2	12042	91.2	77	6.8	1164.8	8.8	1135	100	13207	100	

1. Surface roughened not included.

Table A.9. Rim Elaboration by Cluster (MNV).

	Rim Elaboration																	
	Plain		Incised		Fingnail		Cane		Stick		Can/Seg		Pelnode		UID/O		All	
	Count		Count		Count		Count		Count		Count		Count		Count		Count	
Cluster	N	Pct	N	Pct	N	Pct	N	Pct	N	Pct	N	Pct	N	Pct	N	Pct	N	Pct
1	7	25.0	.	.	2	7.1	9	32.1	1	3.6	3	10.7	4	14.3	2	7.1	28	100
2	43	45.3	10	10.5	6	6.3	24	25.3	7	7.4	.	.	.	.	5	5.3	95	100
All	50	40.7	10	8.1	8	6.5	33	26.8	8	6.5	3	2.4	4	3.3	7	5.7	123	100

Table A.10. Applique Rim Strip Depth by Cluster.

Cluster	Min	Max	Mean	STD	N
1	4.0	13.0	9.9	2.0	32
2	3.0	18.8	10.2	3.5	63

Table A.11. Land and Groove Width by Cluster.

Cluster 1						
No. Obs	Variable	N	Minimum	Maximum	Mean	Std Dev
28	Land	28	1	2.2	1.421	0.325
	Groove	28	0.9	3	1.836	0.536

Cluster 2						
No. Obs	Variable	N	Minimum	Maximum	Mean	Std Dev
16	Land	16	0.7	2	1.381	0.331
	Groove	16	0.1	2.7	1.419	0.648

Appendix B
Santa Catalina de Guale: Tables

Table B.1. Early Convento, Temper.

Temper								All			
Grit				Sand							
Count		Weight		Count		Weight		Count		Weight	
Sum	Pct	Sum	Pct	Sum	Pct	Sum	Pct	Sum	Pct	Sum	Pct
237	96.3	2728.7	98.1	9	3.7	52.6	1.9	246	100	2781.3	100

Frequency missing = 3

Table B.2. Early Convento, Surface Finishes.

Interior Finish												Exterior Finish							
Unbrn		Ibrn		Iebrn		Izrf		Ierf		All		Ubrn		Ebrn		Erf		All	
Count		Count		Count		Count		Count		Count		Count		Count		Count		Count	
N	Pct	N	Pct	N	Pct	N	Pct	N	Pct	N	Pct	N	Pct	N	Pct	N	Pct	N	Pct
46	18.6	190	76.9	8	3.2	1	0.4	2	0.8	247	100	224	90.7	15	6.1	8	3.2	247	100

Unburn = unburnished
Ibrn = interior burnished
Iebrn = interior/exterior burnished

Izrf = interior zoned red filmed
Ierf = interior and exterior red filmed
Ebrn = exterior burnished
Erf = exterior red filmed

Table B.3. Early Convento, Frequency of Dots.

Master Code								All			
Stamped				Dot				All			
Count		Weight		Count		Weight		Count		Weight	
Sum	Pct	Sum	Pct	Sum	Pct	Sum	Pct	Sum	Pct	Sum	Pct
165	93.2	1818.0	85.1	12	6.8	318.3	14.9	177	100	2136.3	100

Table B.4. Late Proveniences, Surface Treatments.

Structure	Interior Finish																	All	
	Unburn		Ibm		Irf		Izrf		Iezrf		Ierf		Izb		Izrb			All	
	Count		Count		Count		Count		Count		Count		Count		Count			Count	
	N	Pct	N	Pct	N	Pct	N	Pct	N	Pct	N	Pct	N	Pct	N	Pct		N	Pct
Church	162	23.3	524	75.5	4	0.58	.	.	.	.	.	.	1	0.14	3	0.43		694	100
Kitchen	164	20.5	628	78.4	6	0.75	2	0.25	.		.		.	.	1	0.12		801	100
Convento	271	27.8	664	68.1	34	3.49	3	0.31	2	0.21	1	0.10	.		.	.		975	100
All	597	24.2	1816	73.5	44	1.78	5	0.20	2	0.08	1	0.04	1	0.04	4	0.16		2470	100

Table B.4 (cont).

Structure	Exterior Finish												All	
	Unbrn		Ebm		Erf		Ezb		Bp		Ezrf			
	Count		Count		Count		Count		Count		Count		Count	
	N	Pct	N	Pct	N	Pct	N	Pct	N	Pct	N	Pct	N	Pct
Church	637	91.8	51	7.35	3	0.43	1	0.14	1	0.14	1	0.14	694	100
Kitchen	770	96.1	24	3.00	4	0.50	·	·	·	·	3	0.37	801	100
Convento	941	96.5	22	2.26	11	1.13	·	·	1	0.10	·	·	975	100
All	2348	100	97	100	18	100	1	100	2	100	4	100	2470	100

Unburn = Unburnished
Ibm =Interior Burnished
Irf = Interior red filmed
Izrf = Interior zoned red filmed
Ierf = Interior exterior red filmed

Ibf = Interior black filmed
Iezrf = Interior Exterior zoned red filmed
Izb = Interior zoned black
Izrb = Interior zoned red and black
Exbm = Exterior burnished

Erf = Exterior red filmed
Ebf = Exterior black filmed
Ezrf = Exterior zoned black filmed
Ezb = Exterior zoned black
Bp = Black pigment

Table B.5. Late Proveniences, Frequency of Sooted Sherds.

	Sooting							All			
	No Soot				Sooted						
	Count		Weight		Count		Weight		Count		Weight	
Structure	Sum	Pct	Sum	Pct	Sum	Pct	Sum	Pct	Sum	Pct	Sum	Pct
Church	697	99.3	8208.2	99.5	5	0.7	44.7	0.5	702	100	8252.9	100
Kitchen	780	96.8	10441.0	93.1	26	3.2	771.9	6.9	806	100	11213.0	100
Convento	978	99.2	7678.8	99.2	8	0.8	61.5	0.8	986	100	7740.3	100
All	2455	98.4	26328.0	96.8	39	1.6	878.1	3.2	2494	100	27206.2	100

Table B.6. Late Proveniences, Temper (Sherd).

Structure	Temper													All			
	Grit				Sand				Grit and Grog								
	Count		Weight		Count		Weight		Count		Weight		Count		Weight	
	Sum	Pct	Sum	Pct	Sum	Pct	Sum	Pct	Sum	Pct	Sum	Pct	Sum	Pct	Sum	Pct
Church	660	95.7	7950.2	97.4	30	4.3	208.8	2.6	·	·	·	·	690	100	8159.0	100
Kitchen	764	98.5	10865.0	98.2	8	1.0	151.2	1.4	4	0.5	48.9	0.4	776	100	11065.1	100
Convento	919	95.6	7465.7	97.2	38	4.0	192.6	2.5	4	0.4	20.3	0.3	961	100	7678.6	100
All	2343	96.5	26281.9	97.7	76	3.1	552.6	2.1	8	0.3	69.2	0.3	2427	100	26903.7	100

Table B.7. Late Proveniences, Temper by Vessel Form.[1]

Frequency Percent Row Pct Col Pct	Temper			
	Grit	Sand	Grit / Grog	Total
Bowl	36 22.64 92.31 24.00	2 1.26 5.13 33.33	1 0.63 2.56 33.33	39 24.53
Straight	32 20.13 91.43 21.33	2 1.26 5.71 33.33	1 0.63 2.86 33.33	35 22.01
X Unrest	5 3.14 100.00 3.33	0 0.00 0.00 0.00	0 0.00 0.00 0.00	5 3.14
X Rest	2 1.26 66.67 1.33	1 0.63 33.33 16.67	0 0.00 0.00 0.00	3 1.89
X Uid	31 19.50 100.00 20.67	0 0.00 0.00 0.00	0 0.00 0.00 0.00	31 19.50
Rsmjar	5 3.14 100.00 3.33	0 0.00 0.00 0.00	0 0.00 0.00 0.00	5 3.14
Carinated Bowl	14 8.81 100.00 9.33	0 0.00 0.00 0.00	0 0.00 0.00 0.00	14 8.81
Brimmed Vessels	25 15.72 92.59 16.67	1 0.63 3.70 16.67	1 0.63 3.70 33.33	27 16.98
Total	150 94.34	6 3.77	3 1.89	159 100.00

1. See Table 6.7 for key to forms.

Table B.8. Late Proveniences, Frequency of Central Dots.

Master Code								All							
Stamp				Dot											
Count		Weight		Count		Weight		Count		Weight					
Sum	Pct	Sum	Pct	Sum	Pct	Sum	Pct	Sum	Pct	Sum	Pct				
1424	94.9	15728.0	85.2	77	5.1	2741.2	14.8	1501	100	18469.2	100				

Table B.9. Late Proveniences, Frequency of Curvilinear Stamping.

	Master Code								All				
	Rectilinear				Curvilinear								
	Count		Weight		Count		Weight		Count		Weight		
	Sum	Pct	Sum	Pct	Sum	Pct	Sum	Pct	Sum	Pct	Sum	Pct	
	1494	99.5	18376.0	99.5	7	0.5	93.2	0.5	1501	100	18469.2	100	

Appendix C
Santa Catalina de Santa María: Tables

Table C.1. Frequency of Rectilinear vs. Curvilinear Stamped Sherds.

Master Code								All			
Rectilinear				Curvilinear							
Count		Weight		Count		Weight		Count		Weight	
Sum	Pct	Sum	Pct	Sum	Pct	Sum	Pct	Sum	Pct	Sum	Pct
11557	98.9	74016.4	98.7	126	1.1	980.6	1.3	11683	100	74997.0	100

Table C.2. Frequency of Sherds with Central Dots.

Master Code								All			
Stamped				Dot							
Count		Weight		Count		Weight		Count		Weight	
Sum	Pct	Sum	Pct	Sum	Pct	Sum	Pct	Sum	Pct	Sum	Pct
11409	97.7	71693.2	95.6	274	2.3	3303.8	4.4	11683	100	74997.0	100

Table C.3. Temper by Structure.

Structure	Temper											
	Grit				Sand				Grit and Grog			
	Count		Weight		Count		Weight		Count		Weight	
	Sum	Pct	Sum	Pct	Sum	Pct	Sum	Pct	Sum	Pct	Sum	Pct
Structure	10044	93.8	62124.0	94.7	526	4.9	2590.3	3.9	66	0.6	382.5	0.6
Kitchen	2966	96.3	19483.0	95.3	87	2.8	689.6	3.4	4	0.1	25.0	0.1
Church	1687	90.7	11858.0	91.4	109	5.9	672.8	5.2	32	1.7	254.1	2.0
ABO Str	328	87.2	1853.1	88.9	44	11.7	179.2	8.6	1	0.3	7.7	0.4
All	15025	93.8	95318.1	94.3	766	4.8	4131.9	4.1	103	0.6	669.3	0.7

Table C.3 (cont).

Structure	Shell and Sand				Grog				Sand and Shell			
	Count		Weight		Count		Weight		Count		Weight	
	Sum	Pct	Sum	Pct	Sum	Pct	Sum	Pct	Sum	Pct	Sum	Pct
Convento	5	0.0	14.7	0.0	30	0.6	229.0	0.3	1	0.0	5.9	0.0
Kitchen	13	0.4	146.9	0.7	1	0.0	5.0	0.0	.	.	.	.
Church	23	1.2	141.7	1.1	3	0.2	15.6	0.1	.	.	.	.
ABO Str	.	.	.		.	.	.		.	.	.	
All	41	0.3	303.3	0.3	34	0.2	249.6	0.2	1	0.0.	5.9.	0.0

Table C.3 (cont).

Structure	Temper												All			
	Grit and Shell				Grit and Limestone				Sand and Limestone								
	Count		Weight		Count		Weight		Count		Weight		Count		Weight	
	Sum	Pct	Sum	Pct	Sum	Pct	Sum	Pct	Sum	Pct	Sum	Pct	Sum	Pct	Sum	Pct
Convento	20	0.2	128.7	0.2	12	0.1	99.8	0.2	3	0.0	13.1	0.0	10707	100	65588.0	100
Kitchen	2	0.1	11.7	0.1	5	0.2	57.4	0.3	3	0.1	28.5	0.1	3081	100	20447.1	100
Church	5	0.3	23.3	0.2	.	.	.	.	1	0.1	2.6	0.0	1860	100	12968.1	100
ABO Str	.	.	.	.	1	0.3	3.8	0.2	2	0.5	41.0	2.0	376	100	2084.8	100
All	27	0.2	163.7	0.2	18	0.1	161.0	0.2	9	0.1	85.2	0.1	16024	100	101088	100

Frequency missing = 208.

Table C.4. Temper by Vessel Form.

Frequency Percent Row Pct Col Pct	Temper							
	Grit	Sand	Grit & Grog	Shell	Shell & Grit	Grit & Limestone	Limestone	Total
Bowl	55 11.53 67.90 13.78	24 5.03 29.63 34.78	1 0.21 1.23 33.33	1 0.21 1.23 33.33	0 0.00 0.00 0.00	0 0.00 0.00 0.00	0 0.00 0.00 0.00	81 16.98
Straight	94 19.71 86.24 23.56	12 2.52 11.01 17.39	1 0.21 0.92 33.33	2 0.42 1.83 66.67	0 0.00 0.00 0.00	0 0.00 0.00 0.00	0 0.00 0.00 0.00	109 22.85
Jar	144 30.19 91.14 36.09	13 2.73 8.23 18.84	1 0.21 0.63 33.33	0 0.00 0.00 0.00	0 0.00 0.00 0.00	0 0.00 0.00 0.00	0 0.00 0.00 0.00	158 33.12
Carinated Bowl	14 2.94 70.00 3.51	6 1.26 30.00 8.70	0 0.00 0.00 0.00	0 0.00 0.00 0.00	0 0.00 0.00 0.00	0 0.00 0.00 0.00	0 0.00 0.00 0.00	20 4.19
Unidentified Colono ware	12 2.52 70.59 3.01	5 1.05 29.41 7.25	0 0.00 0.00 0.00	0 0.00 0.00 0.00	0 0.00 0.00 0.00	0 0.00 0.00 0.00	0 0.00 0.00 0.00	17 3.56
Brimmed Vessel	80 16.77 86.96 20.05	9 1.89 9.78 13.04	0 0.00 0.00 0.00	0 0.00 0.00 0.00	0 0.00 0.00 0.00	0 0.00 0.00 0.00	0 0.00 0.00 0.00	92 19.29
Total	399 83.65	69 14.47	3 0.63	3 0.63	1 0.21	1 0.21	1 0.21	477 100.00

Table C.5. Chi-Square Test, Temper by Vessel Form.

Frequency Expected Deviation Cell Chi-Square	Vessel Form						Total
	Bowl	Straight	Jar	Carinated Bowl	Unidentified Colono	Brimmed Vessel	
Grit	55	93	142	14	12	79	395
	67.252	89.386	131.95	17.026	14.472	74.914	
	-12.25	3.6142	10.05	-3.026	-2.472	4.0862	
	2.2321	0.1461	0.7654	0.5378	0.4222	0.2229	
Sand	24	12	13	6	5	9	69
	11.748	15.614	23.05	2.9741	2.528	13.086	
	12.252	-3.614	-10.05	3.0259	2.472	-4.086	
	12.778	0.8366	4.3816	3.0785	2.4172	1.2759	
Total	79	105	155	20	17	88	464

Statistics for Table of Temper by Vessel Form

Statistics	DF	Value	Prob
Chi-Square	5	29.094	.001

Table C.6. Surface Finish by Structure.

Structure	Unburnished		Interior Burnished		Interior Red Filmed		Interior Zoned Red Filmed		Int/Ext Red Filmed		Interior Black Filmed	
	Count		Count		Count		Count		Count		Count	
	Sum	Pct	Sum	Pct	Sum	Pct	Sum	Pct	Sum	Pct	Sum	Pct
Convento	2597	24.1	7624	70.6	323	3.0	128	1.2	58	0.5	16	0.1
Kitchen	253	8.2	2798	90.7	26	0.8	6	0.2	1	0.0	.	.
Church	354	18.0	1534	77.8	63	3.2	6	0.3	9	0.5	4	0.2
Abo	62	16.4	307	81.2	9	2.4	.	.	.	.	.	.
All	3266	20.1	12263	75.5	421	2.6	140	0.9	68	0.4	20	0.1

Interior or Interior and Exterior Surface

Table C.6 (cont).

Structure	Interior or Interior and Exterior Surface						All	
	Int/Ext Zoned Red Filmed		Interior Zoned Black Filmed		Interior Zoned Black and Red			
	Count		Count		Count		Count	
	Sum	Pct	Sum	Pct	Sum	Pct	Sum	Pct
Convento	49	0.5	1	0.0	2	0.0	10798	10
Kitchen	.	.	1	0.0	.	.	3085	100
Church	.	.	.	.	1	0.1	1971	100
Abo	.	.	.	.	.	.	378	100
All	49	0.3	2	0.0	3	0.0	16232	100

Table C.6 (cont).

Structure	Exterior Surface										All	
	Unburnished		Exterior Burnished		Exterior Red Filmed		Exterior Black Filmed		Exterior Zoned Red Filmed			
	Count		Count		Count		Count		Count			
	Sum	Pct	Sum	Pct	Sum	Pct	Sum	Pct	Sum	Pct	Sum	Pct
Convento	10699	99.1	44	0.4	34	0.3	8	0.1	13	0.1	10798	100
Kitchen	3062	99.3	9	0.3	7	0.2	7	0.2	.	.	3085	100
Church	1934	98.1	23	1.2	13	0.7	.	.	1	0.1	1971	100
Abo	373	98.7	5	1.3	.	.	.	.	.	.	378	100
All	16068	100	81	100	54	100	15	100	14	100	16232	100

Table C.7. Chi-Square Test, Interior Filming by Vessel Form.

Frequency Expected Deviation Cell Chi-Square	Bowl	Straight	Jar	Carinated Bowl	Unidentified Colono ware	Brimmed Vessel	Total
No Film	69 69.283 -0.283 0.0012	94 93.233 0.7673 0.0063	151 135.14 15.855 1.8602	20 17.107 2.8931 0.4893	16 14.541 1.4591 0.1464	58 78.692 -20.69 5.4409	408
Filmed	12 11.717 0.283 0.0068	15 15.767 -0.767 0.0373	7 22.855 -15.86 10.999	0 2.8931 -2.893 2.8931	1 2.4591 -1.459 0.8658	34 13.308 20.692 32.172	69
Total	81	109	158	20	17	92	477

Statistics for Table of Interior Filming by Vessel Form

Statistic	DF	Value	Prob
Chi-Square	5	54.919	<0.001

Table C.8. Sooted Sherds.

Structure	Sooting								All			
	No Sooting				Sooted							
	Count		Weight		Count		Weight		Count		Weight	
	Sum	Pct	Sum	Pct	Sum	Pct	Sum	Pct	Sum	Pct	Sum	Pct
Convento	10753	99.6	65591.0	99.3	45	0.4	441.4	0.7	10798	100	66033.4	100
Kitchen	3079	99.8	20266.0	99.1	6	0.2	192.6	0.9	3085	100	20458.6	100
Church	1960	99.4	13414.0	99.2	11	0.6	107.4	0.8	1971	100	13521.4	100
Abo Str	378	100	2089.1	100	.	.	.	.	378	100	2089.1	100
All	16170	99.6	101361.1	99.3	62	0.4	741.4	0.7	16232	100	102102.5	100

Notes

1. Pottery and Culture Change

1. As originally defined by the Spanish, *La Florida* encompassed all the land north and east of Mexico. The concept, however, was based on a seriously skewed understanding of the geography and the staggering amount of territory this definition embraced. By the time of the first missions, *La Florida* was reduced to what is now the southeastern United States (Milanich 1999:2:88–89). In reality, the amount of territory the Spanish ever controlled was much smaller. With the exception of a few interior forays and the establishment of ephemeral missions or outposts to the west and north, coastal and southern Georgia and northern Florida were the extent of the Spanish dominion.

2. Obviously correlated with this premise is whether pottery factories were established. *Talleres* were apparently rather common in Latin America, and they have been documented in the Caribbean (Cruxent 1990; Ortega and Fondeur 1978; see also Deagan 1985:295, 1983:234). No Spanish colonial pottery factories have been found in the southeastern United States.

3. The proto-Yamassee were inland relations of the Guale living in the province of La Tama in central Georgia. According to Green (1991:4; see also Worth 1995:20), La Tama was occupied by the separate chiefdoms of Altamaha, Ocute, and possibly Ichisi. In any event, the Yamassee began to arrive on the coast in the early 1660s, after their interior villages were attacked by Chichimecos and the chiefdoms fragmented. The term *Yamasis* also appears for the first time in documents in the 1660s. Most researchers believe that as applied, Yamassee came to refer to a "multiethnic confederacy" (Green 1991:3) composed of the refugees from La Tama, Guale, and others from the mission system, as well as individuals from other Southeastern tribes.

4. Hann (1988:245–246) noted little influence by the Spanish on Apalachee pottery production and use. Instead, the Spanish "borrowed from the natives, adopting their cooking utensils as well as the foods that were prepared in them" (Hann 1988:245). Hann (1988:246) did note the appearance of colono-ware forms and, perhaps, improved firing techniques (see also Smith 1951) in Apalachee pottery during the Mission period.

2. Archaeological and Ethnohistoric Perspectives on the Guale Indians

1. It is difficult to give a pithy definition of the Southeastern Ceremonial Complex, largely because those who study it do not agree on a definition, nor do they agree on the material assemblage that represents it (see papers in Galloway 1989). Muller (1989:11) lamented that it was easier to say what the complex was *not* than to "determine its precise role in various societies." In any event, around A.D. 1250 there emerged in the Southeast a series of elaborately decorated artifacts with motifs focused on a narrow range of themes, in partic-ular warfare, fertility, and religion. Many of these artifacts served as badges of status and rank or as amulets. Much of this appears in mortuary contexts. The complex as a whole, or rather the various complexes—there was a good deal of regional diversity in both style and content of Southeastern Ceremonial Complex artifacts—served as a religious mechanism for the validation of the rule of chiefs (Muller 1989:26). Inasmuch as the elite traded extensively in these objects, the complex also had an economic function (Brose 1989:29–30). Brose (1989:27–28) drew an interesting distinction between the function of the complex in prehistory and after contact: "This artifact complex at its precontact apogee was the physical sign of an extravagant devotion to persons, causes, and things, whereas perhaps during and certainly after the initial contact period the artifacts themselves became the direct object of such devotion—in standard usage, a cult."

2. A council house was described by Oviedo (1959:328, quoted in Jones 1978:198) from information furnished by someone from the Ayllón expedition as "very large, and they are made of very tall and graceful pines; and they leave their branches and leaves on the top and afterwards make a row or line of pines for a wall, and another [row] from the other side, leaving in the middle the width of 15 or 30 feet from one line to the other, and a good 300 feet or more in length. At the top they join the branches, and thus there is no need of a roof or covering, notwithstanding the fact that they cover all of the upper part with very well placed mattings, interweaving them in the spaces or open places among the said pines. Inside, there are other pines, crossed with the

facade of the first one, doubling the thickness of the wall. The wall fence is thick and strong, because the timbers are joined. And in such houses there may easily be contained 200 men, living in them as the Indians do, locating their door where it is convenient." Later descriptions consistently refer to council houses as round; the council house at the Irene site was round. The U-shape implied by this description is unusual; the round shape may have gotten lost in translation.

3. Duke's (1993) study comparing Irene and Altamaha phase fine-screen samples and Pearson's (1979) study comparing Savannah and Irene phase materials do not address site seasonality.

4. The Harris Neck site may have been the location of the town of Tolomato (Worth, personal communication 1999), one of the sites in the important Guale-Tolomato chiefdom. Jesuits may have been there in 1573–1574. Nuestra Señora de Guadalupe de Tolomato was established sometime after 1587. The Franciscan friar residing there in 1597 was killed in the Juanillo rebellion (Hann 1990b:29). The mission was also destroyed. Many Tolomatans were relocated to a service town near St. Augustine in the 1620s (Bushnell 1994:119).

5. The "early" assignment is based on the author's assessment of descriptions of rim style in Larsen and Thomas (1986).

6. Except where extraction was particularly laborious (Fewkes 1944).

7. Little work has been done on paddle reconstructions for the Irene phase. More has been done for the earlier and more diverse Swift Creek phase (A.D. 100–750). Two Swift Creek phase paddle reconstructions, along with a pot for scale, can be seen in *Sun Circles and Human Hands* (Fundaburk and Foreman 1957:Plate III).

8. These terms refer to designs acquired by rote learning that are more or less meaningless; to designs used to convey social identities but in which the relationship between the design form and meaning is not necessarily specific; and to a subgroup of symbolic designs that "have a singular, predictable relationship between a referential form and its message" (Plog 1995:370), respectively.

9. Jones (1978:180) reported five hundred people on the expedition, Milanich (1990:10) cited six hundred, and Hoffman (1990:60) said "600 or so."

10. The friars' control over these fields weakened in the 1680s in favor of the military; control reverted to the caciques in the 1690s (Bushnell 1994:153, 174).

11. Worth (1992) makes the same point with reference to the Timucua; see also Saunders 1998.

12. Among the powerful Calusa of southwestern Florida, Spanish missionaries were tolerated only as long as the trade goods lasted (Hann 1991).

13. The *visitador* was a government functionary who periodically visited the missions to report on conditions and resolve disputes.

3. The Pottery of the Guale Indians, A.D. 1300–1702

1. At Santa Elena, South and DePratter (1996:45–46) included a minority check stamped ware with earlier Irene materials but noted an increase in check stamping and a decrease in curvilinear stamping in what they considered the Altamaha phase (A.D. 1575–1715) of the Irene period. The relevance of data from Santa Elena on Parris Island is debatable. Current models locate the area outside of Guale, particularly after 1450. Assemblages bordering Guale might be expected to contain aspects of the same ceramics, but to be more diverse if competition between the ethnic groups is low (Hodder 1982).

2. Caldwell and McCann (1941:42) noted that folded rims were relatively rare at Irene but were common at contemporaneous coastal sites. They may have been including Altamaha wares in this observation, however.

3. Charles Fairbanks apparently held the same opinion (see McMurray 1973:48).

5. The Meeting House Fields Site

1. Some of this randomness may come from long-term, multiple phase occupations in which intrasite settlement patterning becomes blurred. Sites with relatively short occupation spans may show more patterning. Pearson (1984) reported two clusters of middens at the early Irene Red Bird Creek site, each focused on a burial mound. Hale (personal communication, 1999) also noted intrasite settlement patterning on Rose Dhu Island south of Savannah. At that site, there were two U-shaped areas of discrete middens. Hale suggested that in the center of each of the "U's" there was a plaza area that appeared to have been kept relatively free of debris.

2. The Kings Bay date (DePratter 1984:51, Figure 3) does not come from an Irene cultural occupation. Garrison (personal communication, 1999) reported an AMS date of A.D. 1520 ± 60 (1σ cal A.D. 1430 [1450] 1610) from the Groves Creek site (9CH71) on Skidaway Island. The date was run on the single charred cob recovered from the site. The cob was associated with a large, rectangular burned wattle and daub structure. A formal ceramic analysis has not been completed, but ceramics support a late occupation for this feature.

3. Note that these contexts differ in kind from the later mission samples. The Meeting House Fields assemblage comes from only one context, middens, and

these are secondary (disposal) as opposed to primary contexts of use. One 1 × 2 meter unit was excavated in a nonshell area, where houses would presumably be located, but no features were found, and so little pottery was recovered that all further excavations were devoted to middens.

4. Midden E could also have been considered an outlier. The low total for burnished plain distanced it from other middens in this cluster. However, similar values on other surface treatments, particularly incising, argued for inclusion in Cluster 2. In addition, distance values for joining Midden E into Cluster 2 were relatively low.

5. The Red Bird Creek site had an extremely high proportion of burnished plain wares and a correspondingly low number of plain wares as compared to the other, presumably later, sites. Even if the relatively high percentage of burnished plain materials and other ceramics excavated from the burial mound at that site were excluded from the analysis, burnished plain was still more prevalent than plain pottery, at 13.5 percent and 2.8 percent, respectively. The rim assemblage from Red Bird Creek is consistent with an early Irene site; the reason for the high percentage of burnished plain at that site is unknown.

6. The sample of the site materials was small enough to miss rare artifacts.

6. Mission Santa Catalina de Guale, St. Catherines Island, Georgia

1. Such use wear could have resulted from ceremonies associated with interment.

7. Mission Santa Catalina de Santa María, Amelia Island, Florida

1. The number of inhabitants was recorded as forty natives and five Spanish at the time of the attack (Hita Salazar in Bushnell 1994:146). The number of Guale may refer to men only, as was common at the time.

2. The population of the "four places" on Sapelo Island was 86 men and their families. As will be seen, not all of these families actually moved to the Santa María.

3. A number of Sápala apparently defected during their move, which coincided with a pirate raid in 1684. The Tupiqui moved to a separate mission on Amelia Island, perhaps due to political strife with the Sápala (Worth 1995:45).

4. In the documentary record, Santa Catalina is used to refer to the *doctrina,* or administrative center, but Santa María is often used to refer to the mission

and Guale town. To avoid confusion with the St. Catherines Island mission, I will refer to the 1684–1702 occupation on Amelia Island as Santa María.

5. For the record, the last remaining Yamassee in Spanish Florida also lived at Santa María (Hann 1990a:82).

6. Like Mission Santa Catalina, the Santa María church had subfloor burials.

7. These buff-colored, sandy, grog-tempered wares have been attributed to the Mocama, a linguistic division of the northern Timucuan peoples living between St. Augustine and the southern end of St. Simons Island. The ware is, however, clearly a historic phenomenon, and its development along the coast remains a mystery.

8. In principle, the support of soldiers was shared among all of the neighboring towns that "benefitted" from the presence of the garrison. It seems clear from visitation records, however, that the community in which the soldiers were stationed was most affected.

9. This enumeration of colono-ware forms includes only vessel sherds recovered from the study area. Other forms were present, including a relatively large number of candlestick holders from both the church and the convento excavations.

8. Continuity and Change

1. The Yamassee who settled along the Georgia coast and into Florida made pottery indistinguishable, at least at the type level, from the Guale. In other words, they made Altamaha/San Marcos pottery.

2. Smith (1984) has questioned many of Wallace's methods and interpretations, particularly as regards the question of contemporaneity between these sites. It may be that much of this data needs to be reconsidered.

3. Pearson (1977a:82) addressed the issue of curation or heirlooming of these early artifacts and dismissed the possibility.

4. I have reexamined the collections from Wallace's excavations and noted San Marcos sherds throughout the mound fill.

5. There is evidence suggesting that Mission period Guale used earlier mounds. At Johns Mound on St. Catherines Island (Larsen and Thomas 1982), two bundle burials associated with Altamaha pottery were found in a St. Catherines/Irene phase burial mound. One of these burials was also accompanied by elements of a domestic pig, suggesting that there was a European occupation on the island before this interment.

6. At the Kent Mound site, also on St. Simons Island, Cook (1978) recovered some "protohistoric San Marcos" vessels with a burial. Attributes of these vessels that were considered indicative of Spanish influence were bell shapes,

loop handles, and red filming. All other pottery from the mound was Irene. In a later article (Cook and Snow 1983), only one of these vessels is mentioned, an Irene filfot stamped vessel with elaborate Southeastern Ceremonial Complex incised designs on the neck and shoulder. The vessel form, a restricted, almost collared, jar, was referred to as Altamaha, and Spanish influenced, but there are no Spanish precedents per se. Historic artifacts located elsewhere in the mound were used to date the jar to the early sixteenth century (Cook and Snow 1983:5). However, because there were no folded rims or Altamaha-like stamping at the Kent Mound (Cook 1978:131–132), Kent Mound materials are not germane to this discussion of change.

References Cited

Adair, J.
1930 [1775] *The History of the American Indians.* Promontory Press, New York.

Adams, W. Y.
1979 On the Argument from Ceramics to History: A Challenge Based on Evidence from Medieval Nubia. *Current Anthropology* 20(4):727–744.

Alexander, M.
1976 *Discovering the New World: Based on the Works of Theodore de Bry,* edited by M. Alexander. Harper and Row, New York.

Anderson, D. G.
1989 The Mississippian in South Carolina. In *Studies in South Carolina Archaeology: Essays in Honor of Robert L. Stephenson,* edited by A. C. Goodyear III and G. T. Hanson, pp. 101–132. Occasional Papers of the South Carolina Institute of Archaeology and Anthropology, Anthropological Studies 9, University of South Carolina, Columbia.
1994 *The Savannah River Chiefdoms: Politcal Change in the Late Prehistoric Southeast.* University of Alabama Press, Tuscaloosa.

Anderson, D. G., and J. W. Joseph
1988 *Prehistory and History along the Upper Savannah River: Technical Synthesis of Cultural Resource Investigations.* Richard B. Russell Multiple Resource Area Vol. 1. Interagency Archaeological Services, National Park Service, Atlanta, Georgia.

Arnade, C. W.
1959 *The Seige of St. Augustine in 1702.* University of Florida Monographs, Social Sciences No. 3. University Press of Florida, Gainesville.

Arnold, D. E.

1984   Social Interaction and Ceramic Design: Community-wide Correlates in Quinua, Peru. In *Pots and Potters: Current Approaches in Ceramic Archaeology,* edited by P. M. Rice, pp. 133–161. UCLA Institute of Archaeology Monograph 24. University of California Press, Los Angeles.

1985   *Ceramic Theory and Cultural Process.* Cambridge University Press, Cambridge.

Ashley, K. A., and V. Rolland

1997   Grog Tempered Pottery in the Mocama Province. *Florida Anthropologist* 50(2):51–66.

Axtell, J.

1988a Some Thoughts on the Ethnohistory of Missions. In *After Columbus: Essays in the Ethnohistory of Colonial North America,* edited by J. Axtell, pp. 47–57. Oxford University Press, New York.

1988b Were Indian Conversions *Bona Fide?* In *After Columbus: Essays in the Ethnohistory of Colonial North America,* edited by J. Axtell, pp. 100–124. Oxford University Press, New York.

Binford, L. R.

1962   Archaeology as Anthropology. *American Antiquity* 28(2):217–225.

1963   "Red Ochre" Caches from the Michigan Area: A Possible Case of Cultural Drift. *Southwestern Journal of Anthropology* 19:89–108.

Borremans, N. T.

1985   Archaeology of the Devil's Walkingstick Site: A Diachronic Perspective of Aboriginal Life on a Tidal River in Southeast Georgia. Unpublished Master's thesis, University of Florida, Gainesville.

Braithwaite, M.

1982   Decoration as Ritual Symbol: A Theoretical Proposal and an Ethnographic Study in Southern Sudan. In *Symbolic and Structural Archaeology,* edited by I. Hodder, pp. 80–88. Cambridge University Press, Cambridge.

Braley, C. O.

1990   The Lamar Ceramics of the Georgia Coast. In *Lamar Archaeology: Mississippian Chiefdoms in the Deep South,* edited by M. Williams and G. Shapiro, pp. 94–103. University of Alabama Press, Tuscaloosa.

Braley, C. O., L. D. O'Steen, and I. R. Quitmeyer

1986   *Archaeological Investigations at 9McI41, Harris Neck National Wildlife Refuge, McIntosh County, Georgia.* Southeastern Archaeological Services, Inc., Athens, Georgia.

Braudel, Fernand
1981   *The Structures of Everyday Life: The Limits of the Possible.* Translated by
        Siân Reynolds. Harper and Row, New York.

Braun, D. P.
1995   Style, Selection, and Historicity. In *Style, Society, and Person: Archaeo-
        logical and Ethnological Perspectives,* edited by C. Carr and J. E. Neitzel,
        124–141. Plenum Press, New York.

Brewer, M. A.
1985   Pottery from Wamassee Head. *Early Georgia* 13:15–28.

Brose, D. S.
1989   From the Southeastern Ceremonial Complex to the Southern Cult:
        "You Can't Tell the Players without a Program." In *The Southeastern
        Ceremonial Complex: Artifacts and Analysis,* edited by P. Galloway, pp.
        27–40. University of Nebraska Press, Lincoln.

Bushnell, A.
1981   *The King's Coffer: Proprietors of the Spanish Florida Treasury 1656–1702.*
        University of Florida Press, Gainesville.

1986   *Santa María in the Written Record.* Florida State Museum Depart-
        ment of Anthropology Miscellaneous Project Report Series No. 21.
        Gainesville.

1990   The Sacramental Imperative: Catholic Ritual and Indian Sedentism
        in the Provinces of Florida. In *Columbian Consequences Volume 2:
        Archaeological and Historical Perspectives on the Spanish Borderlands East,*
        edited by D. H. Thomas, pp. 475–490. Smithsonian Institution Press,
        Washington, D.C.

1994   *Situado and Sabana: Spain's Support System for the Presidio and Mission
        Provinces of Florida.* Anthropological Papers of the American Museum
        of Natural History No. 74. University of Georgia Press, Athens.

Caldwell, J. R.
1943   Cultural Relations of Four Indian Sites of the Georgia Coast. Unpub-
        lished Ph.D. dissertation, University of Chicago.

1971   Chronology of the Georgia Coast. *Southeastern Archaeological Confer-
        ence Bulletin* 13:88–92.

Caldwell, J. R., and C. McCann
1941   *Irene Mound Site, Chatham County, Georgia.* University of Georgia
        Press, Athens.

Carr, C.
1995a   Building a Unified Middle-Range Theory of Artifact Design: Historical
        Perspectives and Tactics. In *Style, Society, and Person: Archaeological and*

Ethnological Perspectives, edited by C. Carr and J. E. Neitzel, pp. 151–170. Plenum Press, New York.

1995b A Unified Middle-Range Theory of Artifact Design. In *Style, Society, and Person: Archaeological and Ethnological Perspectives,* edited by C. Carr and J. E. Neitzel, pp. 171- 258. Plenum Press, New York.

Carr, C., and J. E. Neitzel

1995 Integrating Approaches to Material Style in Theory and Philosophy. In *Style, Society, and Person: Archaeological and Ethnological Perspectives,* edited by C. Carr and J. E. Neitzel, pp.3–20. Plenum Press, New York.

Charlton, T. H.

1968 Post-Conquest Aztec Ceramics: Implications for Archaeological Interpretation. *Florida Anthropologist* 21:96–101.

Charlton, T. H., and P. Fournier G.

1993 Urban and Rural Dimensions of the Contact Period: Central Mexico, 1521–1620. In *Ethnohistory and Archaeology: Approaches to Postcontact Change in the Americas,* edited by J. D. Rogers and S. M. Wilson, pp. 210–220. Plenum Press, New York.

Cook, Fred C.

1978 The Kent Mound: A Study of the Irene Phase on the Lower Georgia Coast. Unpublished Master's thesis, Department of Anthropology, Florida State University, Tallahassee.

1980a Aboriginal Mortality on the Georgia Coast during the Early Historic Period. *South Carolina Antiquities* 12(1):36–42.

1980b Chronological and Functional Reexamination of the Irene Ceramic Complex. In *Excursions in Southeastern Geology: The Archaeology-Geology of the Georgia Coast,* edited by J. D. Howard, C. B. DePratter, and R. W. Frey, pp. 160–169. The Geological Society of America, Guidebook 20. Georgia Department of Natural Resources, Atlanta.

1986 *Origin and Change of Irene Rim Decoration in Coastal Georgia.* Chesopiean 4(24):2–22.

Cook, F. C., and C. E. Pearson

1989 The Southeastern Ceremonial Complex on the Georgia Coast. In *The Southeastern Ceremonial Complex: Artifacts and Analysis,* edited by P. Galloway, pp. 147–165. University of Nebraska Press, Lincoln.

Cook, F. C., and F. Snow

1983 Southeastern Ceremonial Complex Symbolism on the Georgia Coast during the Late Irene Phase at Two 16th Century Spanish Contact Sites. *Chesopiean* 21(3):2–14.

Crook, M. R.

1978 Mississippian Period Community Organization on the Georgia Coast. Unpublished Ph.D. dissertation, University of Florida, Gainesville.

1980 Spatial Association and Distribution of Aggregate Village Sites in a Southeastern Atlantic Coastal Area. *The Sapelo Papers: Researches in the History and Prehistory of Sapelo Island, Georgia*, edited by D. P. Juengst, pp. 77–88. West Georgia College Studies in the Social Sciences 19. West Georgia College, Carrolton.

1981 Space, Time, and Subsistence at Bourbon Field: Final Summary Report of Investigations Submitted to the National Geographic Society and the Georgia Department of Natural Resources. Photocopy on file, West Georgia College, Carrolton.

1986 *Mississippi Period Archaeology of the Georgia Coastal Zone.* Laboratory of Archaeology Series Report No. 23. Georgia Archaeological Research Design Papers No. 1. University of Georgia, Athens.

1990 Regional Chronologies, Georgia/South Carolina Coast. In *Lamar Archaeology: Mississippian Chiefdoms in the Deep South,* edited by M. Williams and G. Shapiro, p. 36. University of Alabama Press, Tuscaloosa.

Cruxent, J.M.

1990 The Origin of La Isabela: First Spanish Colony in the New World. In *Columbian Consequences Volume 2: Archaeological and Historical Perspectives on the Spanish Borderlands East,* edited by D. H. Thomas, pp. 251–259. Smithsonian Institution Press, Washington, D.C.

Cusick, J.

1989 A Study of Postcontact Stylistic Change in Taino Ceramics at En Bas Saline, Haiti. Unpublished Master's thesis, University of Florida, Gainesville.

David, N., J. Sterner, and K. Gavua

1988 Why Pots are Decorated. *Current Anthropology* 29(3):365–379.

Deagan, K.

1983 *Spanish St. Augustine: The Archaeology of a Colonial Creole Community.* Academic Press, New York.

1985 Spanish-Indian Interaction in Sixteenth Century Florida and the Caribbean. In *Cultures in Contact: The European Impact on Native Cultural Institutions in Eastern North America, A.D. 1000–1800,* edited by W. Fitzhugh, pp. 281–318. Smithsonian Institution Press, Washington, D.C.

1988 The Archaeology of the Spanish Contact Period in the Caribbean. *Journal of World Prehistory* 2(2):187–233.

1990a Sixteenth Century Spanish-American Colonization in the Southeastern United States and the Caribbean. In *Columbian Consequences Volume 2: Archaeological and Historical Perspectives on the Spanish Borderlands East,* edited by D. H. Thomas, pp. 225–250. Smithsonian Institution Press, Washington, D.C.

1990b Accommodation and Resistance: The Process and Impact of Spanish Colonization in the Southeast. In *Columbian Consequences Volume 2: Archaeological and Historical Perspectives on the Spanish Borderlands East,* edited by D. H. Thomas, pp. 297–314. Smithsonian Institution Press, Washington, D.C.

Deetz, J.

1965 *The Dynamics of Stylistic Change in Arikara Ceramics.* Illinois Studies in Anthropology No. 4. University of Illinois Press, Urbana.

1968 The Inference of Residence Rules from Archaeological Data. In *New Perspectives in Archeology,* edited by S. R. Binford and L. R. Binford, pp. 41–48. Aldine Publishing Co., Chicago.

DePratter, C. B.

1979 Ceramics. In *The Anthropology of St. Catherines Island 2. The Refuge-Deptford Mortuary Complex,* edited by D. H. Thomas and C. S. Larsen, pp. 109–132. Anthropological Papers Vol. 56, Pt. 1. American Museum of Natural History, New York.

1984 Irene Manifestations on the Northern Georgia Coast. *Early Georgia* 12(1–2):44–58.

1991 *W.P.A. Archaeological Excavations in Chatham County, Georgia: 1937–1942.* University of Georgia Laboratory of Archaeology Series Report Number 29. University of Georgia, Athens.

1994 The Chiefdom of Cofitachequi. In *The Forgotten Centuries: Indians and Europeans in the American South, 1521–1704,* edited by C. Hudson and C. C. Tesser, pp. 197–226. University of Georgia Press, Athens.

DePratter, C. B., and J. D. Howard

1980 Indian Occupation and Geologic History of the Georgia Coast: A 5000 Year Summary. In *Excursions in Southeastern Geology: The Archaeology-Geology of the Georgia Coast,* edited by J. D. Howard, C. B. DePratter, and R. W. Frey, pp. 1–65. Geological Society of America, Guidebook 20. Georgia Department of Natural Resources, Atlanta.

DesJean, T.

1985 The South Bunker Area. In *Aboriginal Subsistence and Settlement Archaeology of the Kings Bay Locality: 1. The Kings Bay and Devils Walking-*

stick Sites, edited by W. H. Adams, pp. 125–151. University of Florida Department of Anthropology Report of Investigations No. 1. Gainesville.

Dobyns, H.

1983   *Their Number Become Thinned: Native American Population Dynamics in Eastern North America.* University of Tennessee Press, Knoxville.

Duke, J. A.

1993   Change in Vertebrate Use between the Irene Phase and the Seventeenth Century on St. Catherines Island, Georgia. Unpublished Master's thesis, Department of Anthropology, University of Georgia, Athens.

Dunlop, Captain

1929   Journal Capt. Dunlop's Voyage to the Southward, 1687. *South Carolina Historical and Genealogical Magazine* 30(3):127–133.

Durham, W. H.

1990   Advances in Evolutionary Culture Theory. *Annual Review of Anthropology* 19:187–210.

Emerson, Thomas E.

1989   Water, Serpents, and the Underworld: An Exploration into Cahokian Symbolism. In *The Southeastern Ceremonial Complex: Artifacts and Analysis,* edited by P. Galloway, pp. 45–92. University of Nebraska Press, Lincoln.

1997   *Cahokia and the Archaeology of Power.* University of Alabama Press, Tuscaloosa.

Fewkes, V. J.

1944   Catawba Pottery Making with Notes on Pamunkey Pottery Making, Cherokee Pottery Making, and Coiling. *Proceedings of the American Philosophical Society* 88(2):69–124.

Foster, G.

1960   *Culture and Conquest: America's Spanish Heritage.* Viking Fund Publications in Anthropology No. 27. New York.

Friedrich, M. H.

1970   Design Structure and Social Interaction: Archeological Implications of an Ethnographic Analysis. *American Antiquity* 35(3):332–343.

Fundaburk, E. L., and M. D. F. Foreman (editors)

1957   *Sun Circles and Human Hands: The Southeastern Indians Art and Industries.* Southern Publications, Fairhope, Alabama.

Galloway, P.

1995   *Choctaw Genesis, 1500–1700.* University of Nebraska Press, Lincoln.

Galloway, P. (editor)

1989   *The Southeastern Ceremonial Complex: Artifacts and Analysis.* University of Nebraska Press, Lincoln.

Gannon, M. V.

1965   *The Cross in the Sand.* University of Florida Press, Gainesville.

Garcia-Arevalo, M.

1978   *Influencia de la Dieta Indo-Hispanica in la Cerámica Taína.* Boletín del Museo del Hombre Dominicano 9. Santo Domingo.

1990   Transculturation in Contact Period and Contemporary Hispaniola. In *Columbian Consequences Volume 2: Archaeological and Historical Perspectives on the Spanish Borderlands East,* edited by D. H. Thomas, pp. 269–280. Smithsonian Institution Press, Washington, D.C.

Garcilaso de la Vega, the Inca

1993   [1605] *La Florida: History of the Adelantado Hernando de Soto, Governor and Captain-General of the Kingdom of La Florida, and of other Heroic Gentlemen, Spaniards and Indians.* Translated by Charmion Shelby. In *The DeSoto Chronicles: The Expedition of Hernando De Soto to North America in 1539–1543,* edited by L. A. Clayton, V. J. Knight Jr., and E. C. Moore. University of Alabama Press, Tuscaloosa.

Geiger, M.

1937   *The Franciscan Conquest of Florida (1573–1618).* Catholic University of America, Washington, D.C.

Green, W. G.

1991   The Search for Altamaha: The Archaeology of an Early 18th Century Yamasee Indian Town. Unpublished Master's thesis, Department of Anthropology, University of South Carolina, Columbia.

Hally, D. J.

1990   Upper Savannah River Phase Characteristics. In *Lamar Archaeology: Mississippian Chiefdoms in the Deep South,* edited by M. Williams and G. Shapiro, pp. 52–55. University of Alabama Press, Tuscaloosa.

Hally, D. J., and J. L. Rudolph

1986   *Mississippi Period Archaeology of the Georgia Piedmont.* Georgia Archaeological Research Design Papers No. 2. Laboratory of Archaeology Series Report No. 24. Athens.

Hally, D. J., M. T. Smith, and J. B. Langford

1990   The Archaeological Reality of de Soto's Coosa. In *Columbian Consequences Volume 2: Archaeological and Historical Perspectives on the Spanish Borderlands East,* edited by D. H. Thomas, pp. 121–138. Smithsonian Institution Press, Washington, D.C.

Hann, J.

1986a Demographic Patterns and Changes in Mid-Seventeenth Century Timucua and Apalachee. *Florida Historical Quarterly* 64:371–392.

1986b *Translation of the Ecija Voyages of 1605 and 1609 and the González Derrotero of 1609.* Florida Archaeology No. 2. Florida Bureau of Archaeological Research, Tallahassee.

1987 Twilight of the Mocamo and Guale Aborigines as Portrayed in the 1695 Spanish Visitation. *Florida Historical Quarterly* 46(1):1–24.

1988 *Apalachee: The Land between Two Rivers.* University of Florida Press, Gainesville.

1990a [1701] Visitation of Guale and Mocama. Ms. on file, San Luis Historical and Archaeological Site, Tallahassee, Florida.

1990b Summary Guide to Spanish Florida Missions and Visitas with Churches in the Sixteenth and Seventeenth Centuries. *The Americas* 46(4):1–99.

1991 *Missions to the Calusa.* University of Florida Press, Gainesville.

1996 *A History of the Timucua Indians and Missions.* University Press of Florida, Gainesville.

Hardin, K.

1986 The Santa Maria Mission Project. *Florida Anthropologist* 39(1–2):75–83.

Hardin, M. A.

1977 Individual Style in San José Pottery Painting: The Role of Deliberate Choice. In *The Individual in Prehistory,* edited by J. N. Hill and J. Gunn, pp. 109–136. Academic Press, New York.

1984 Models of Decoration. In *The Many Dimensions of Pottery: Ceramics in Archaeology and Anthropology,* edited by S. E. van der Leeuw and A. C. Pritchard, pp. 573–614. CINGULA 7. Institute for Pre-and Proto-History, University of Amsterdam, Amsterdam.

Harn, A. D.

1980 *The Prehistory of Dickson Mounds: The Dickson Excavation.* Dickson Mounds Museum Anthropological Studies. Reports of Investigations No. 35. Illinois State Museum, Springfield.

Hegmon M.

1992 Archaeological Research on Style. *Annual Review of Anthropology* 21:417–434.

Hemmings, D., and K. Deagan

1973 *Excavations on Amelia Island in Northeast Florida.* Contributions of the Florida State Museum, Anthropology and History, No. 18. Florida State Museum, Gainesville.

Hill, J. N.

1985   Style: A Conceptual Evolutionary Framework. In *Decoding Prehistoric Ceramics,* edited by B. A. Nelson, pp. 362–385. Southern Illinois University Press, Carbondale.

Hill, J. N., and J. Gunn

1977   *The Individual in Prehistory: Studies in the Variability in Style in Prehistoric Technologies.* Academic Press, New York.

Hodder, I.

1982   *Symbols in Action: Ethnoarchaeological Studies of Material Culture.* Cambridge University Press, Cambridge.

1986   *Reading the Past.* Cambridge University Press, Cambridge.

Hoffman, K.

1990   Archaeological Excavations at the Florida National Guard Headquarters (Site SA-42A), St. Augustine, Florida. Ms. on file, Florida Museum of Natural History, Gainesville.

1997   Cultural Development in *La Florida. Historical Archaeology* 31(1):24–35.

Hoffman, P.

1984   The Chicora Legend and Franco-Spanish Rivalry in *La Florida. Florida Historical Quarterly* 62:419–438.

1990   *A New Andalucia and a Way to the Orient: The American Southeast during the Sixteenth Century.* Louisiana State University Press, Baton Rouge.

Howard, James H.

1968   *The Southeastern Ceremonial Complex and Its Interpretation.* Missouri Archaeological Society Memoir No. 6. Oklahoma State University, Stillwater, Oklahoma.

Hudson, C.

1976   *The Southeastern Indians.* University of Tennessee Press, Knoxville.

1984   *Elements of Southeastern Indian Religion.* Institute of Religious Iconography, State University Groningen. E. J. Brill, Leiden.

Hutchinson, D. L., C. S. Larsen, M. J. Schoeninger, and L. Norr

1998   Regional Variation in the Pattern of Maize Adoption and Use in Florida and Georgia. *American Antiquity* 63(3):397–416.

Irwin, G.

1974   Carved Paddle Decoration of Pottery and Its Capacity for Inference in Archaeology: An Example from the Solomon Islands. *Journal of the Polynesian Society* 83(3):368–371.

Johnson, J. K., and G. Lehmann

1996   Sociopolitical Devolution in Northeast Mississippi and the Timing of the de Soto Entrada. In *Bioarchaeology of Native American Adaptation in the Spanish Borderlands,* edited by B. J. Baker and L. Kealhofer, pp. 38–55. University Press of Florida, Gainesville.

Jones, G. D.
1978   The Ethnohistory of the Guale Coast through 1684. In *The Anthropology of St. Catherines Island: Natural and Cultural History,* edited by D. H. Thomas, G. D. Jones, and R. S. Durham, pp. 178–209. Anthropological Papers Vol. 55, Pt. 2. American Museum of Natural History, New York.

Kimber, E.
1974   [1745] *Itinerant Observations in America.* Collections of the Georgia Historical Society Vol. IV. Reprint Co., Spartanburg, North Carolina.

Kosso, P.
1991   Method in Archaeology: Middle-Range Theory as Hermeneutics. *American Antiquity* 56(4):621–627.

Kubler, George
1961   On the Colonial Extinction of the Motifs of Pre-Columbian Art. In *Essays in Pre-Columbian Art and Archaeology,* edited by S. K. Lothrop, pp. 14–34. Harvard University Press, Cambridge.

Larsen, C. S.
1990   Biological Interpretation and the Context for Contact. In *The Archaeology of Mission Santa Catalina de Guale: Biocultural Interpretations of a Population in Transition,* edited by C. S. Larsen, pp. 11–25. Anthropological Papers No. 68. American Museum of Natural History, New York.
1994   In the Wake of Columbus: Native Population Biology in the Postcontact Americas. *Yearbook of Physical Anthropology* 37:109–154.

Larsen, C. S., and D. H. Thomas
1982   *The Anthropology of St. Catherines Island: 4. The St. Catherines Period Mortuary Complex.* Anthropological Papers Vol. 57, Pt. 4. American Museum of Natural History, New York.
1986   *The Anthropology of St. Catherines Island: 5. The South End Mound Complex.* Anthropological Papers Vol. 63, Pt. 1. American Museum of Natural History, New York.

Larson, L. H., Jr.
1953   Coastal Mission Survey. Unpublished ms. on file, Georgia Historical Commission, Atlanta.
1955   An Unusual Figurine from the Georgia Coast. *Florida Anthropologist* 8:75–81.

1958   Southern Cult Manifestations of the Georgia Coast. *American Antiquity* 23:426–430.

1978   Historic Guale Indians of the Georgia Coast and the Impact of the Spanish Mission Effort. In *Tacachale,* edited by J. T. Milanich and S. Proctor, pp. 120–140. University Presses of Florida, Gainesville.

1980a   *Aboriginal Subsistence Technology on the Southeastern Coastal Plain during the Late Prehistoric Period.* University Presses of Florida, Gainesville.

1980b   The Spanish on Sapelo. In *The Sapelo Papers: Researches in the History and Prehistory of Sapelo Island, Georgia,* edited by D. P. Juengst, pp. 35–45. West Georgia College Studies in the Social Sciences 19. West Georgia College, Carrollton.

1984   Irene Manifestations in the McIntosh County Tidewater Area. *Early Georgia* 12(1–2):64–70.

Lathrap, D. W.

1976   Shipibo Tourist Art. In *Ethnic and Tourist Arts: Cultural Expressions from the Fourth World,* edited by N. H. H. Graburn, pp. 197–207. University of California Press, Berkeley.

Laudonnière, R.

1975   [1586] *Three Voyages.* Translated by C. Bennett. University Presses of Florida, Gainesville.

McMurray, J. A.

1973   The Definition of the Ceramic Complex at San Juan del Puerto. Unpublished Ph.D. dissertation, University of Florida, Gainesville.

Maschner, H. D. G. (editor)

1996   *Darwinian Archaeologies.* Plenum Press, New York.

Matter, R. A.

1972   The Spanish Missions of Florida: The Friars vs the Governors in the "Golden Age," 1606–1690. Unpublished Ph.D. dissertation, University of Washington, Seattle.

Milanich, J. T.

1986   Comments. In *Mississippi Period Archaeology of the Georgia Coastal Zone,* by M. R. Crook, pp. 58–61. Laboratory of Archaeology Series Report No. 23. Georgia Archaeological Research Design Papers No. 1. University of Georgia, Athens.

1990   The European Entrada into *La Florida.* In *Columbian Consequences Volume 2: Archaeological and Historical Perspectives on the Spanish Borderlands East,* edited by D. H. Thomas, pp. 3–30. Smithsonian Institution Press, Washington, D.C.

1994   Franciscan Missions and Native Peoples in Spanish Florida. In *The*

Forgotten Centuries: Indians and Europeans in the American South, 1521–1704, edited by C. Hudson and C. C. Tesser, pp. 276–303. University of Georgia, Athens.

1995   *Florida Indians and the Invasion from Europe.* University Press of Florida, Gainesville.

1999   *Laboring in the Fields of the Lord: Spanish Missions and Southeastern Indians.* Smithsonian Institution Press, Washington, D.C.

Milanich, J. T., and W. C. Sturtevant

1972   *Francisco Pareja's 1613 Confessionario: A Documentary Source for Timucuan Ethnography.* Florida Division of Archives, History, and Records, Tallahassee.

Milner, G. R.

1980   Epidemic Disease in the Postcontact Southeast: A Reappraisal. *Mid-Continental Journal of Archaeology* 5:39–56.

Moore, C. B.

1897   Certain Aboriginal Mounds of the Georgia Coast. *Journal of the Academy of Natural Sciences of Philadelphia* 11(1):1–138.

Muller, J.

1989   The Southern Cult. In *The Southeastern Ceremonial Complex: Artifacts and Analysis,* edited by P. Galloway, pp. 11–26. University of Nebraska Press, Lincoln.

Nicklin, K.

1971   Stability and Innovation in Pottery Manufacture. *World Archaeology* 3(1):13–48.

Oré, L. G. de

1936   *The Martyrs of Florida (1513–1616).* Translated and edited by M. Geiger. Franciscan Studies 19. Joseph W. Wagner, New York.

Ortega, E., and C. Fondeur

1978   *Estudio de la Cerámica del Periodo Indo-Hispano de la Antigua Concepción de la Vega.* Fundación Ortega Alvarez. Serie Científica 1. Santo Domingo.

Otto, J., and R. Lewis

1974   *A Formal and Functional Analysis of San Marcos Pottery from Site SA 16–23, St. Augustine.* Florida Department of State, Bureau of Historic Sites and Properties Bulletin 4. Tallahassee.

Oviedo y Valdés, Gonzalo Fernández de

1959   *Historia general y natural de las Indias,* vol. 4. Biblioteca de Autores Españolas, Tomo CXX. Ediciones Atlas, Madrid.

Patrik, L.

1985 Is There an Archaeological Record? In *Advances in Archaeological Method and Theory*, vol. 8, edited by M. B. Schiffer, pp. 1–26. Academic Press, New York.

Pauketat, T. R., and T. E. Emerson

1991 The Ideology of Authority and the Power of the Pot. *American Anthropologist* 93:919–941.

Pearson, C. E.

1977a Evidence of Early Spanish Contact on the Georgia Coast. *Historical Archaeology* 11:74–83.

1977b *Analysis of Late Prehistoric Settlement on Ossabaw Island, Georgia.* Laboratory of Archaeology Series, Report No. 12. University of Georgia, Athens.

1978 Analysis of Late Mississippian Settlements on Ossabaw Island, Georgia. In *Mississippian Settlement Systems*, edited by B. D. Smith, pp. 53–80. Academic Press, New York.

1979 Patterns of Mississippian Period Adaptation in Coastal Georgia. Unpublished Ph.D. dissertation, Department of Anthropology, University of Georgia, Athens.

1980 Late Prehistoric Settlement Systems on Ossabaw Island, Georgia. In *Excursions in Southeastern Geology: The Archaeology-Geology of the Georgia Coast,* by J. D. Howard, C. B. DePratter, and R. W. Frey, pp. 179–191. Guidebook 20. Department of Natural Resources, Atlanta, Georgia.

1984 Red Bird Creek: Late Prehistoric Material Culture and Subsistence in Coastal Georgia. *Early Georgia* 12 (1–2):1–40.

Piatek, B.

1985 Non-local Aboriginal Ceramics from Early Historic Contexts in St. Augustine. *Florida Anthropologist* 38(1–2):81–89.

Plog, S.

1980 *Stylistic Variation in Prehistoric Ceramics: Design Analysis in the American Southwest.* Cambridge University Press, New York.

1983 Analysis of Style in Artifacts. *Annual Review of Anthropology* 12:125–142.

1995 Approaches to Style: Complements and Contrasts. In *Style, Society, and Person: Archaeological and Ethnological Perspectives,* edited by C. Carr and J. E. Neitzel, pp. 369–387. Plenum Press, New York.

Quimby, G. I.

1966 *Indian Culture and European Trade Goods.* University of Wisconsin Press, Milwaukee.

Quimby, G. I., and A. Spoehr

1951 Acculturation and Material Culture-1. *Fieldiana* 36(6):107–147.

Quinn, D. B.

1979   *New American World: A Documentary History of North America to 1612,* vol. 2. Arno Press, New York.

Ramenofsky, A. F.

1987   *Vectors of Death: The Archaeology of European Contact.* University of New Mexico Press, Albuquerque.

Ramenofsky, A. F., and P. Galloway

1997   Disease and the Soto Entrado. In *The Hernando de Soto Expedition: History, Historiography, and "Discovery" in the Southeast,* edited by P. Galloway, pp. 259–282. University of Nebraska Press, Lincoln.

Redman, C. L.

1978   Multivariate Artifact Analysis: A Basis for Multidimensional Interpretations. In *Social Archaeology: Beyond Subsistence and Dating,* edited by C. L. Redman, M. J. Berman, E. V. Curtin, W. T. Langhorne Jr., N. M. Versaggi, and J. C. Wanser, pp. 159–192. Academic Press, New York.

Reitz, E. J.

1990   Zooarchaeological Evidence of Subsistence at La Florida Missions. In *Columbian Consequences Volume 2: Archaeological and Historical Perspectives on the Spanish Borderlands East,* edited by D. H. Thomas, pp. 543–554. Smithsonian Institution Press, Washington, D.C.

Reitz, E. J., and M. C. Scarry

1985   *Reconstructing Historic Subsistence with an Example from Sixteenth Century Spanish Florida.* Society for Historical Archaeology Special Publication No. 3. Braun-Brumfield, Inc., Ann Arbor.

Rice, P. M.

1984   Change and Conservatism in Pottery-Producing Systems. In *The Many Dimensions of Pottery: Ceramics in Archaeology and Anthropology,* edited by S. E. van der Leeuw and A. C. Pritchard. CINGULA 7. Institute for Pre- and Proto-History, University of Amsterdam, Amsterdam.

1987   *Pottery Analysis: A Sourcebook.* University of Chicago Press, Chicago.

Ross, M.

1923   French Intrusions and Indian Uprisings in Georgia and South Carolina (1577–1580). *Georgia Historical Quarterly* 7(3):251–281.

1924   The French on the Savannah 1605. *Georgia Historical Quarterly* 8(3): 167–194.

Russo, M.

1991   A Method for the Measurement of Season and Duration of Oyster Collection: Two Case Studies from the Prehistoric Southeast U.S. Coast. *Journal of Archaeological Science* 18:205–221.

Saunders, R.

1985   The Artesian Well Area. In *Aboriginal Subsistence and Settlement Archaeology of the Kings Bay Locality: 1. The Kings Bay and Devils Walkingstick Sites,* edited by W. H. Adams, pp. 257–294. University of Florida Department of Anthropology Report of Investigations No. 1. Gainesville.

1986a   Attribute Variability in Late Swift Creek Phase Ceramics from Kings Bay, Georgia. Unpublished Master's thesis, University of Florida, Gainesville.

1986b   The Archaeological Assessment of Acculturation: A Case Study Using Spanish Missions of the American Southwest. Unpublished manuscript on file with the author.

1986c   Pottery Manufacture and Design Symbolism of Late Swift Creek Phase Ceramics at Kings Bay, Georgia. In *Ceramic Notes,* vol. 3, edited by P. M. Rice, pp. 145–198. Occasional Publications of the Ceramic Technology Laboratory, Florida Museum of Natural History, Gainesville.

1990   Ideal and Innovation: Spanish Mission Architecture in the Southeast. In *Columbian Consequences Volume 2: Archaeological and Historical Perspectives on the Spanish Borderlands East,* edited by D. H. Thomas, pp. 527–542. Smithsonian Institution Press, Washington, D.C.

1991   Architecture of the Missions Santa Maria and Santa Catalina, Amelia Island, Florida. *Florida Anthropologist* 44(3–4):126–138.

1992   Continuity and Change in Guale Indian Pottery, A.D. 1350–1702. Unpublished Ph.D. dissertation, Department of Anthropology, University of Florida, Gainesville.

1993   Architecture of the Missions Santa María and Santa Catalina de Amelia. In *The Spanish Missions of La Florida,* edited by B. G. McEwan, pp. 35–61. University Press of Florida, Gainesville.

1998   Forced Relocation, Power Relations, and Culture Contact in the Missions of *La Florida.* In *Studies in Culture Contact: Interaction, Culture Change, and Archaeology,* edited by J. G. Cusick, pp. 402–429. Center for Archaeological Investigations, Southern Illinois University, Carbondale.

2000a   The Guale Indians of the Lower Atlantic Coast: Change and Continuity. In *Indians of the Greater Southeast during the Historic Period,* edited by B. G. McEwan. University Press of Florida, Gainesville.

2000b   Seasonality, Sedentism, Subsistence, and Disease in the Protohistoric: Archaeological vs. Ethnohistoric Data along the Lower Atlantic Coast. In *Protohistory and Archaeology: Advances in Interdisciplinary Research,* edited by C. B. Wesson and M. A. Rees. University of Alabama Press, Tuscaloosa.

2001   The Lost Colony of San Miguel de Gualdape, Past and Present. In *The Search for San Miguel,* edited by D. H. Thomas. Anthropological Papers No. 76. American Museum of Natural History, New York.

Saunders, R., and M. R. Russo

1988   Meeting House Fields: Irene Phase Material Culture and Seasonality of St. Catherines Island. Report prepared for the American Museum of Natural History, New York.

Scarry, M. C., and E. J. Reitz

1990   Herbs, Fish, Scum, and Vermin: Subsistence Strategies in Sixteenth Century Spanish Florida. In *Columbian Consequences Volume 2: Archaeological and Historical Perspectives on the Spanish Borderlands East,* edited by D. H. Thomas, pp. 343–356. Smithsonian Institution Press, Washington, D.C.

Schoeninger, M. J., N. J. van der Merwe, K. Moore, J. Lee-Thorpe, and C. S. Larsen

1990   Decrease in Diet Quality between the Prehistoric and Contact Periods on St. Catherines Island, Georgia. In *The Archaeology of Mission Santa Catalina de Guale: Biocultural Interpretations of a Population in Transition,* edited by C. S. Larsen, pp. 78–93. Anthropological Papers No. 68. American Museum of Natural History, New York.

Scott, J. C.

1985   *Weapons of the Weak: Everyday Forms of Peasant Resistance.* Yale University Press, New Haven.

Sears, W. H.

1959   A-296—A Seminole Site in Alachua County. *Florida Anthropologist* 7:25–30.

Shapiro, G. N.

1984   Ceramic Vessels, Site Permanence, and Group Size: A Mississippian Example. *American Antiquity* 49(4):696–712.

1987   *Archaeology at San Luis: Broad Scale Testing, 1984–1985.* Florida Archaeology (3). Florida Bureau of Archaeological Research, Tallahassee.

Shepard, A. O.

1980   *Ceramics for the Archaeologist.* Carnegie Institution of Washington, Washington, D.C.

Silver, T.

1990   *A New Face on the Countryside: Indians, Colonists, and Slaves in the South Atlantic Forests, 1500–1800.* Cambridge University Press, Cambridge.

Smith, B. (translator)

1968 *Narratives of de Soto in the Conquest of Florida: As Told by A Gentleman of Elvas and in a Relation by Luys Hernandez de Biedma.* Palmetto Books, Gainesville, Florida.

Smith, G.

1986 Non-European Pottery at the Sixteenth Century Spanish Site of Puerto Real, Haiti. Unpublished Master's thesis, University of Florida, Gainesville.

Smith, H. G.

1948 Two Historical Archaeological Periods in Florida. *American Antiquity* 13(4):313–319.

1949 *Two Archaeological Sites in Brevard County Florida.* Florida Anthropological Society Publications No. 1. University Press of Florida, Gainesville.

1951 A Spanish Mission Site in Jefferson County, Florida. In *Here They Once Stood,* by M. F. Boyd, H. G. Smith, and J. W. Griffin, pp. 107–136. University Presses of Florida, Gainesville.

Smith, M. T.

1987 *Archaeology of Aboriginal Culture Change in the Interior Southeast.* University Presses of Florida, Gainesville.

Smith, M. T., and D. G. Hally

1992 Chiefly Behavior: Evidence from Sixteenth Century Spanish Accounts. In *Lords of the Southeast: Social Inequality and the Native Elites of Southeastern North America,* edited by A. W. Barker and T. R. Pauketat, pp. 99–110. Archaeological Papers of the American Anthropological Association No. 3. American Anthropological Association, Washington, D.C.

Smith, M. T., and M. Williams

1990 Piedmont Oconee River. In *Lamar Archaeology: Mississippian Chiefdoms in the Deep South,* edited by M. Wiliams and G. Shapiro, pp. 60–63. University of Alabama Press, Tuscaloosa.

Smith, R. L.

1984 Coastal Mississippian Period Sites at Kings Bay, Georgia: A Model-Based Archeological Analysis. Unpublished Ph.D. dissertation, University of Florida, Gainesville.

Snow, F.

1977 *An Archaeological Survey of the Ocmulgee Big Bend Region.* Occasional Papers from South Georgia No. 3. South Georgia College, Douglas.

1990 Pine Barrens Lamar. In *Lamar Archaeology: Mississippian Chiefdoms in the Deep South,* edited by M. Williams and G. Shapiro, pp. 82–93. University of Alabama Press, Tuscaloosa.

South, S.

1977   *Method and Theory in Historical Archeology.* Academic Press, New York.

1988   Santa Elena: Threshold of Conquest. In *The Recovery of Meaning,* edited by M. Leone and P. B. Potter Jr., pp. 27–71. Anthropological Society of Washington. Smithsonian Institution Press, Washington, D.C.

1990   From Thermodynamics to a Status Artifact Model: Spanish Santa Elena. In *Columbian Consequences Volume 2: Archaeological and Historical Perspectives on the Spanish Borderlands East,* edited by D. H. Thomas, pp. 329–341. Smithsonian Institution Press, Washington, D.C.

South, S., and C. B. DePratter

1996   *Discovery at Santa Elena: Block Excavation 1993.* South Carolina Institute of Archaeology and Anthropology Research Manuscript Series 222. University of South Carolina, Columbia.

Speck, Frank G.

1909   *Ethnology of the Yuchi Indians.* University of Pennsylvania Anthropological Publications of the University Museum Vol. 1, No. 1. University Museum, Philadelphia.

Spicer, E. H.

1961   Types of Contact and Processes of Change. In *Perspectives in American Indian Culture Change,* edited by E. H. Spicer, pp. 517–544. University of Chicago Press, Chicago.

Spielmann, K. A., M. J. Schoeninger, and K. Moore

1990   Plains-Pueblo Interdependence and Human Diet at Pecos Pueblo, New Mexico. *American Antiquity* 55(4):745–765.

Stahle, D. W., M. K. Cleaveland, D. B. Blanton, M. D. Therrell, and D. A. Gay

1998   The Lost Colony and Jamestown Droughts. *Science* 280:564–567.

Stuiver, M., G. W. Pearson, and T. Braziunas

1986   Radiocarbon Age Calibration of Marine Samples Back to 9000 CAL YR BP. *Radiocarbon* 28:980–1021.

Stuiver, M., and P. J. Reimer

1986   A Computer Program for Radiocarbon Age Calibration. *Radiocarbon* 28:1022–1030.

Sturtevant, W. C.

1962   Spanish-Indian Relations in Southeastern North America. *Ethnohistory* 9(1):41–94.

Swanton, J. R.

1922   *Early History of the Creek Indians and Their Neighbors.* Bureau of American Ethnology Bulletin 73. Smithsonian Institution, Washington, D.C.

1946   *The Indians of the Southeastern United States.* Bureau of American Ethnology Bulletin 137. Smithsonian Institution, Washington, D.C.

Thomas, D. H.

1987   *The Archaeology of Mission Santa Catalina de Guale: 1. Search and Discovery.* Anthropological Papers Vol. 63, Pt. 2. American Museum of Natural History, New York.

1988a Saints and Soldiers at Santa Catalina: Hispanic Designs for Colonial America. In *The Recovery of Meaning in Historical Archaeology,* edited by M. P. Leone and P. B. Potter Jr., pp. 73–140. Smithsonian Institution Press, Washington, D.C.

1988b *St. Catherines: An Island in Time.* Georgia History and Culture Series. Georgia Endowment for the Humanities, Atlanta.

1993   *Historic Indian Period Archaeology of the Georgia Coastal Zone.* Georgia Archaeological Research Design Paper No. 8, Laboratory of Archaeology Series Report No. 31. University of Georgia, Athens.

Tschopik, H.

1950   An Andean Ceramic Tradition in Historical Perspective. *American Antiquity* 15(3):196–218.

VanPool, C. S., and T. L. VanPool

1999   The Scientific Nature of Postprocessualism. *American Antiquity* 64(1): 33–54.

Walker, K. J.

1985   The Protohistoric and Historic Indian Occupation at Kings Bay: An Overview. In *Aboriginal Subsistence and Settlement Archaeology of the Kings Bay Locality: 1. The Kings Bay and Devils Walkingstick Sites,* edited by W. H. Adams, pp. 55–72. University of Florida Department of Anthropology Report of Investigations No. 1. Gainesville.

Wallace, A. F. C.

1966   *Religion: An Anthropological View.* Random House, New York.

Wallace, R. L.

1975   An Archeological, Ethnohistoric, and Biochemical Investigation of the Guale Aborigines of the Georgia Coastal Strand. Unpublished Ph.D. dissertation, University of Florida, Gainesville.

Waring, A. J.

1968   The Southern Cult and Muskogean Ceremonial. In *The Waring Papers: The Collected Works of Antonio J. Waring,* edited by S. Williams, pp.

30–69. Papers of the Peabody Museum of Archaeology and Ethnology Vol. 58. Harvard University, Cambridge.

Waring, A. J., and P. Holder

1968   A Prehistoric Ceremonial Complex in the Southeastern United States. In *The Waring Papers: The Collected Works of Antonio J. Waring,* edited by S. Williams, pp. 9–29. Papers of the Peabody Museum of Archaeology and Ethnology Vol. 58. Harvard University, Cambridge.

Weisman, B. R.

1989   *Like Beads on a String: A Culture History of the Seminole Indians in North Peninsular Florida.* University of Alabama Press, Tuscaloosa.

Weissner, P.

1985   Style or Isochrestic Variation? A Reply to Sackett. *American Antiquity* 50:160–166.

Wenhold, L. L. (translator and editor)

1936   *A 17th Century Letter of Gabriel Díaz Vara Calderón, Bishop of Cuba, Describing the Indians and Indian Missions of Florida.* Smithsonian Miscellaneous Collections 95(16). Publication 3398. Washington, D.C.

Willey, G. R.

1982   *Archeology of the Florida Gulf Coast.* Reprinted. Originally published 1949. Smithsonian Miscellaneous Collections Vol. 113. Florida Book Store, Inc., Gainesville, Florida.

Willoughby, C. C.

1897   An Analysis of the Decoration upon Pottery from the Mississippi Valley. *Journal of American Folklore* 36(10):9–20.

Wobst, H. M.

1977   Stylistic Behavior and Information Exchange. In *Papers for the Director: Research Essays in Honor of James B. Griffin,* edited by C. E. Cleland, pp. 317–342. University of Michigan Museum of Anthropology Anthropological Papers 61, Ann Arbor.

Worth, J. E.

1992   *The Timucuan Missions of Spanish Florida and the Rebellion of 1656.* Unpublished Ph.D. dissertation, Department of Anthropology, University of Florida, Gainesville.

1995   *The Struggle for the Georgia Coast: An Eighteenth-Century Spanish Retrospective on Guale and Mocama.* Anthropological Papers of the American Museum of Natural History No. 75. University of Georgia Press, Athens.

1998a   *The Timucuan Chiefdoms of Spanish Florida: 1. Assimilation.* University Press of Florida, Gainesville.

1998b *The Timucuan Chiefdoms of Spanish Florida: 2. Resistance and Destruction.* University of Florida Press, Gainesville.

Zubillaga, F.

1946 *Monumenta Antiquae Floridae (1566–1572).* Monumenta Historica Societatis Iesu, Rome.

Index